The College History Series

MOUNT UNION COLLEGE

The College History Series

Mount Union College

Lyle Crist

ARCADIA
PUBLISHING

ISBN 978-0-7385-0801-6

Published by Arcadia Publishing
Charleston, South Carolina

Printed in the United States of America

Library of Congress Catalog Card Number: 2001087306

For all general information contact Arcadia Publishing at:
Telephone 843-853-2070
Fax 843-853-0044
E-mail sales@arcadiapublishing.com
For customer service and orders:
Toll-Free 1-888-313-2665

Visit us on the Internet at www.arcadiapublishing.com

Contents

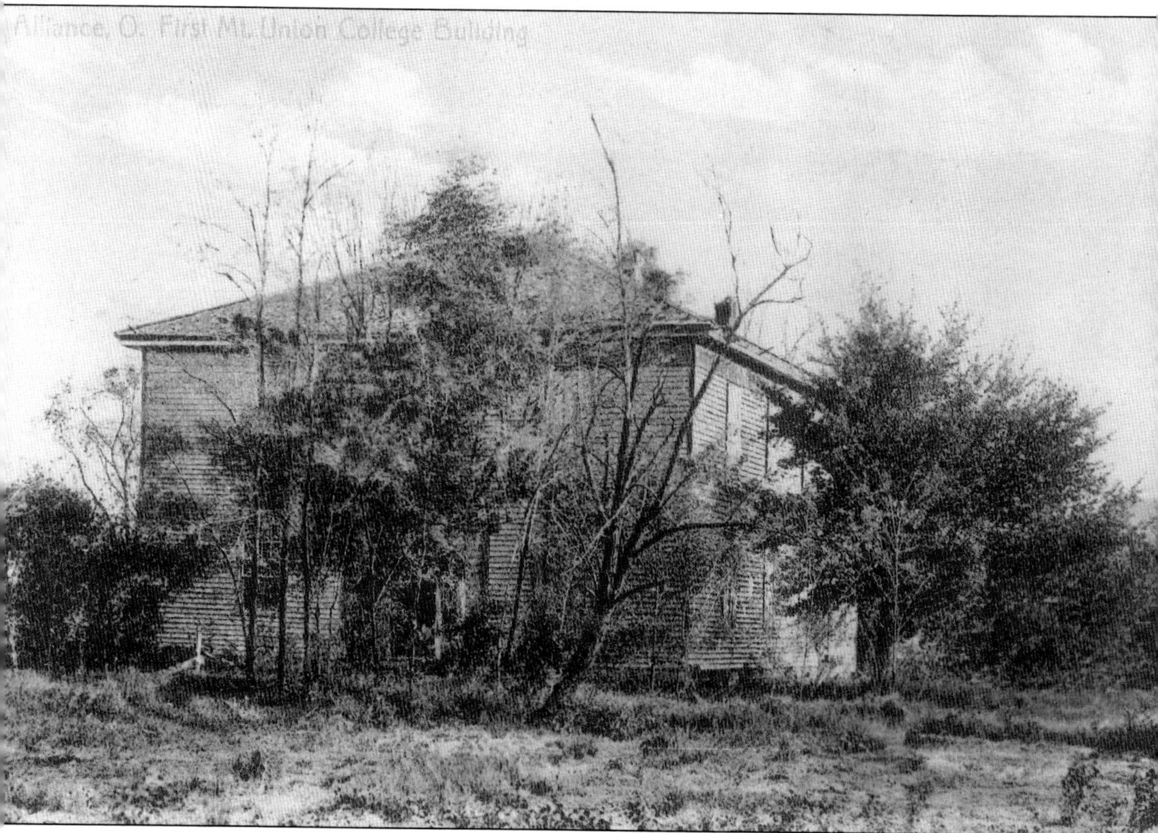

Pictured is the very first Mount Union College building.

INTRODUCTION

In the 1830s, "Mount Union" was the name for a new village; surveys showed that the locality was among highest in Ohio. Thus all agreed to "Mount"—so "Union" was in order when the subscription school opened.

Orville Nelson Hartshorn came to the area after completing his freshman year at Allegheny college in Meadville, PA. "Subscription School" opened October 20, 1846, with six pupils, one of which was Hartshorn's brother.

The school was originally in a carding mill. After one year, Hartshorn returned to Allegheny and finished school in 1849, then returned to Mt. Union. The school was then known as the "Mount Union Seminary." Hartshorn wanted to continue to build the school, and felt that some day it would be a college.

By 1851 enrollment had increased enough that enlarged grounds and a new building were needed. The seminary building was located at the eastern end of what is now Founders Park, opposite where the Memorial Hall used to be. Get this: closing exercises for 1851, like those of 1850, were held on July Tuition charges which varied from $3 to $4 depending on the classes selected.

A classmate with Hartshorn at Allegheny was Oscar Chapman, and Principal Hartshorn's brother E.N. Hartshorn in 1857 was made a professor of natural science. Hartshorn wanted a Christian basis for the school and so chapels were held each morning, and on Sundays all students were expected to go to church.

The charter as a College came in 1858 and the school was for the first time known as "Mount Union College." The First commencement exercises were then held. Forty-four students were in attendance in 1957.

Co-education was dramatic main aspect of the college, and by 1873, the graduation class consisted of 195 graduates; 28 of whom were women.

In 1866 President Hartshorn said that 1,090 students had served as volunteers in the Union army during Civil War.

Enrollment numbered more than 700 students by 1868. The cornerstone for

Chapman Hall was laid July 4th, 1862. Use of the new building began in the spring term of 1864. Some years later it was known as "Chapman" to commemorate Ira Chapman's work. But it wasn't known as Chapman Hall at that time.

The first college sport played was baseball. The Morgan Gymnasium was built on campus in 1891.

Enrollment by 1870 was nearly 700. Degrees for women were identified slightly differently: "M.L.A.," did it refer to Master of Liberal Arts? It did, actually, refer to "Mistress of Liberal Arts" offered in the 1870s. M.E.L. was the degree Mistress of English Literature.

Orville Hartshorn had been head of the institution for 41 years. Tamerlane Pliny Marsh became president in the years 1888–1898 and then President Riker was in charge from 1898 to 1908.

Among the possibilities, a Ph.D. degree was offered by 1872. Also, there was a military program at Mount which consisted of drill parading and lectures on military tactics and theory.

William Henry McMaster became the fourth president in 1908—just nine years after he had graduated from Mount Union himself.

In 1911 Scio College in southern Ohio was merged with Mount Union.

Among new buildings at Mount Union then were Elliott Hall, for which the cornerstone was laid in 1913. Also Lamborn Science Hall was underway in September, 1912.

But then the entrance of the United States into World War I minimized any new structural improvements. The cornerstone for Soldiers Memorial Hall ceremonies were held in 1921. Enrollment reached over 500 by 1927.

Charles Burgess Ketcham became the fifth president; he had a bachelor's degree from Ohio Wesleyan, a divinity degree from Drew University, and a master of arts from Columbia University. He had taught at Mount Union and had also served as an army chaplain, then had been a pastor in four Ohio cities.

The 1945-46 post-war enrollment nearly doubled that of the previous year. Returning veterans in fall of 1946 brought total enrollment to 902. Over 400 of the students were veterans.

Married veterans of World War II were placed in some 30 white trailers and the campus area was known as "White Hollow." A new library was dedicated in 1950.

Carl Bracy was named president following the death of Dr. Ketcham.

In expanding activities on and off campus, the College choir expanded appearances. First they traveled to Oslo, Norway, in 1961. Then in 1966 the choir performed in Alaska, Japan, India, Grcccc, Italy, England, and France.

On campus there was a new men's residence hall in 1960 and then the Hoover-Price Campus Center was opened in 1962. The Cope Music Hall was completed in 1964

Through the college's history, campus enrichment has never ceased and enrollment has now reached some 2,000.

One

The Mount Union of Old

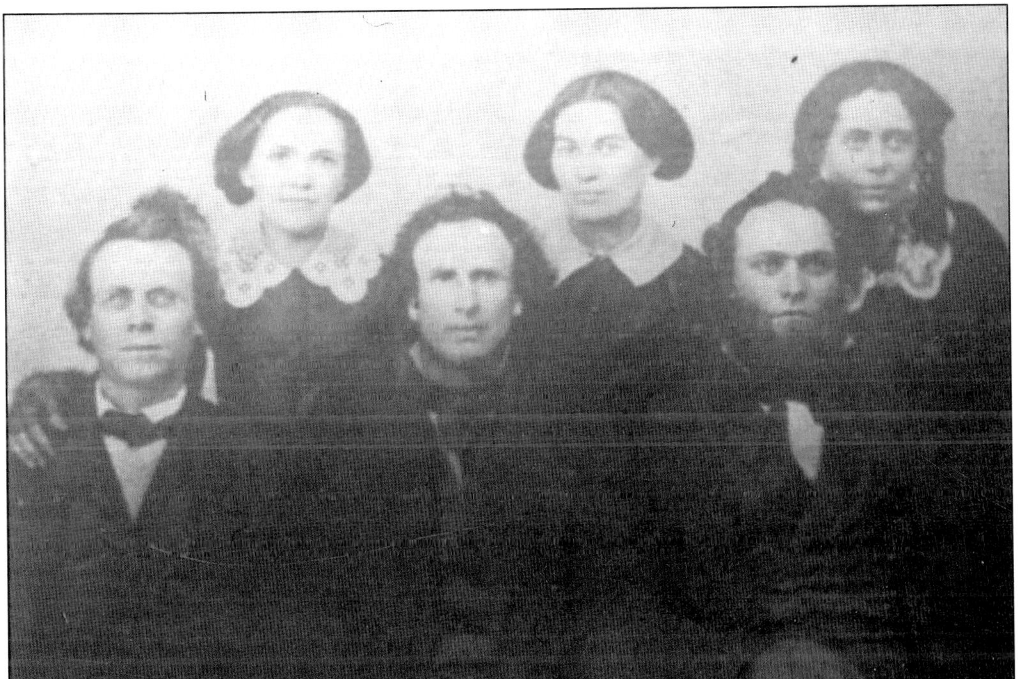

The founders of the College are pictured, from left to right, with their wives: Mrs. Chapman, Prof. I.O. Chapman, Mrs. Hartshorn, Dr. O.N. Hartshorn, Mrs. Clark, and Dr. G.W. Clark.

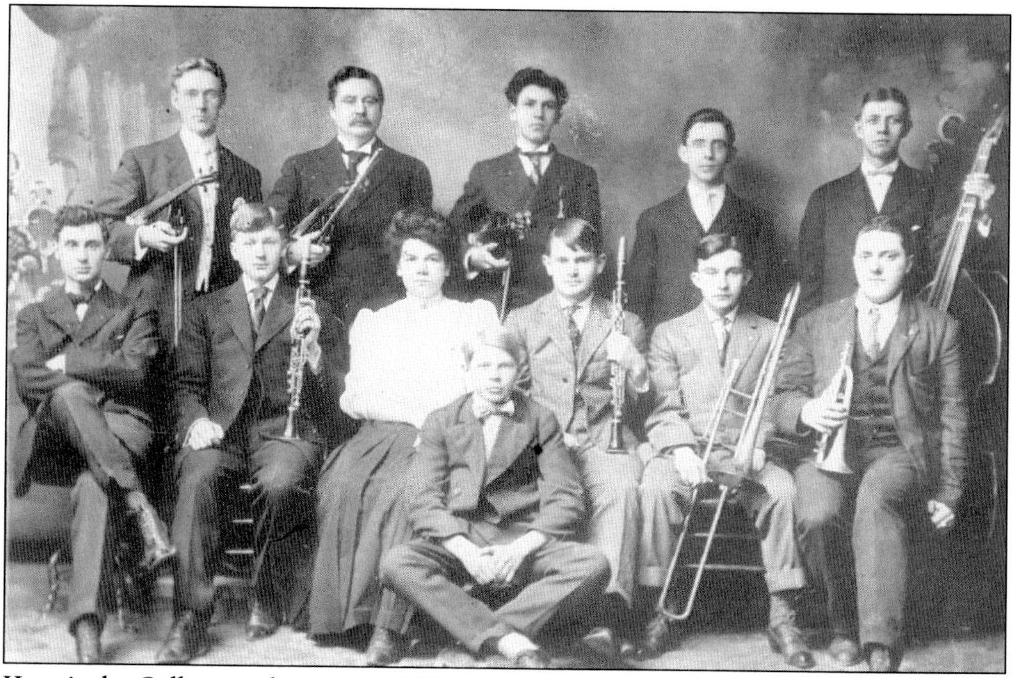

Here is the College orchestra in 1908.

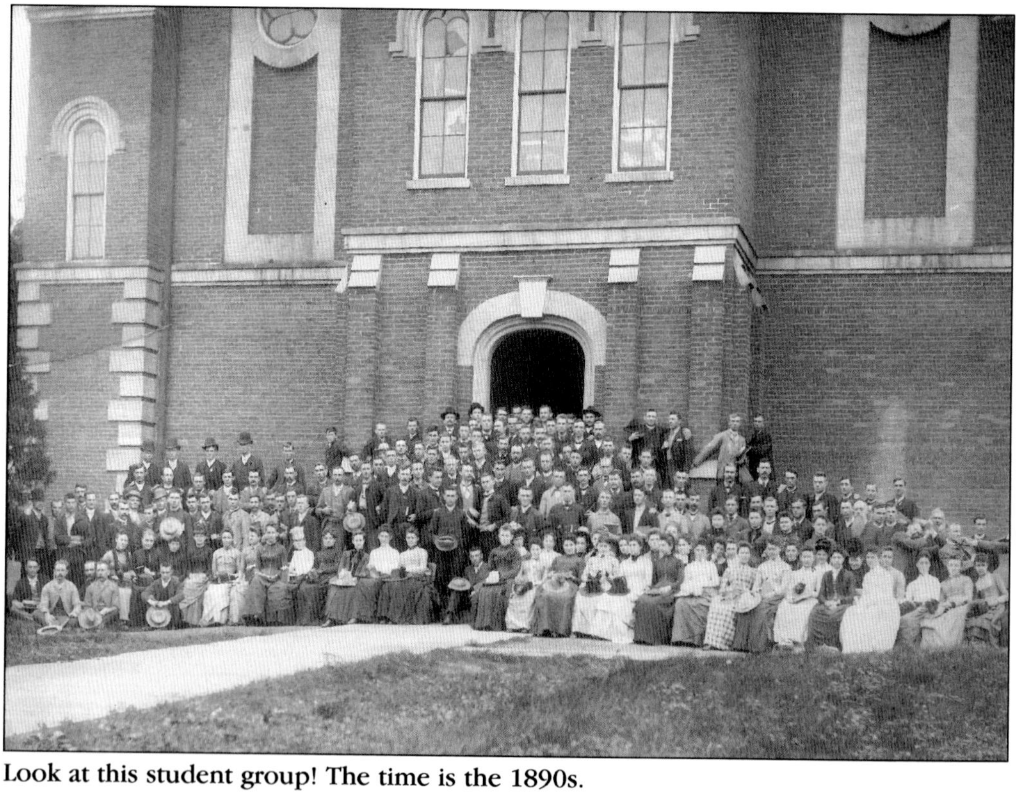

Look at this student group! The time is the 1890s.

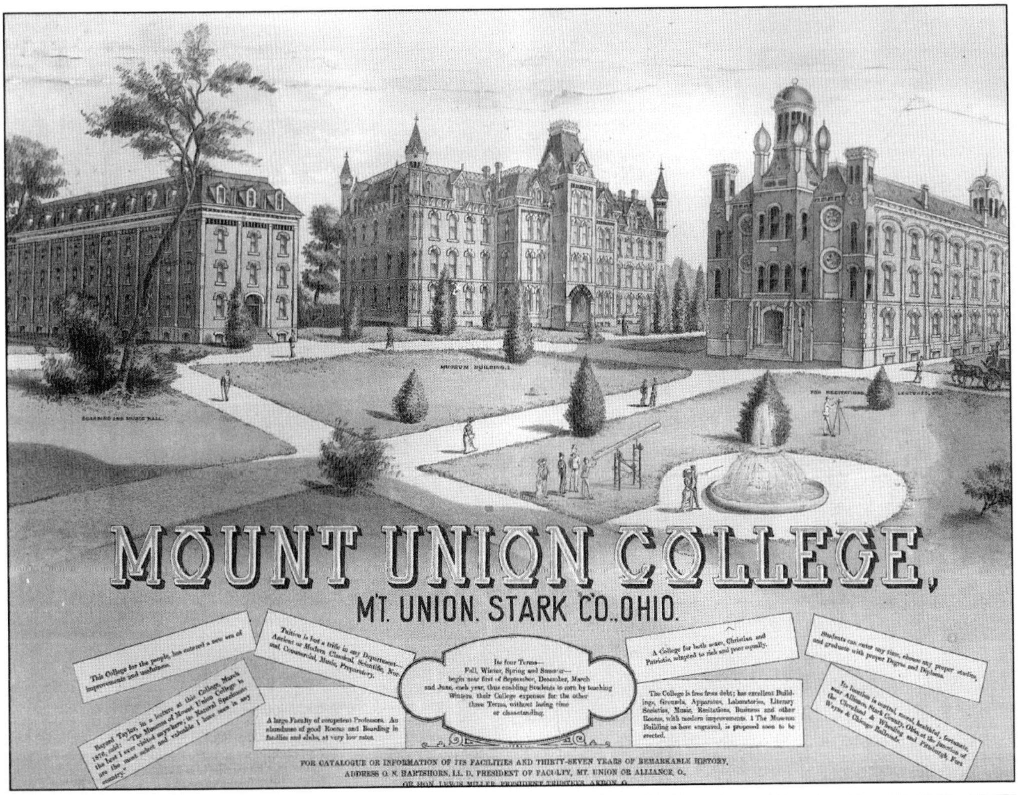

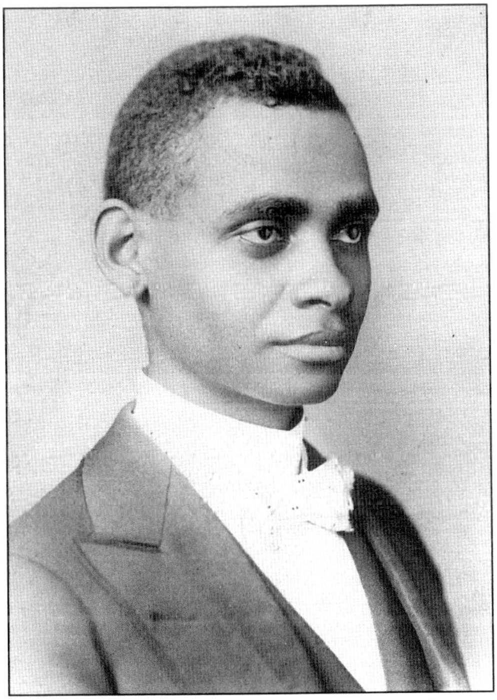

Wayne Manzilla was the first African American graduate from Mt. Union.

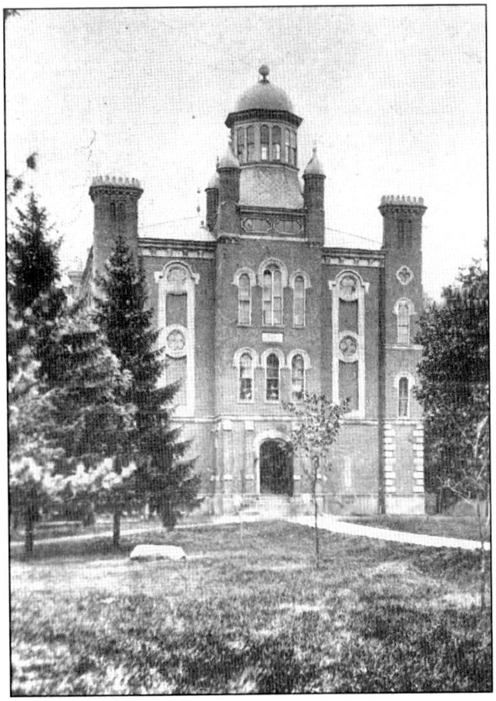

Here is a view of the Main College Building built in 1863.

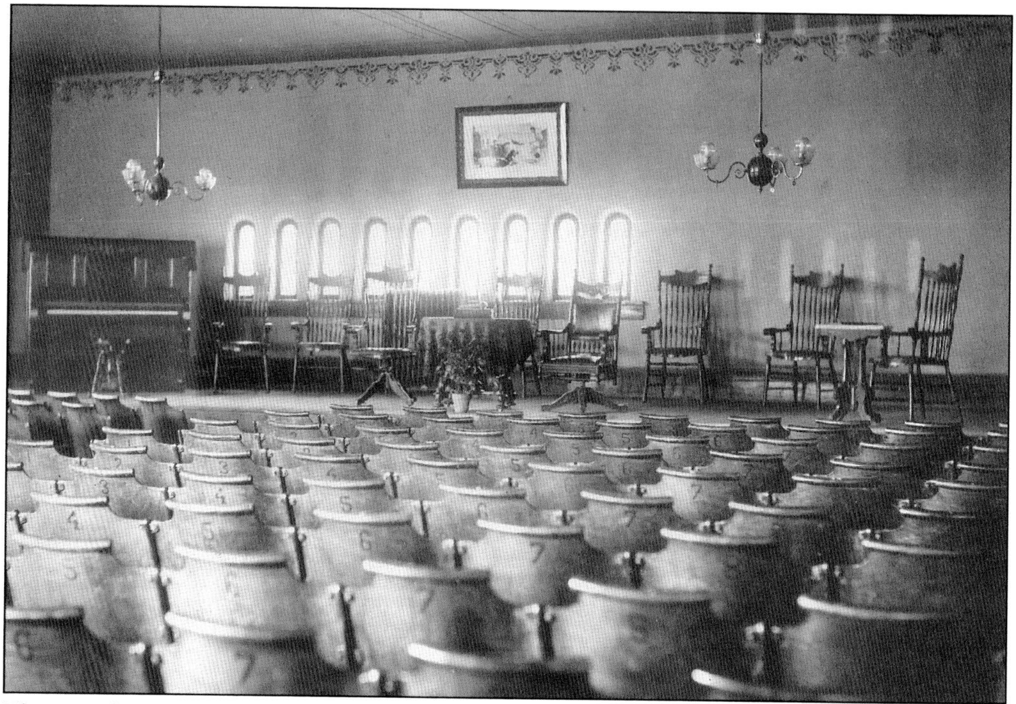

This is the Literary Hall of Scio College around 1900. Scio merged later with Mount Union.

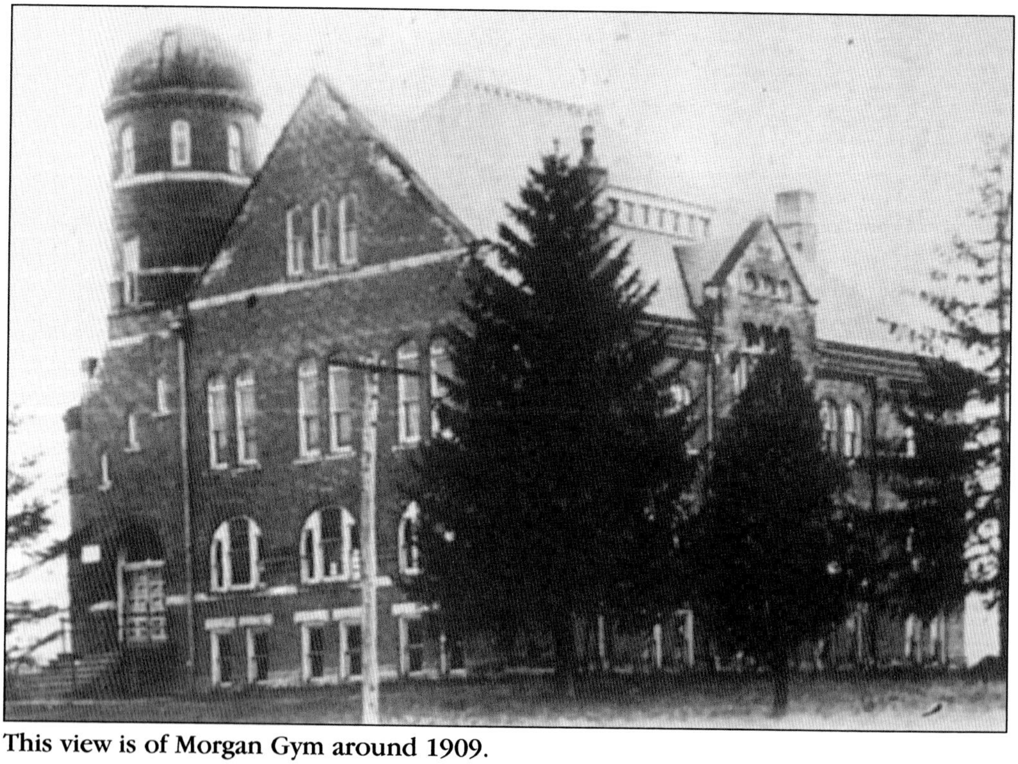

This view is of Morgan Gym around 1909.

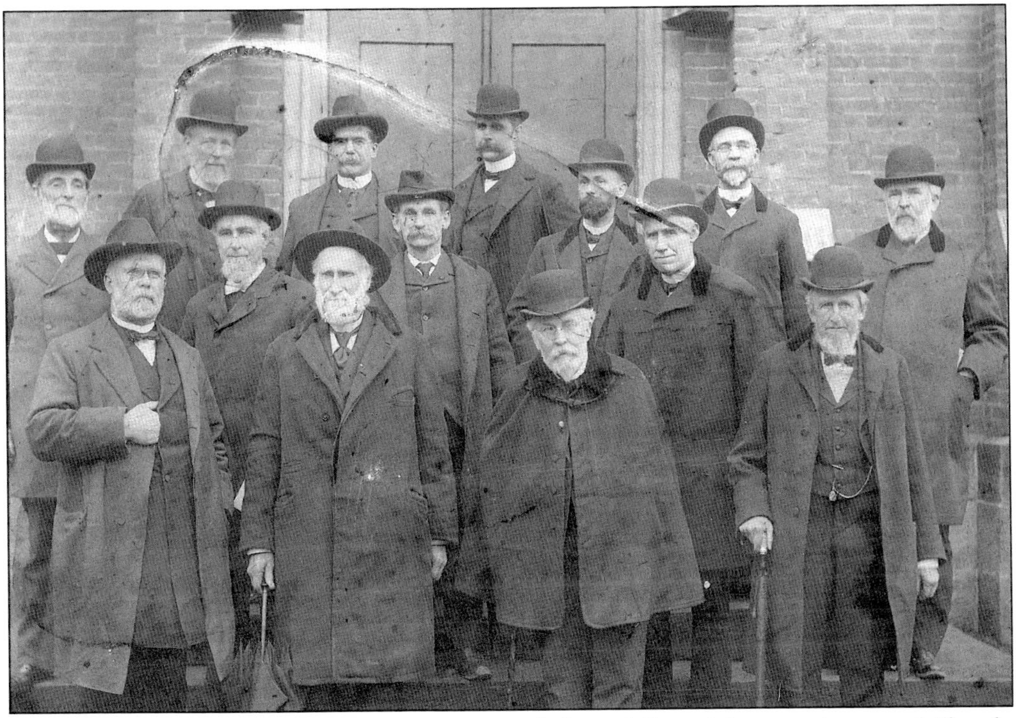

Here are the college trustees for 1901.Pictured, from left to right, are: (top row) Shunk, Carr, Moore, Laughrey, Ramseyraer, and Arter; (front row) Keyes, Sweeny, Hartshorn, Scranton, Marsh, Fording, and Stull.

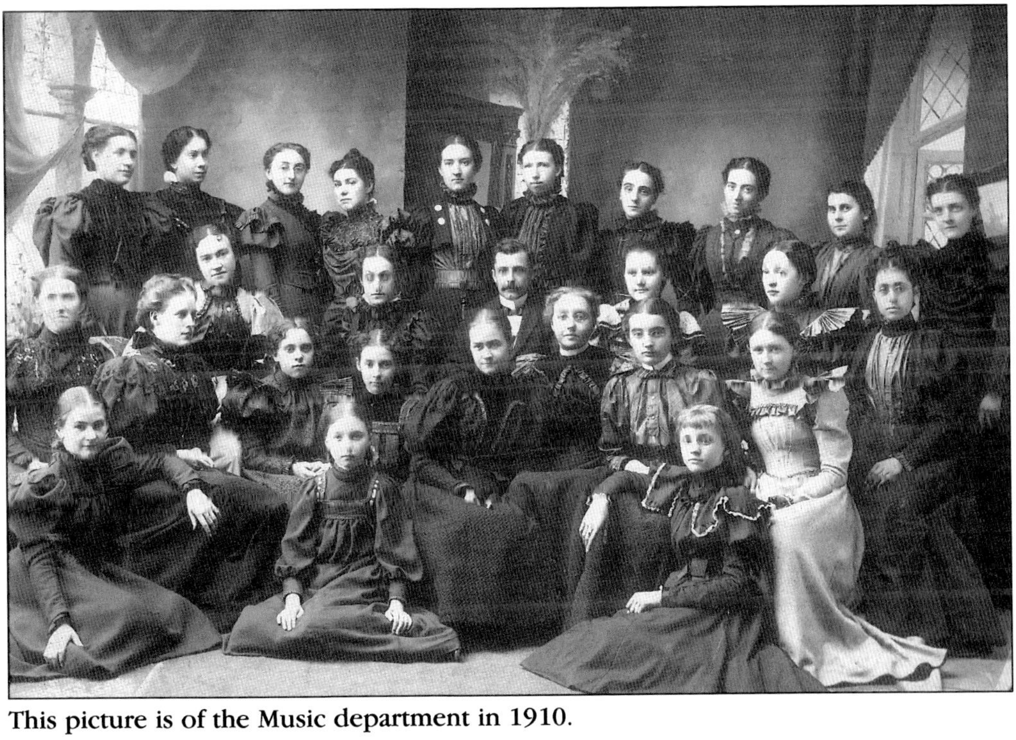

This picture is of the Music department in 1910.

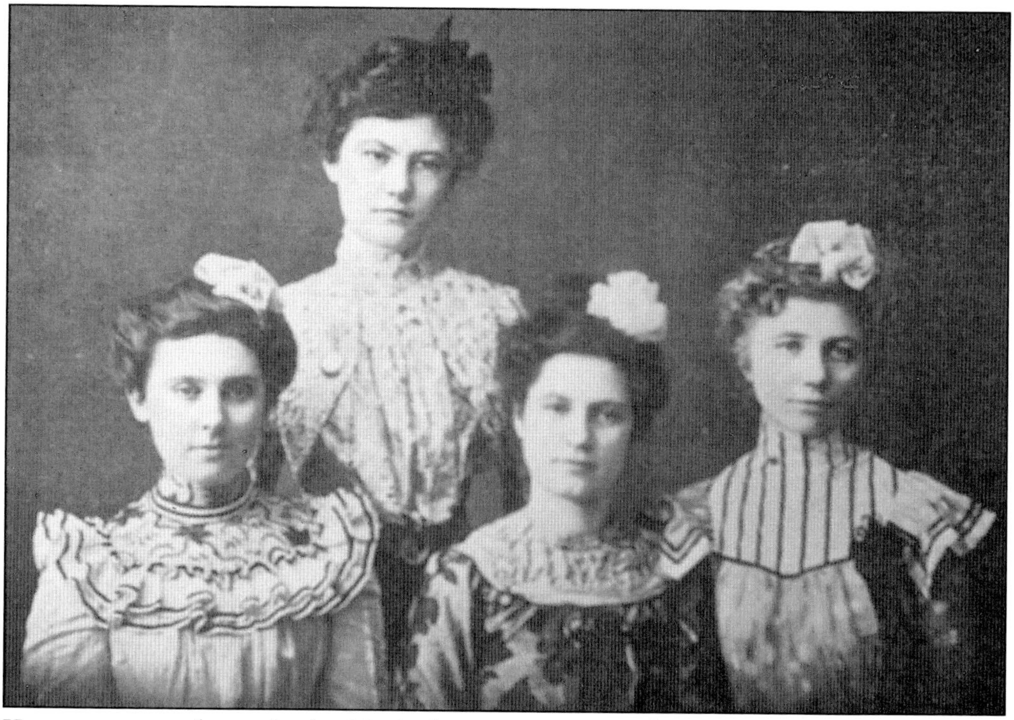

Here we see graduates in the Music department in 1906.

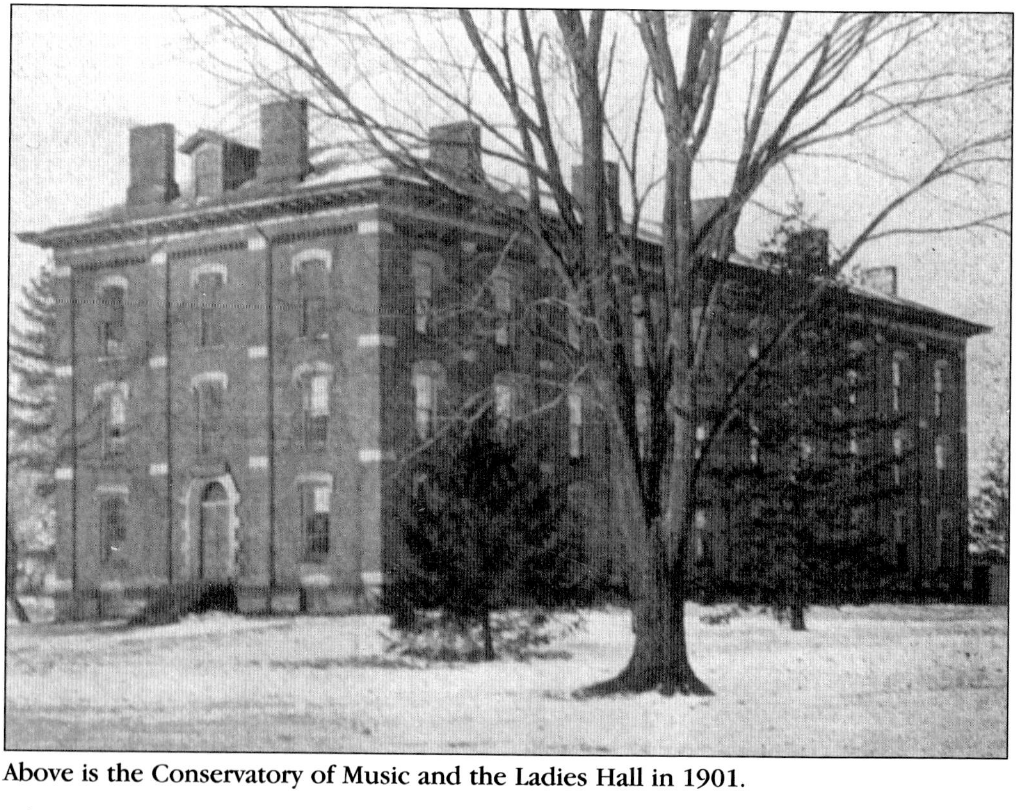

Above is the Conservatory of Music and the Ladies Hall in 1901.

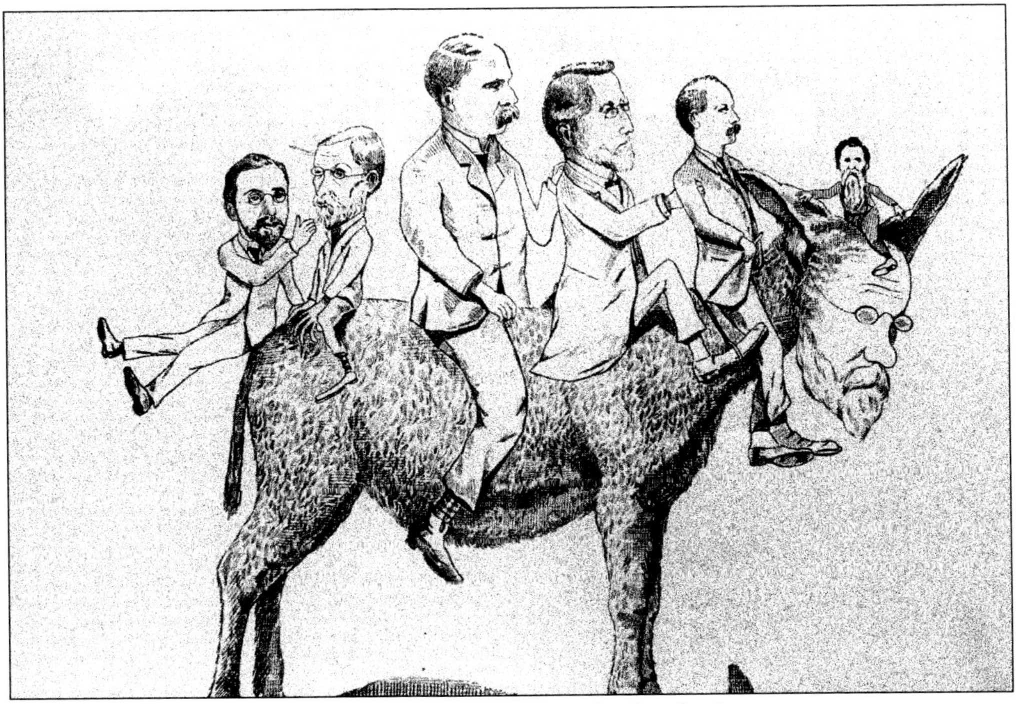

A film cartoon of 1902 states, "I think I can carry the faculty!"

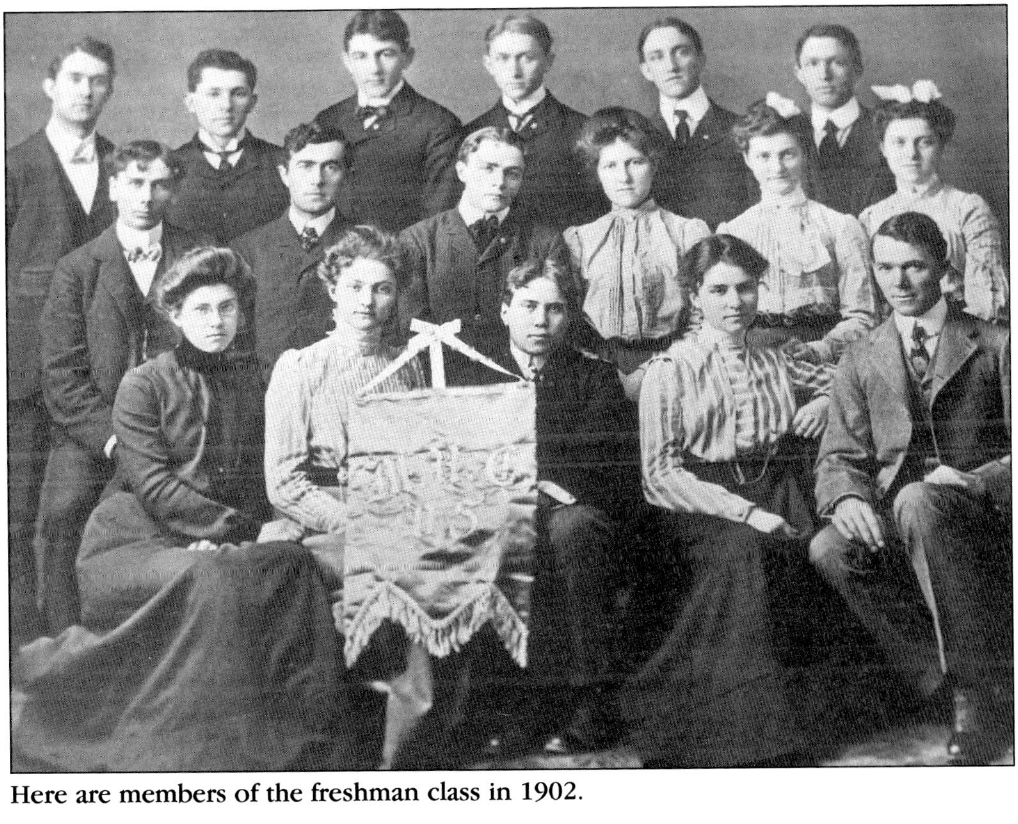

Here are members of the freshman class in 1902.

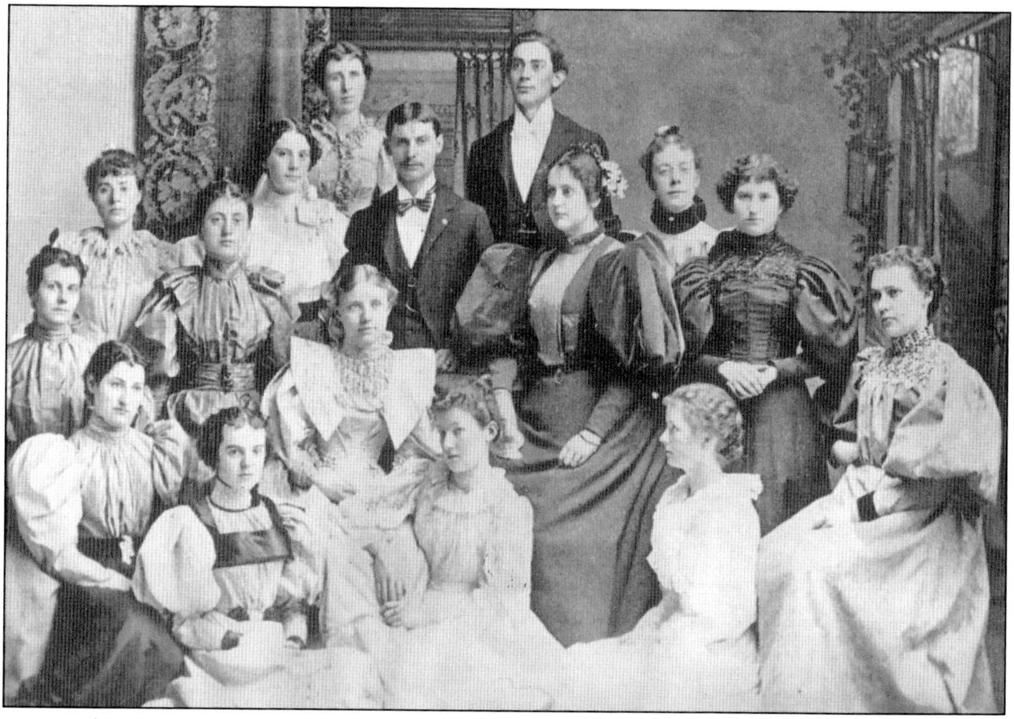

Pictured is the Conservatory of Music in 1905.

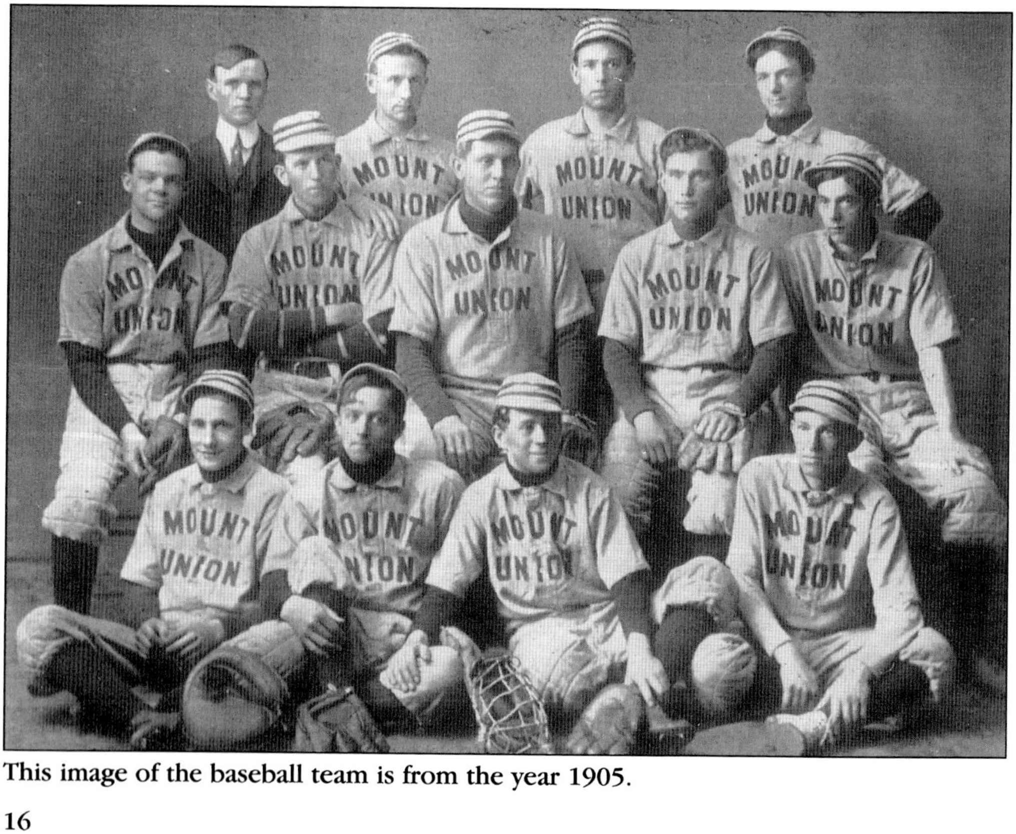

This image of the baseball team is from the year 1905.

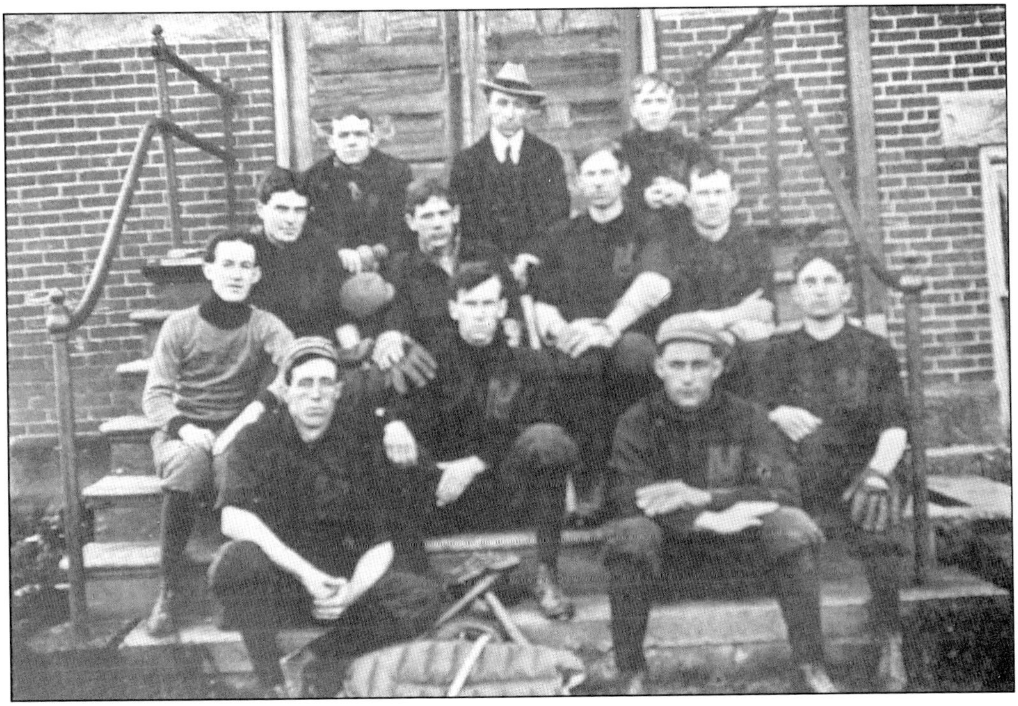

Pictured above is the baseball team of 1901. Below is an image of the basketball squad of 1905.

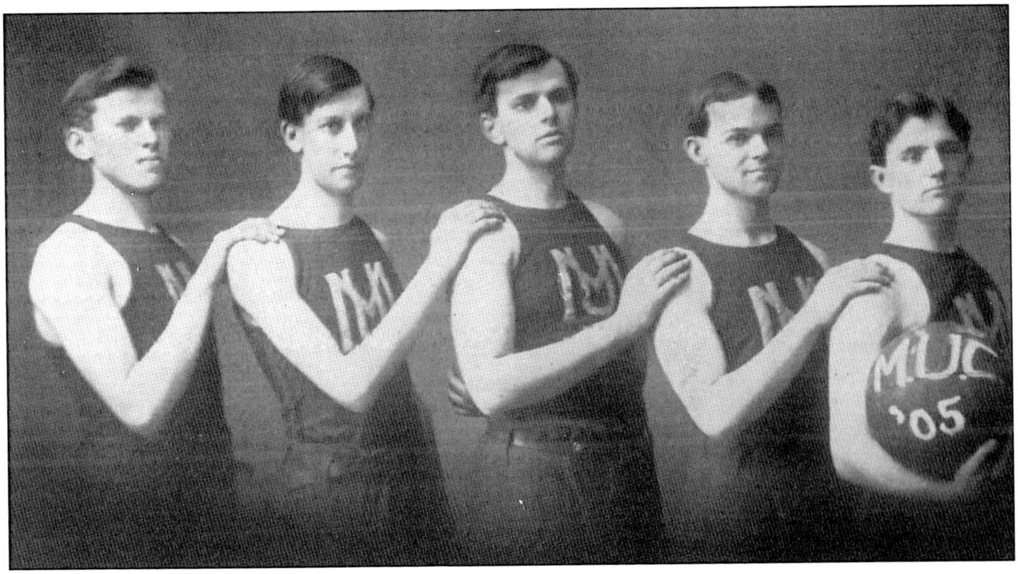

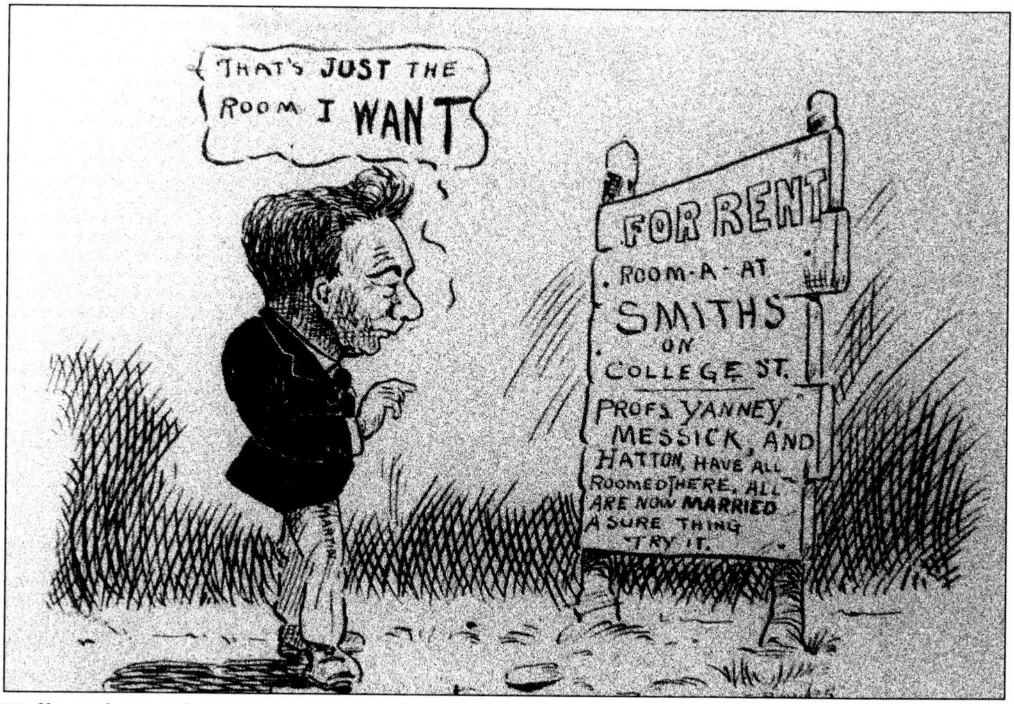

Well, we know that cartooning has long been a way of saying special things. Here's one, on campus, in 1907.

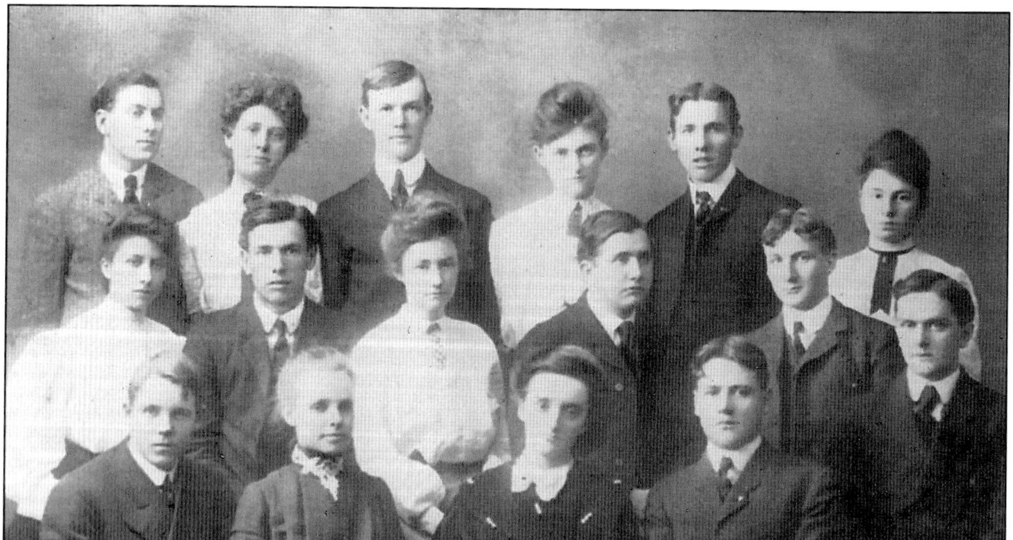

Here we see a group of sophomores, pictured from left to right: (back row) W.H. Seawright, Agnes Graham, C.F. Matthias, Lucille Strong, Arthur Oyster, Alice Snyder; (middle row) Ella Horn, W.H. Reinoehl, Mayme Davis, W.A. Wafls, H.H. Myers, and S.F. Hawkins; (front row) J.V. Kaho, Cora Haines, Lora Murphy, and S.C. Millard.

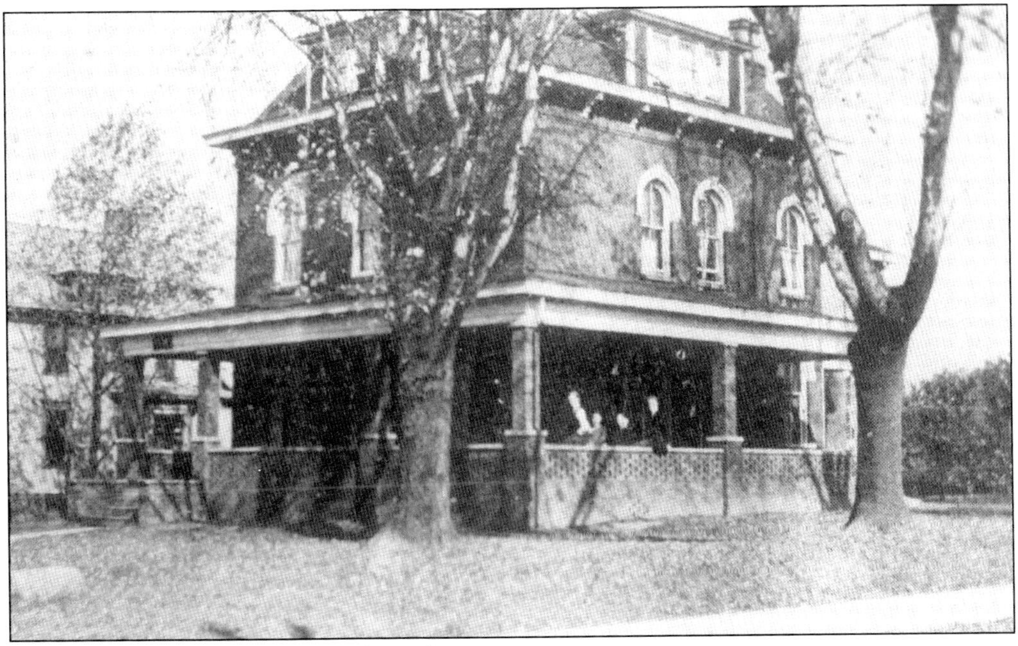

Here is the Sigma Nu house of 1916 . . .

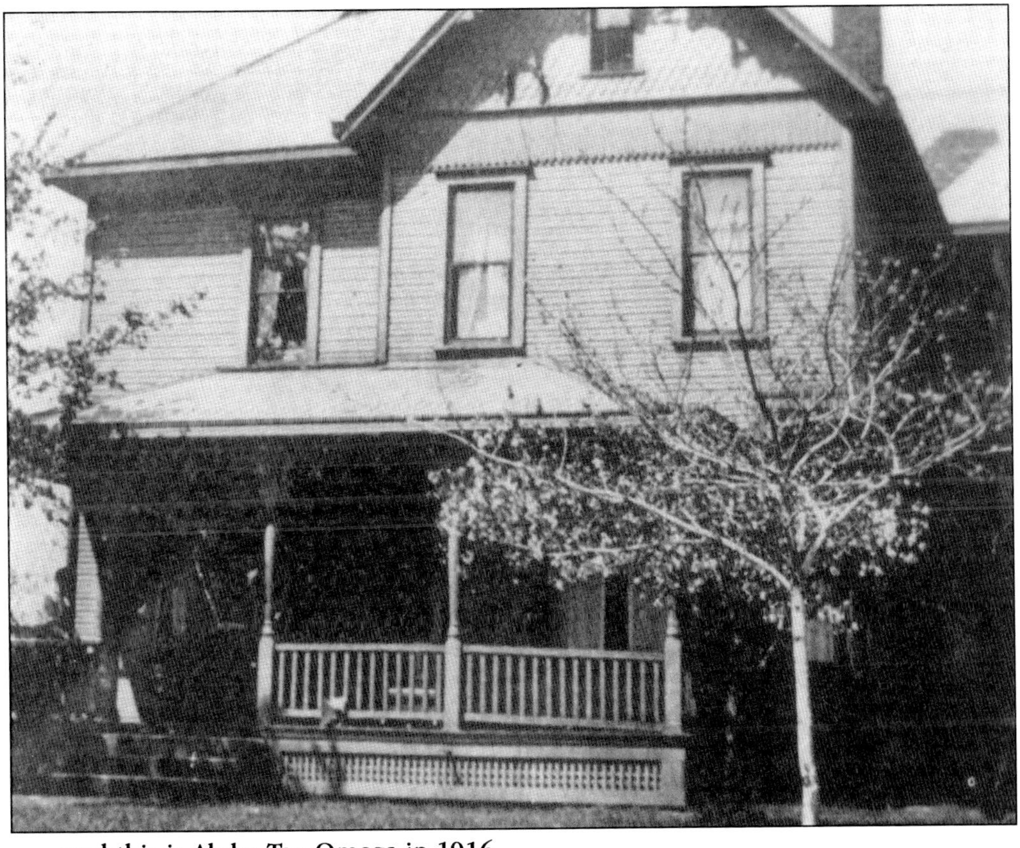

. . . and this is Alpha Tau Omega in 1916.

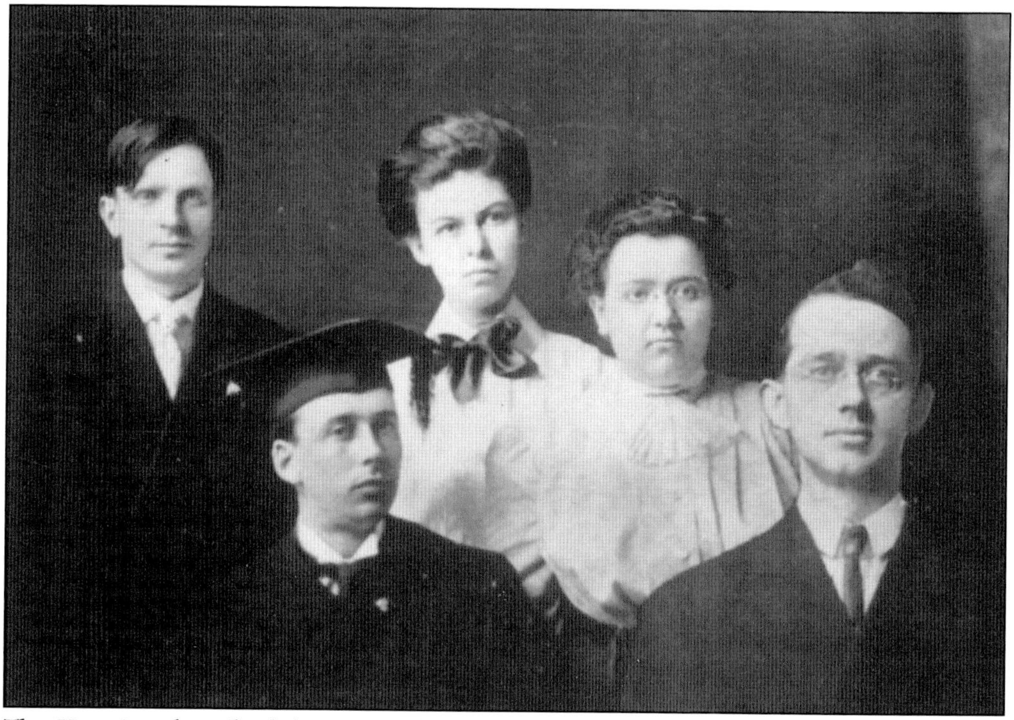

The *Unonian* described this as a volunteer band of 1909.

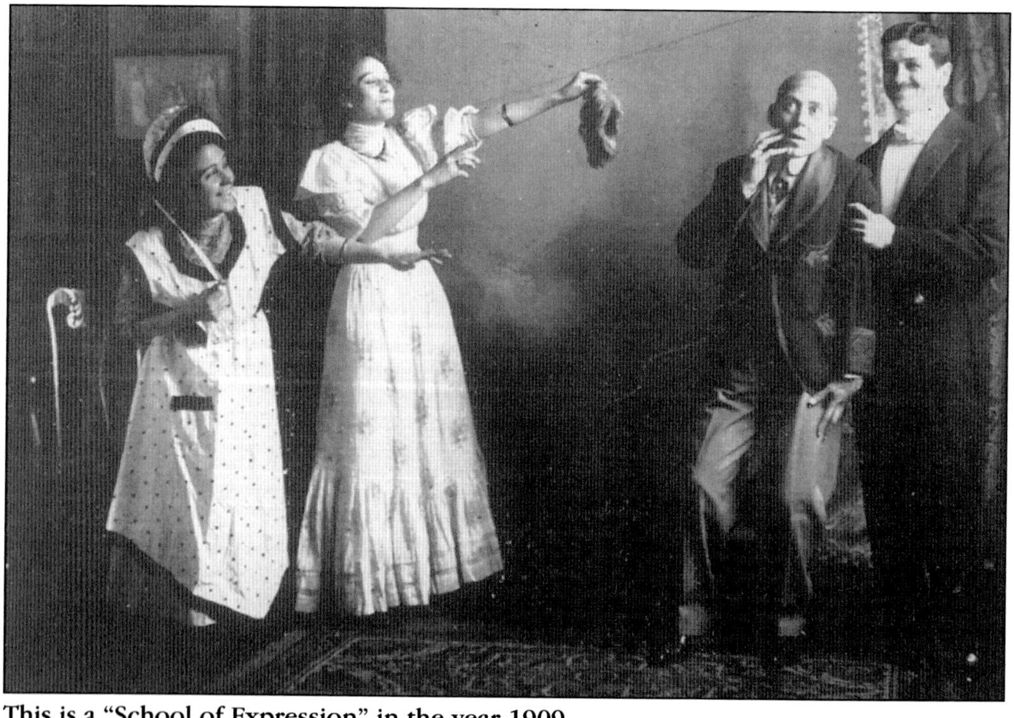

This is a "School of Expression" in the year 1909.

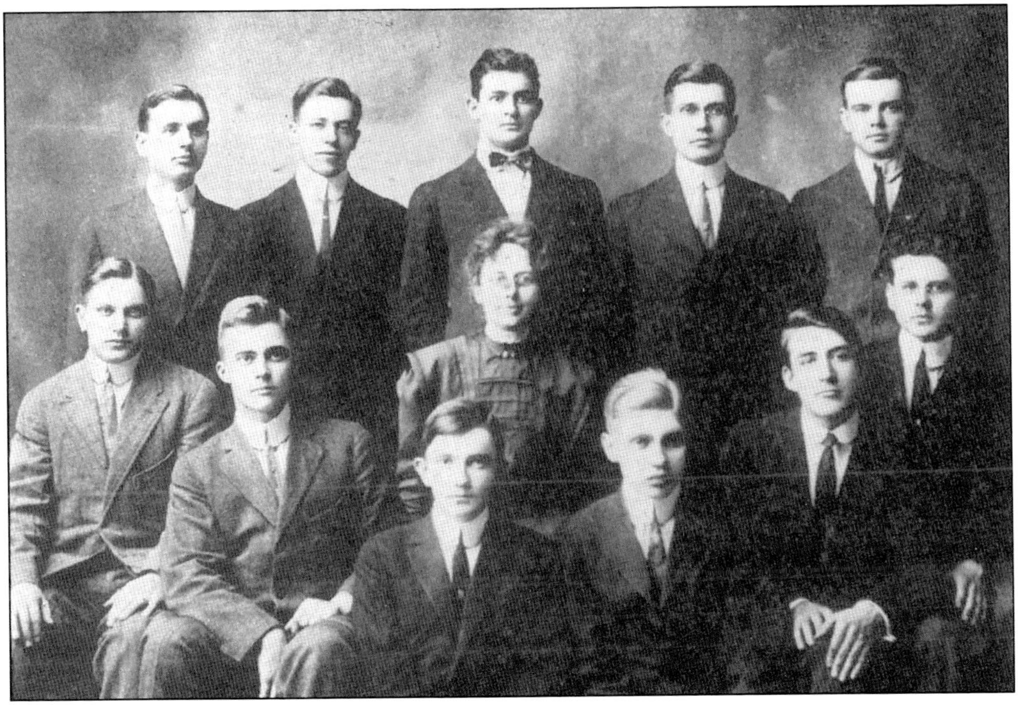

Here is the Men's Glee Club in 1912!

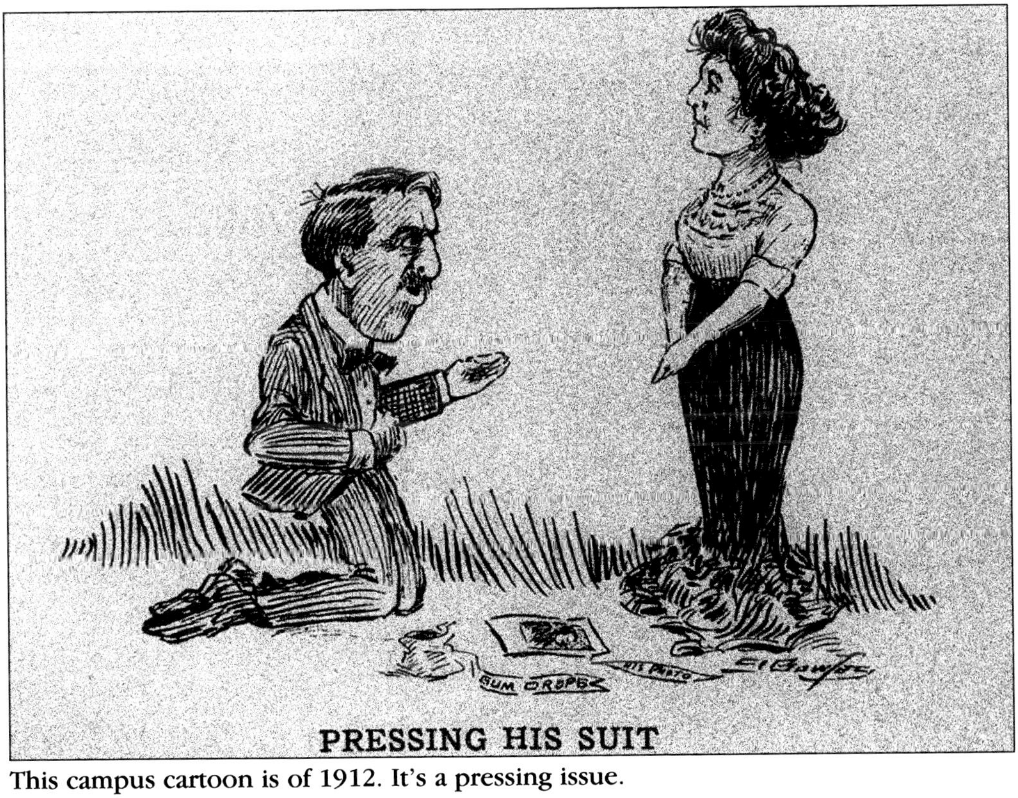

This campus cartoon is of 1912. It's a pressing issue.

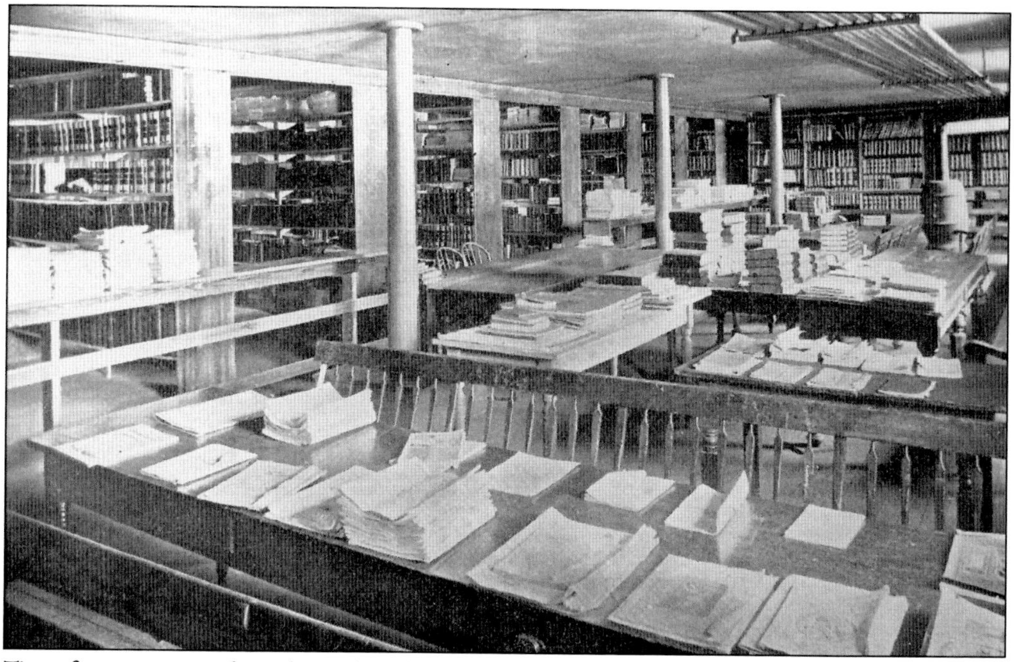

Time for some good study in the library reading room. This photo was taken in 1902.

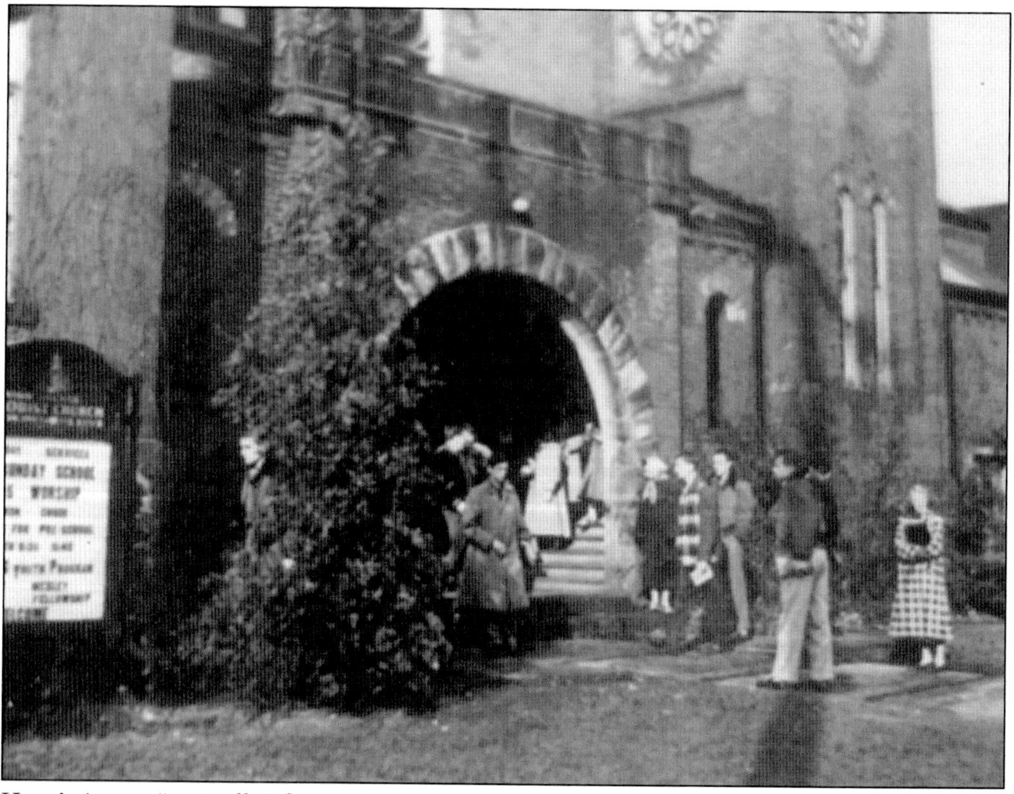

Here's just a "typically" fine view of students entering the Methodist Church, located by campus buildings and very active over the years.

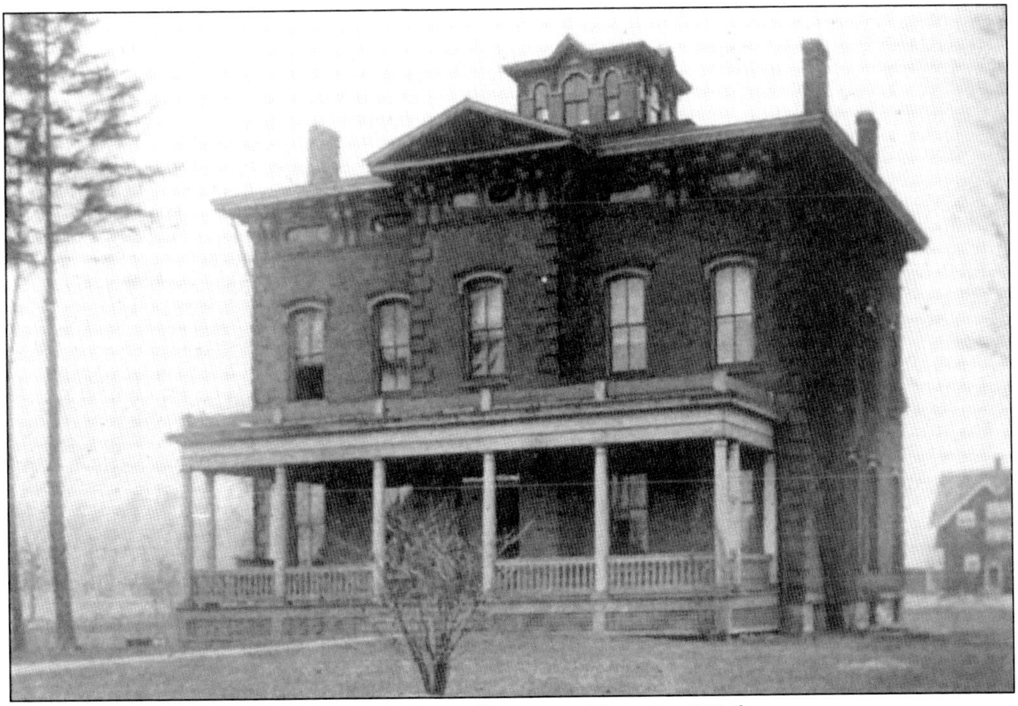

Here's a view of the residence of the college president in 1916.

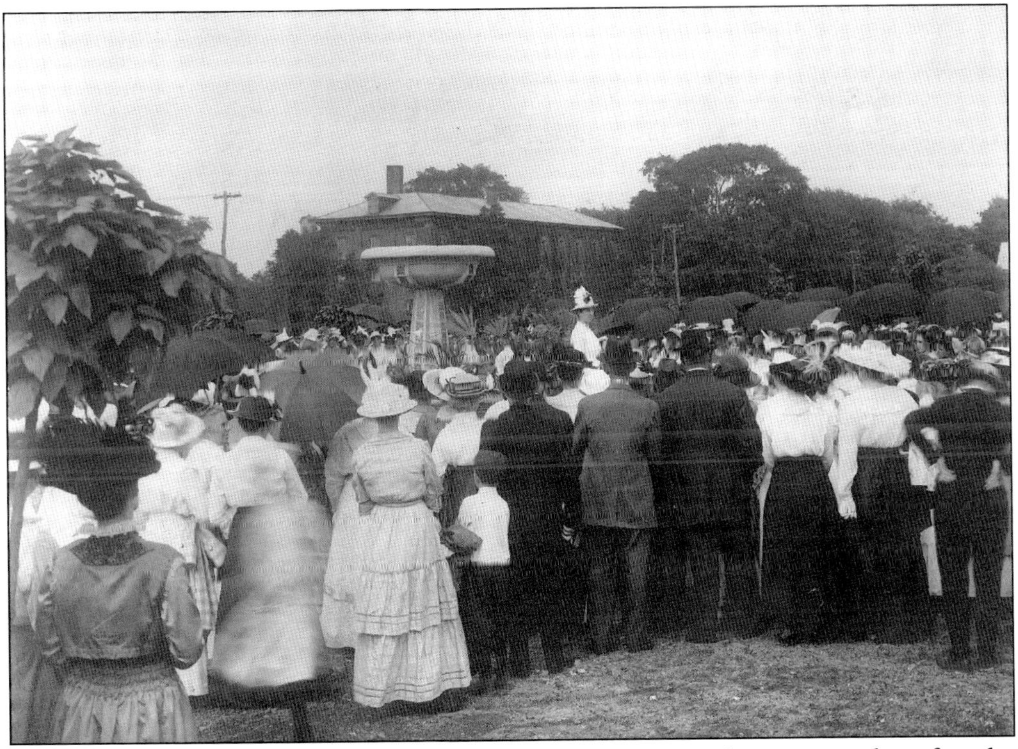

We see here the "Arethusa Fountain" on campus. The photo was taken for the "Founders Park" dedication in 1916.

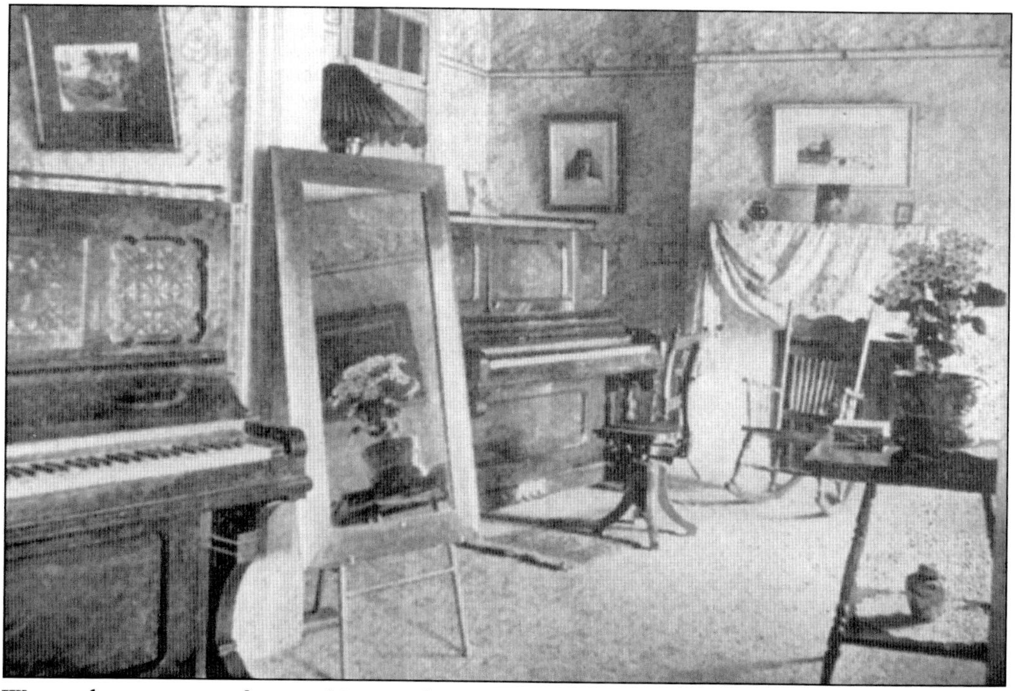

We see here a room for teaching in the conservatory. The year is 1897.

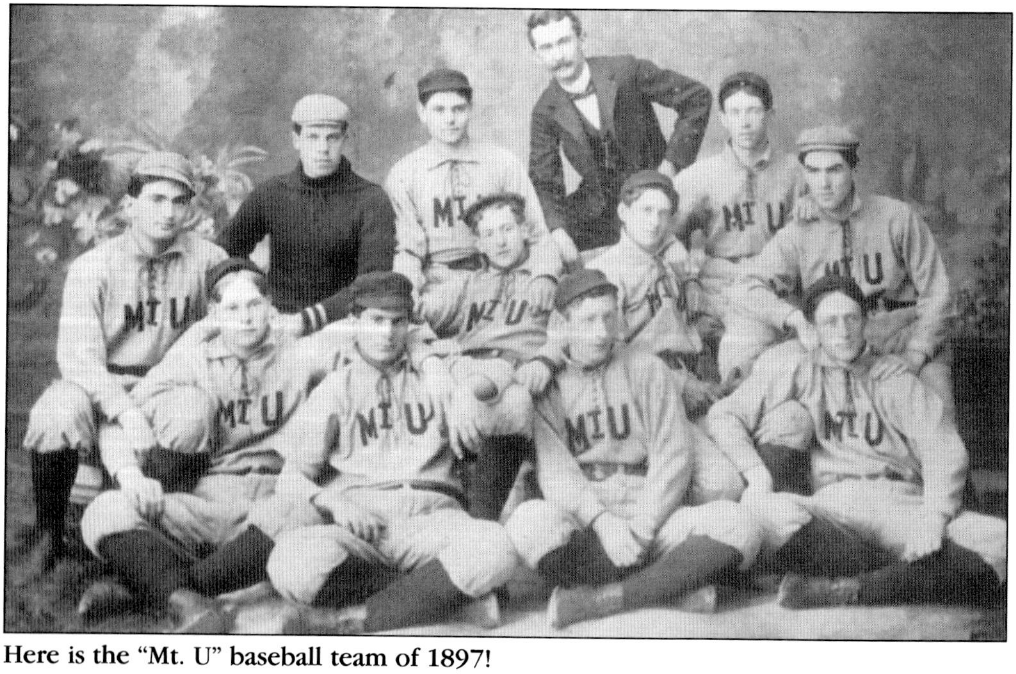

Here is the "Mt. U" baseball team of 1897!

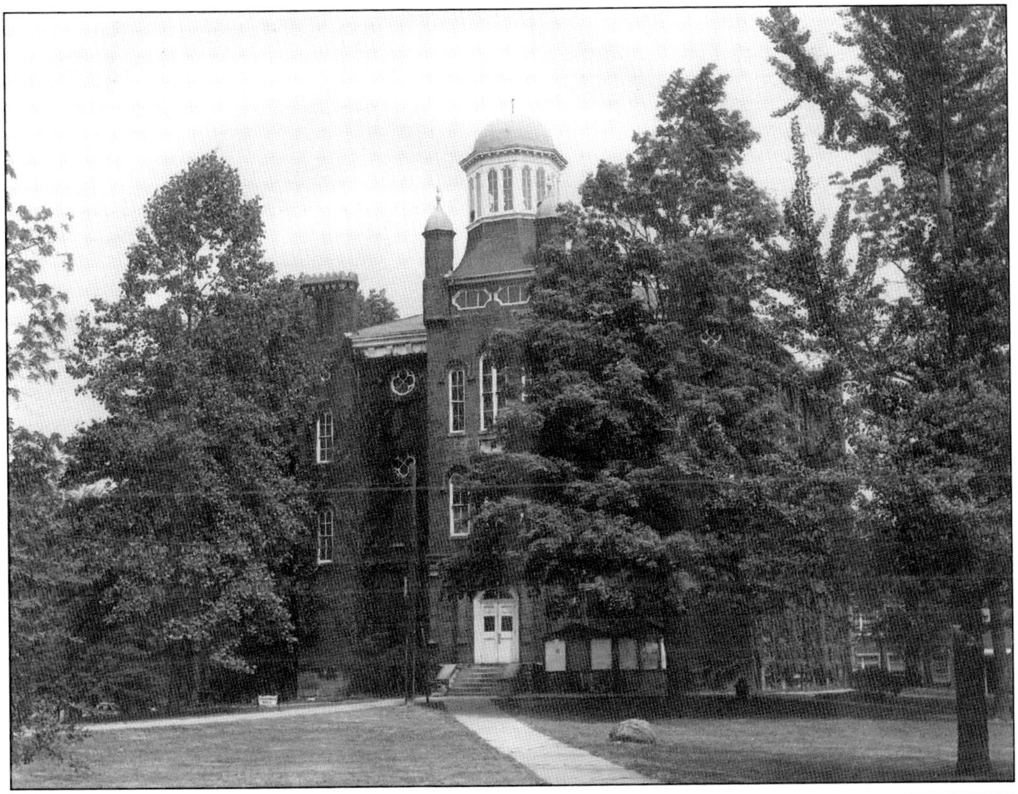

A building that has spanned more years on campus than any other, Chapman Hall is pictured in a typical view many years after the early-century photos. More will be coming.

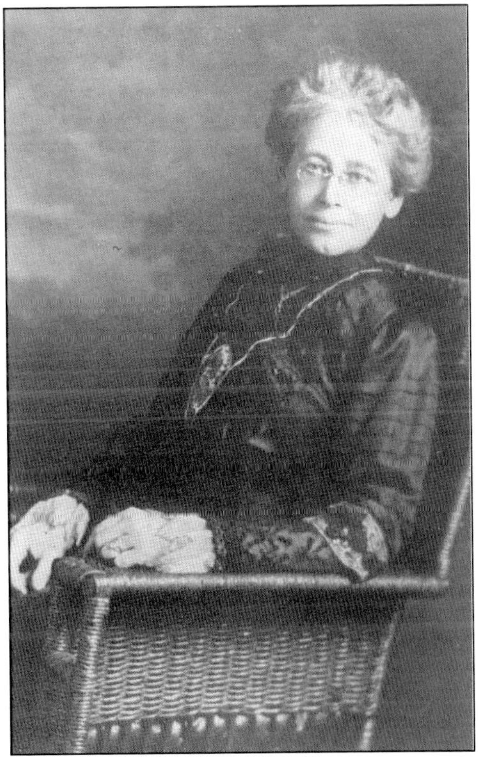

Here we see the Dean of Women from the year 1913. Her name is Mrs. Harriett Newhall Marsh.

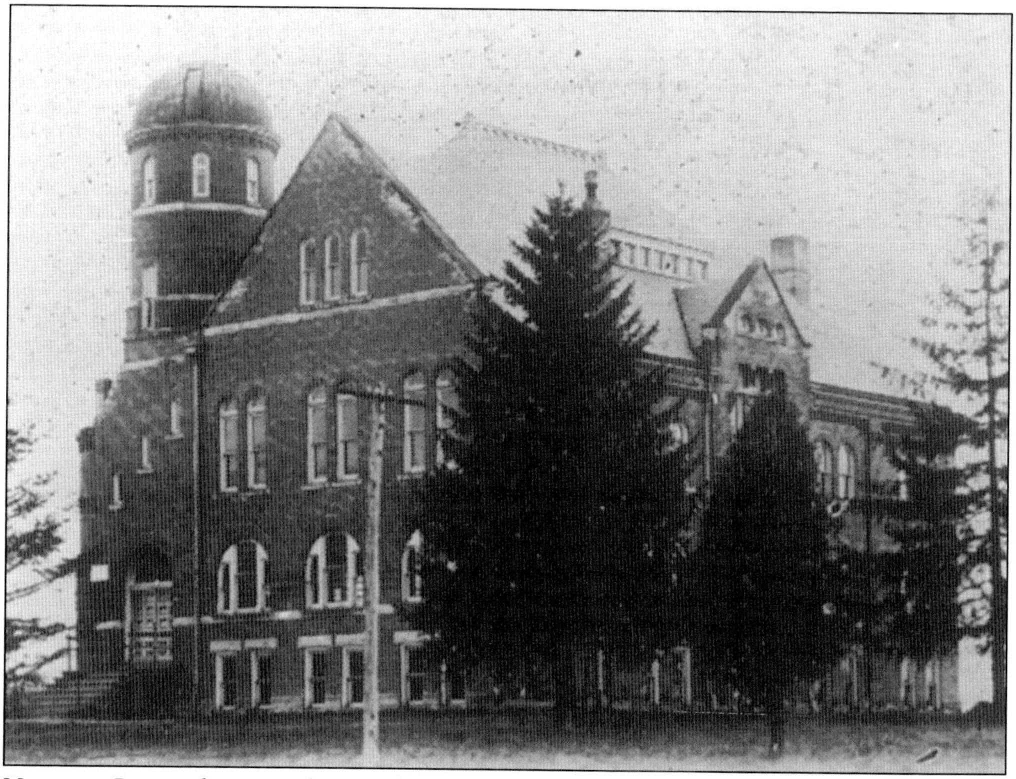

Morgan Gym—always a busy place for many campus activities—is seen in this 1909 image.

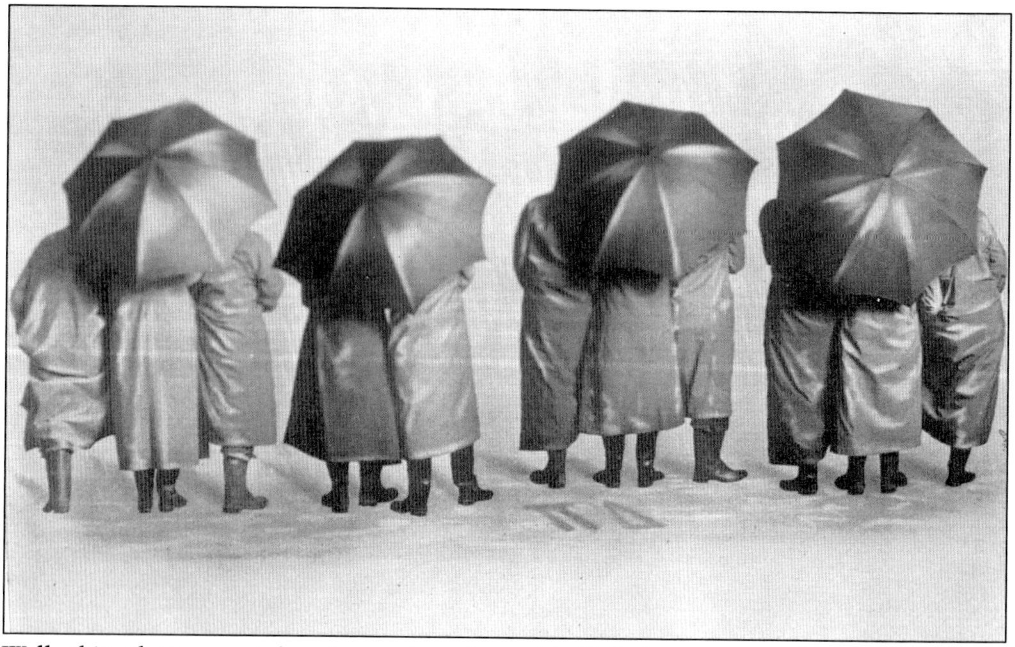

Well, this photo was taken in conjunction with Pi Delta, a group founded in 1906. However, not all were rainwalkers.

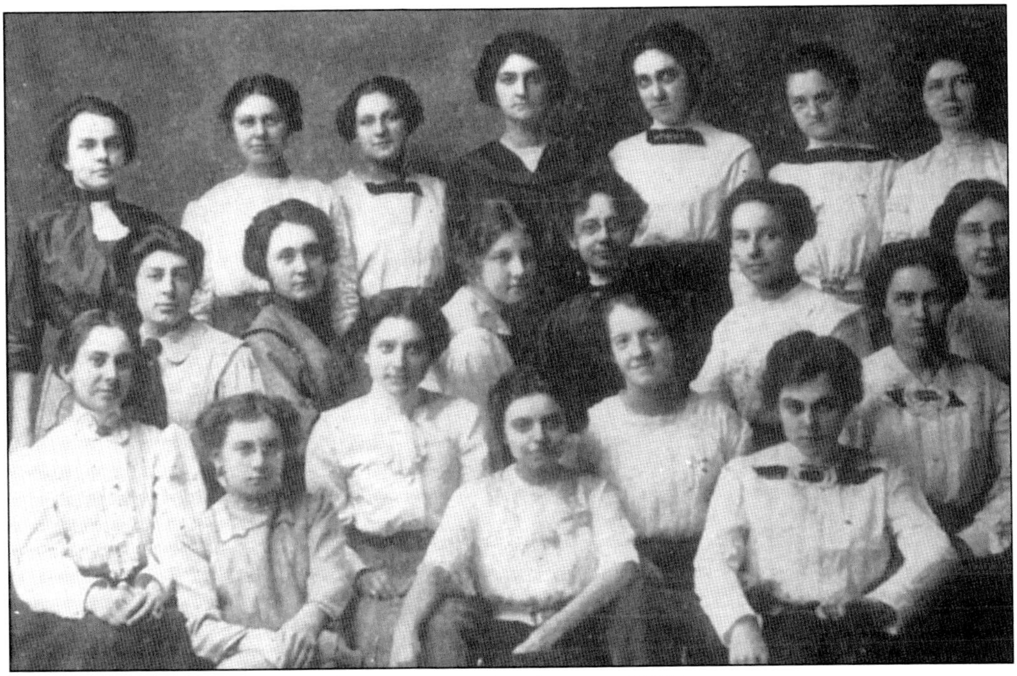

Here is the Ladies' Glee Club on campus in the year 1912.

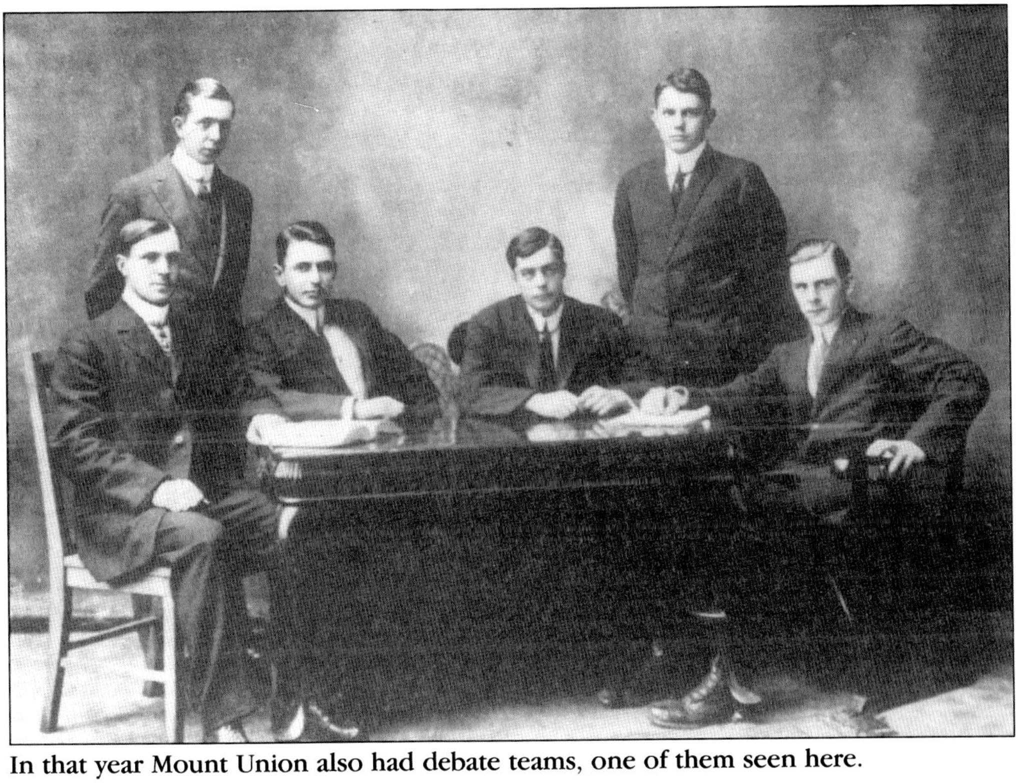

In that year Mount Union also had debate teams, one of them seen here.

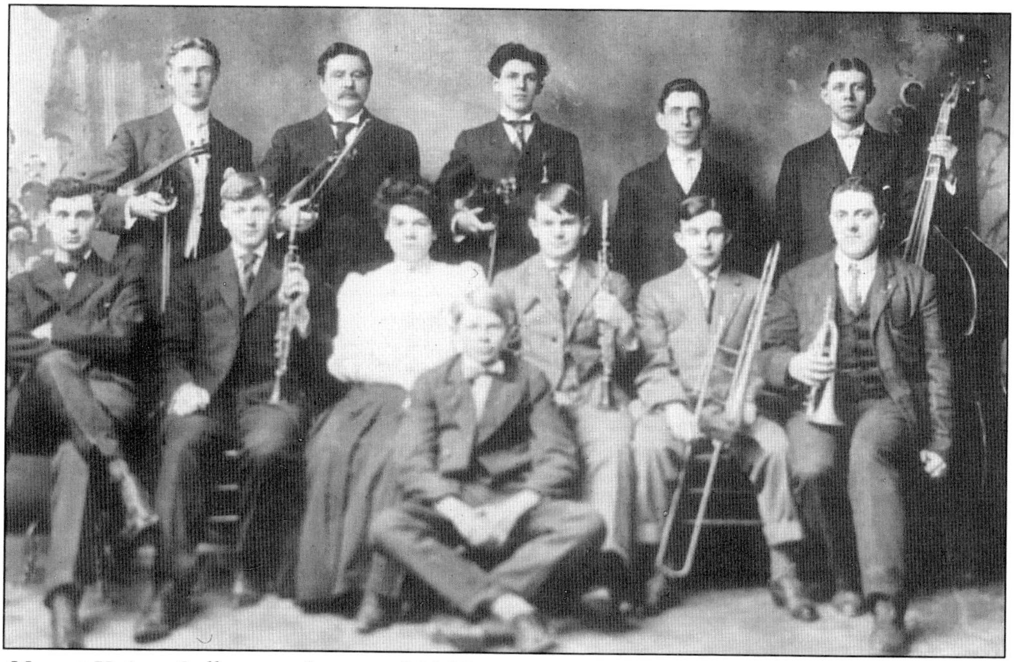

Mount Union College orchestra of 1908.

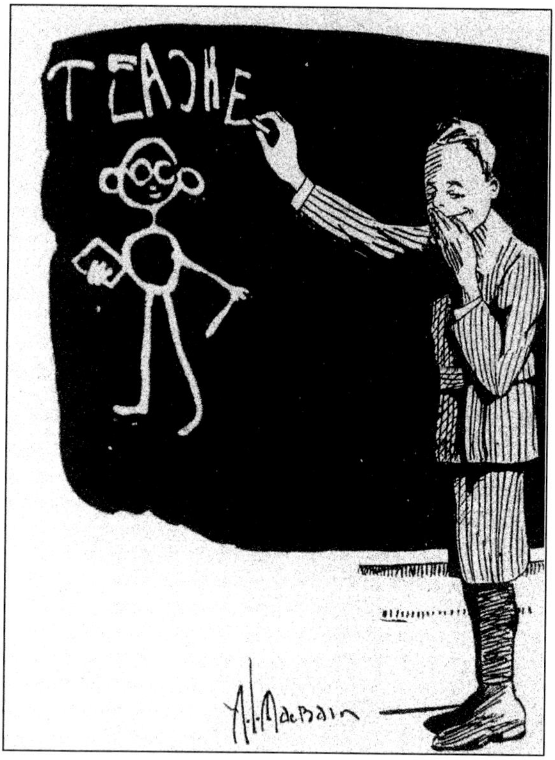

Here we have a cartoon of that era. Easy to make a silly picture of a teacher, but very, very hard to know how to spell the word!

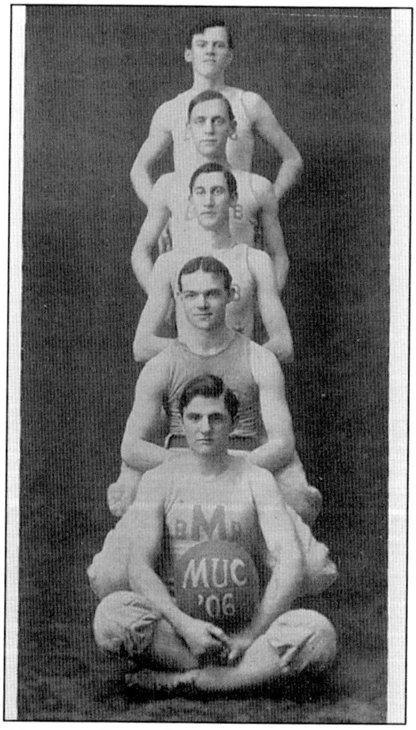

Next is the college basketball team of 1906. From bottom to top are Hact, Capt. Smith, Rickard, Riker, and Vaughn.

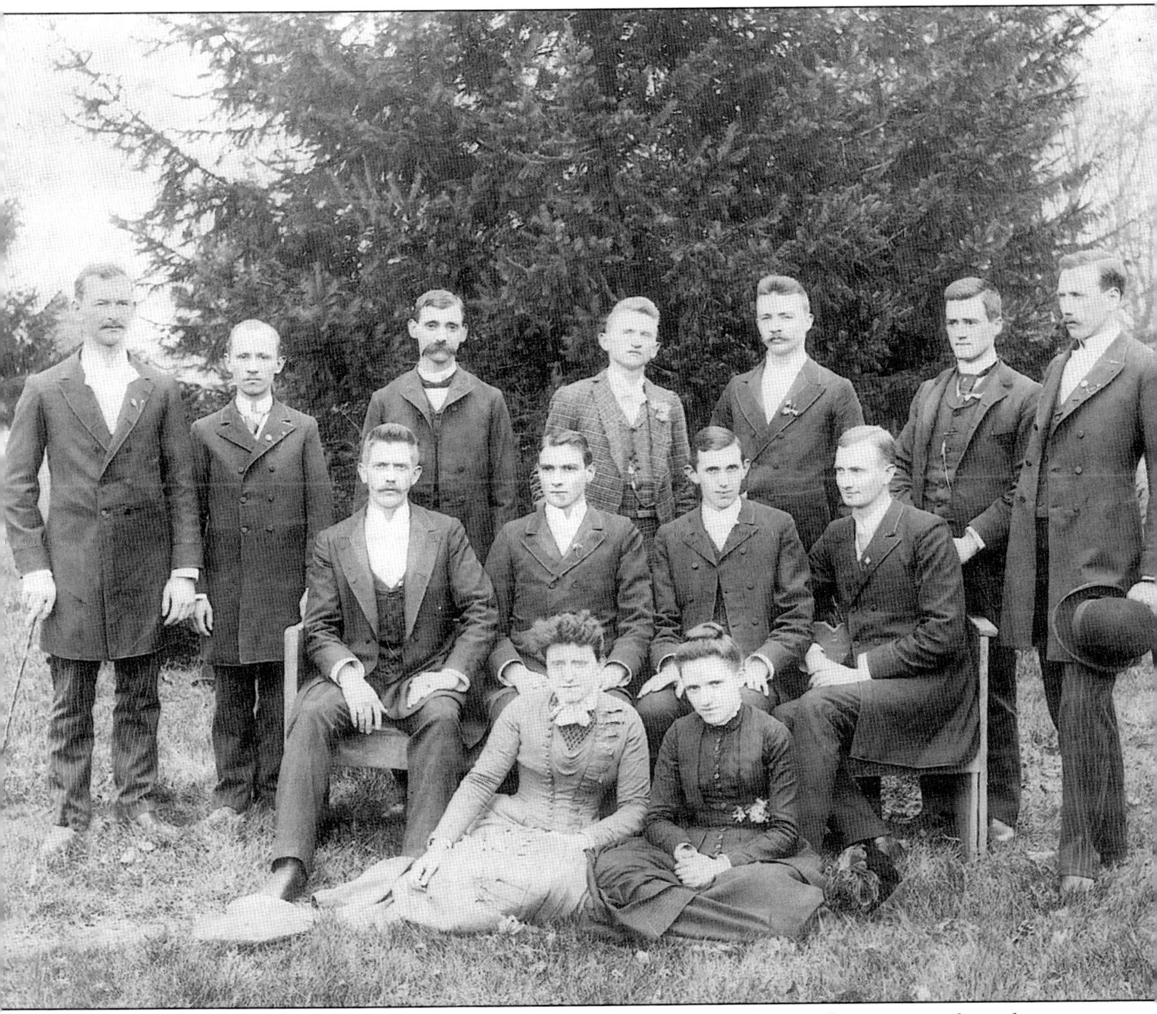

This photo is labeled "Student Body, 1880's, 1890's." Names of most in the photo are as follows: (in standing back row), King, Pek (?), Hartshorn, Bowman, (?), Miller; (middle row) Sage, Pifer, Morgan, Earsman; (seated) Telrow, Anna Keeler.

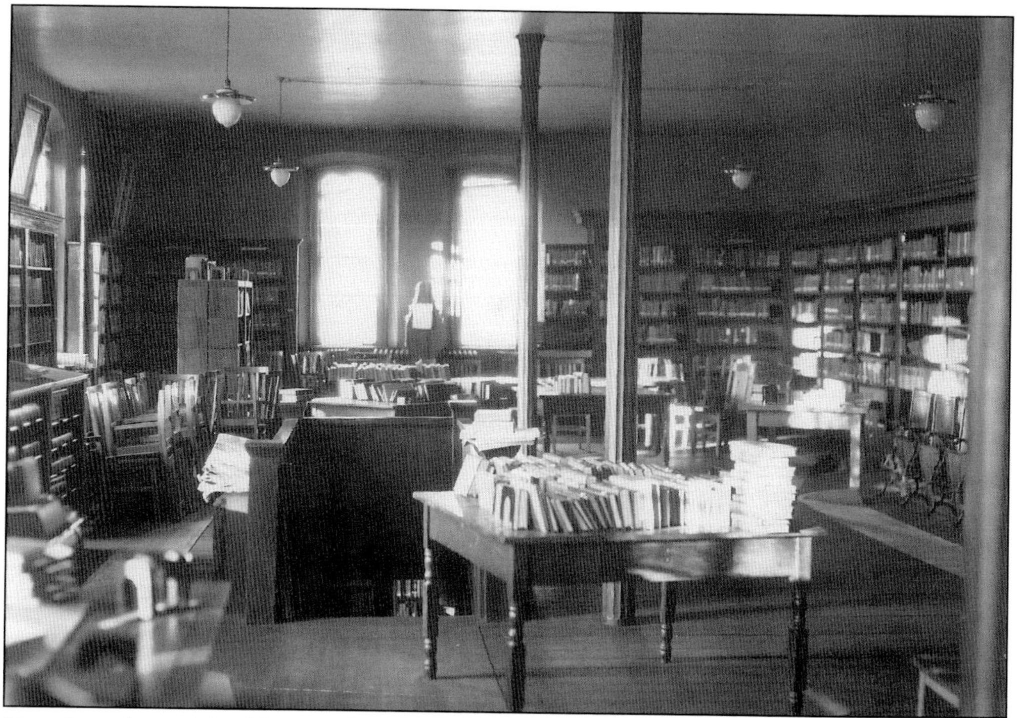

Here is a view of the library which was in Chapman Hall. Why are there no students in the photo? It was taken during the Thanksgiving vacation!

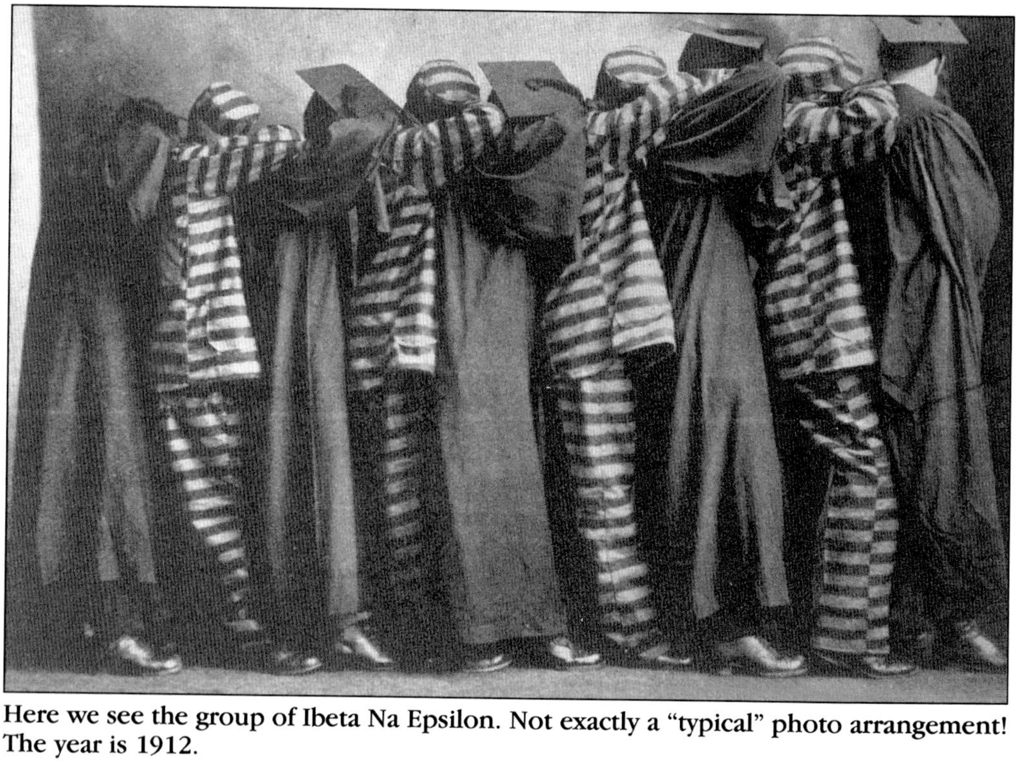

Here we see the group of Ibeta Na Epsilon. Not exactly a "typical" photo arrangement! The year is 1912.

Two

SWINGING INTO THE 20TH CENTURY

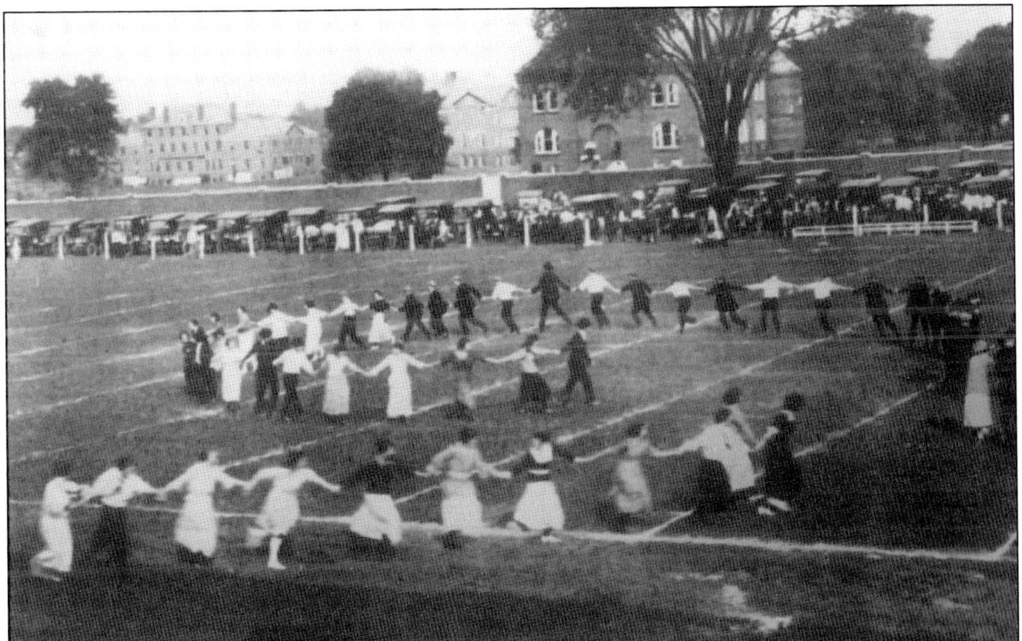

Well, it is the football field, but a slightly different type of "game." The year is 1921.

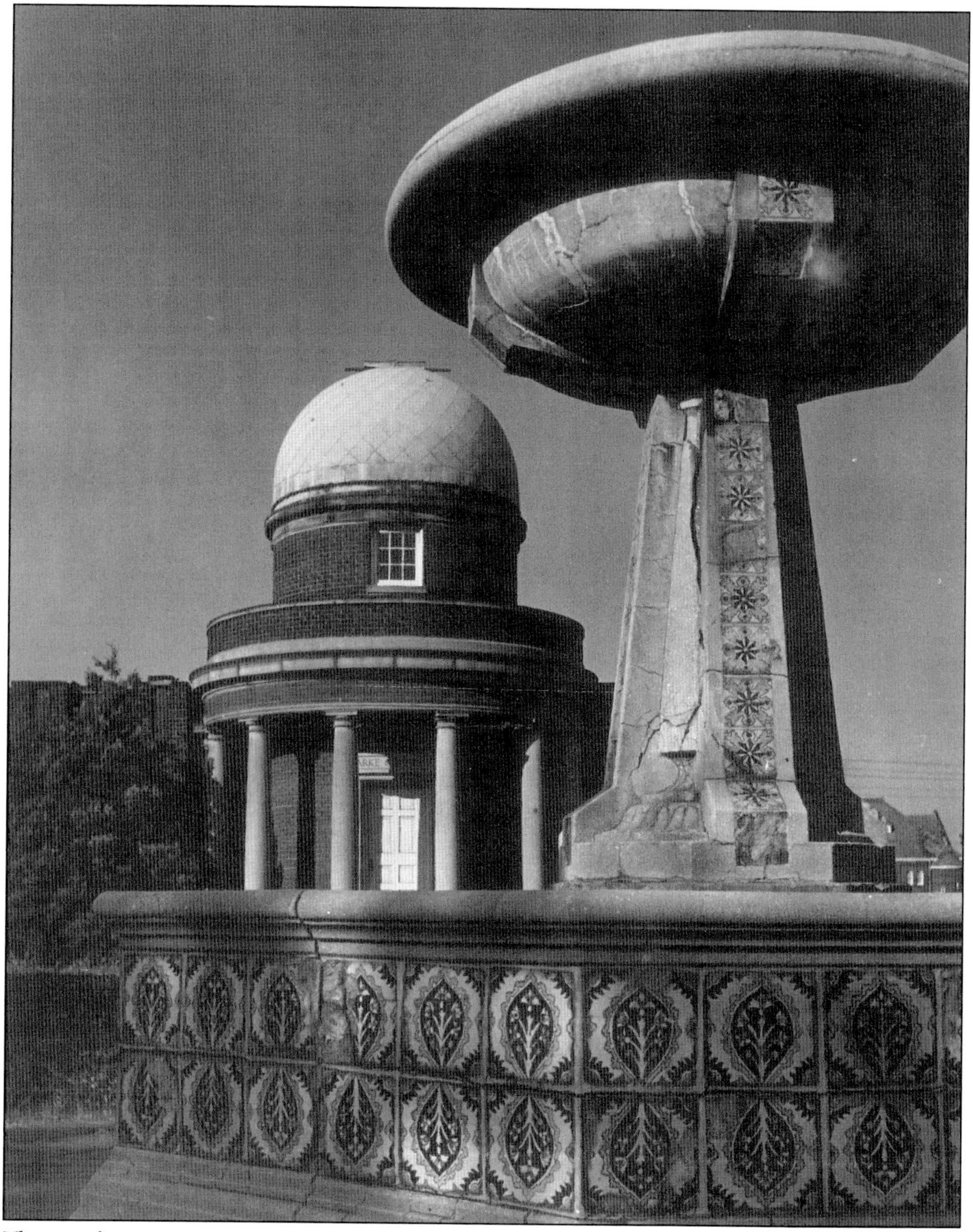

The Arethusa Fountain and the Observatory are seen in this 1920s image.

Here is a photo of President W.H. McMaster in the year 1927.

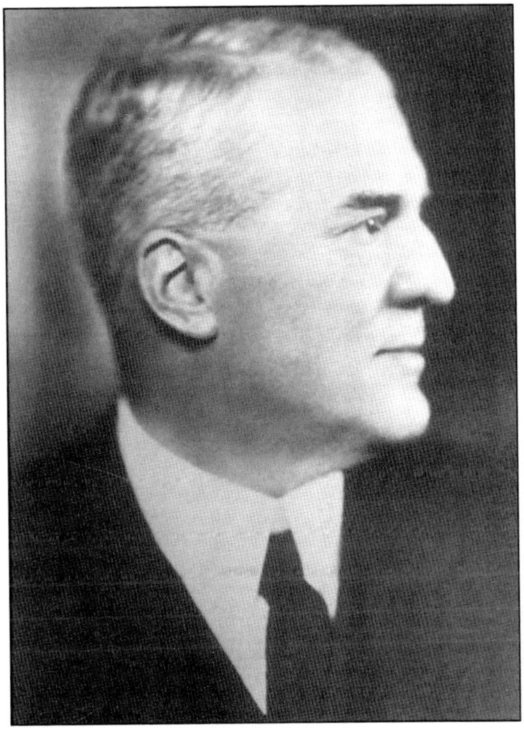

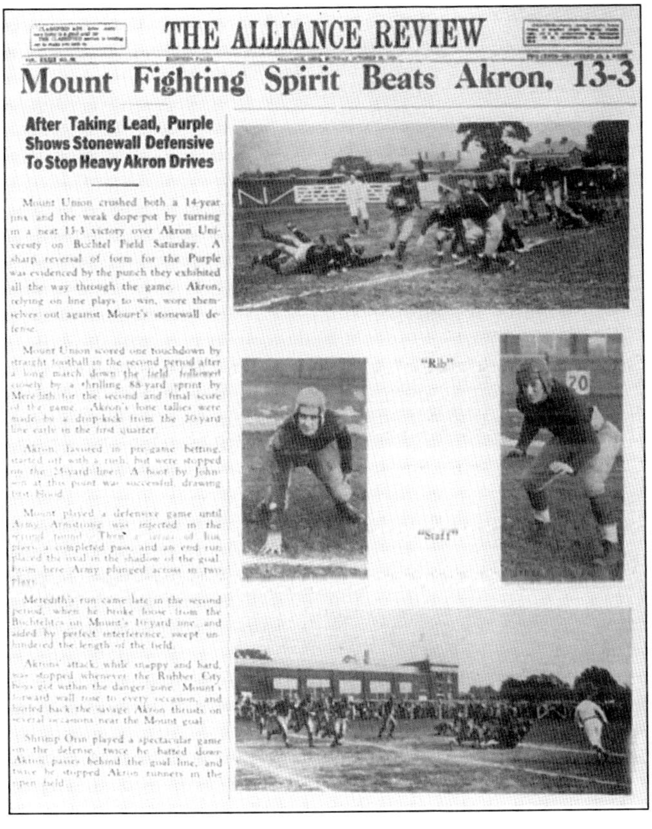

THE ALLIANCE REVIEW

Mount Fighting Spirit Beats Akron, 13-3

After Taking Lead, Purple Shows Stonewall Defensive To Stop Heavy Akron Drives

Mount Union crushed both a 14-year jinx and the weak dope-pot by turning in a neat 13-3 victory over Akron University on Buchtel Field Saturday. A sharp reversal of form for the Purple was evidenced by the punch they exhibited all the way through the game. Akron, relying on line plays to win, wore themselves out against Mount's stonewall defense.

Mount Union scored one touchdown by straight football in the second period after a long march down the field followed closely by a thrilling 88-yard sprint by Meredith for the second and final score of the game. Akron's lone tallies were made by a drop-kick from the 30-yard line early in the first quarter.

Akron, favored in pre-game betting, started off with a rush, but were stopped on the 25-yard line. A boot by Johnson at this point was successful, drawing first blood.

Mount played a defensive game until Army Armstrong was injected in the second round. Then a series of line plays, a completed pass, and an end run placed the oval in the shadow of the goal. From here Army plunged across in two plays.

Meredith's run came late in the second period, when he broke loose from the Buchtelites on Mount's [illegible]-yard line, and aided by perfect interference, swept unhindered the length of the field.

Akron's attack, while snappy and hard, was stopped whenever the Rubber City boys got within the danger zone. Mount's forward wall rose to every occasion, and hurled back the savage Akron thrusts on several occasions near the Mount goal.

Shrimp Onn played a spectacular game on the defense, twice he batted down Akron passes behind the goal line, and twice he stopped Akron runners in the open field.

"Rib"

"Staff"

A local paper and a local win, 1922.

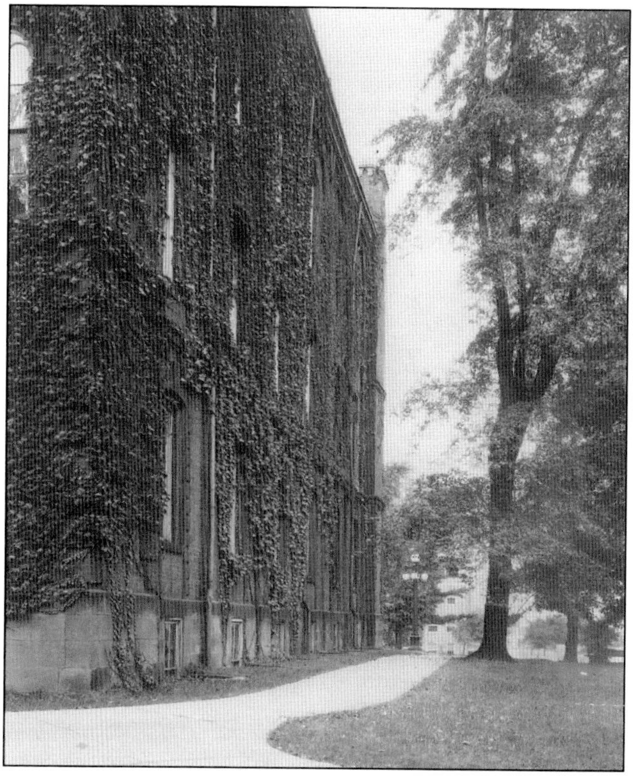

This is, obviously, a view of a side of Chapman Hall taken in the 1930s.

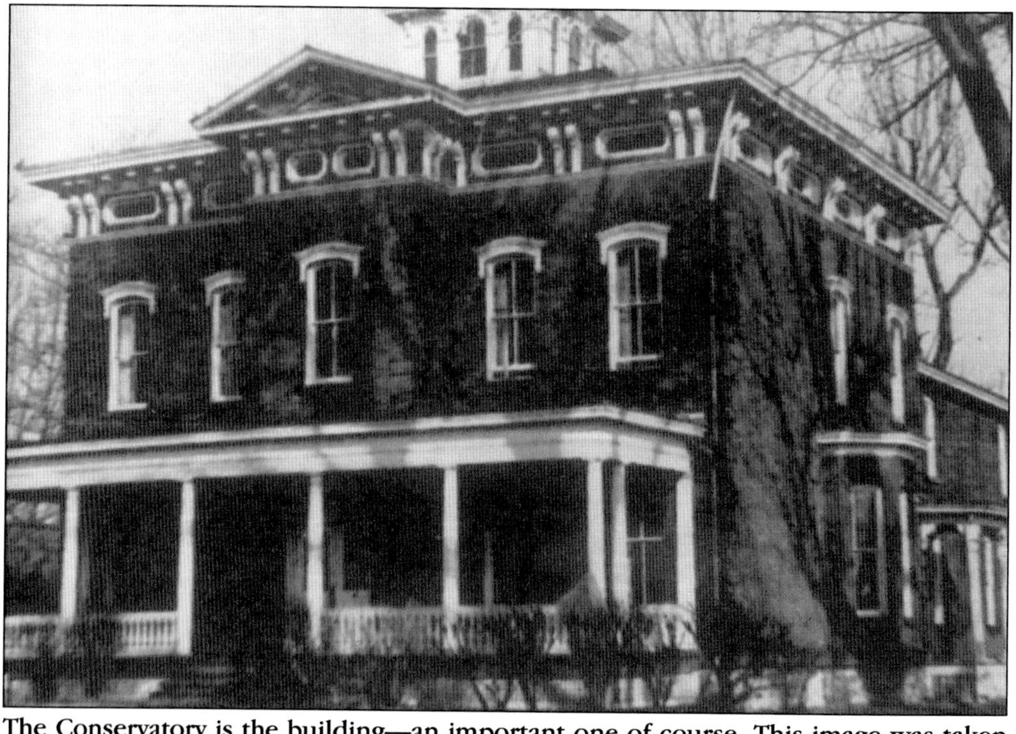

The Conservatory is the building—an important one of course. This image was taken in 1950.

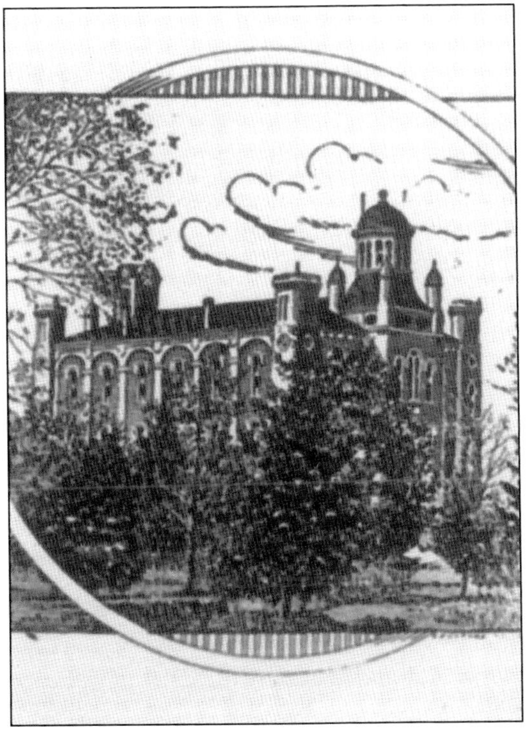

This frequently used photo and sketch of Chapman Hall goes all the way back to 1901.

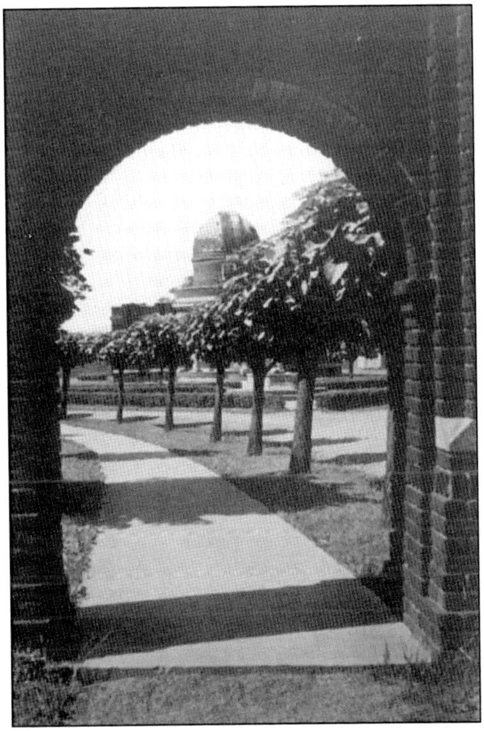

Here is a view of the observatory, taken from one of several "openings" on campus. The year is 1927.

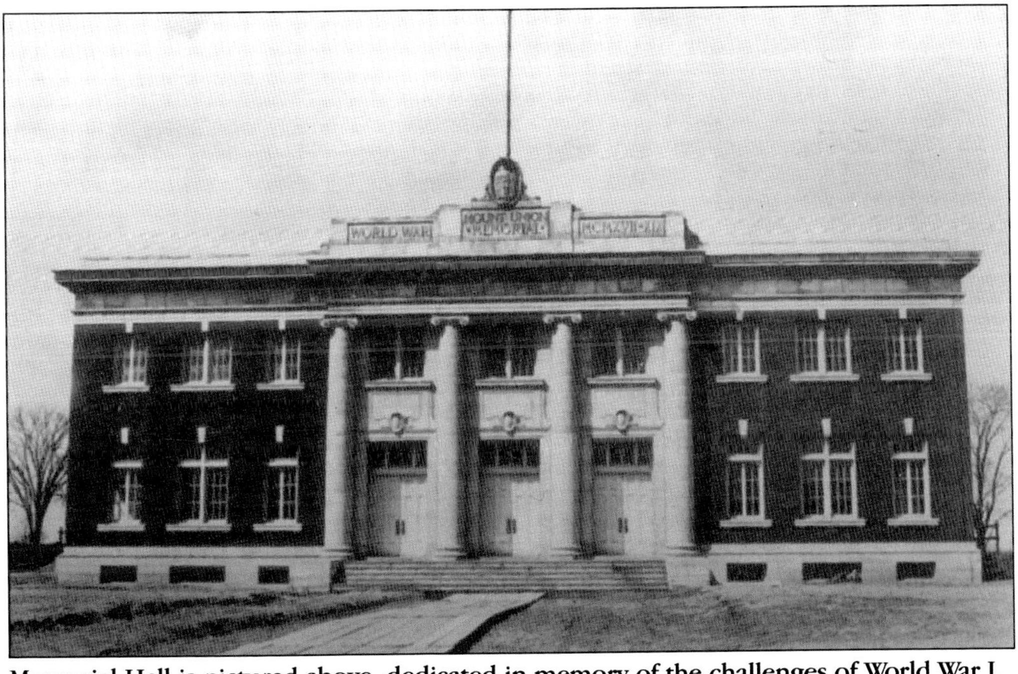

Memorial Hall is pictured above, dedicated in memory of the challenges of World War I.

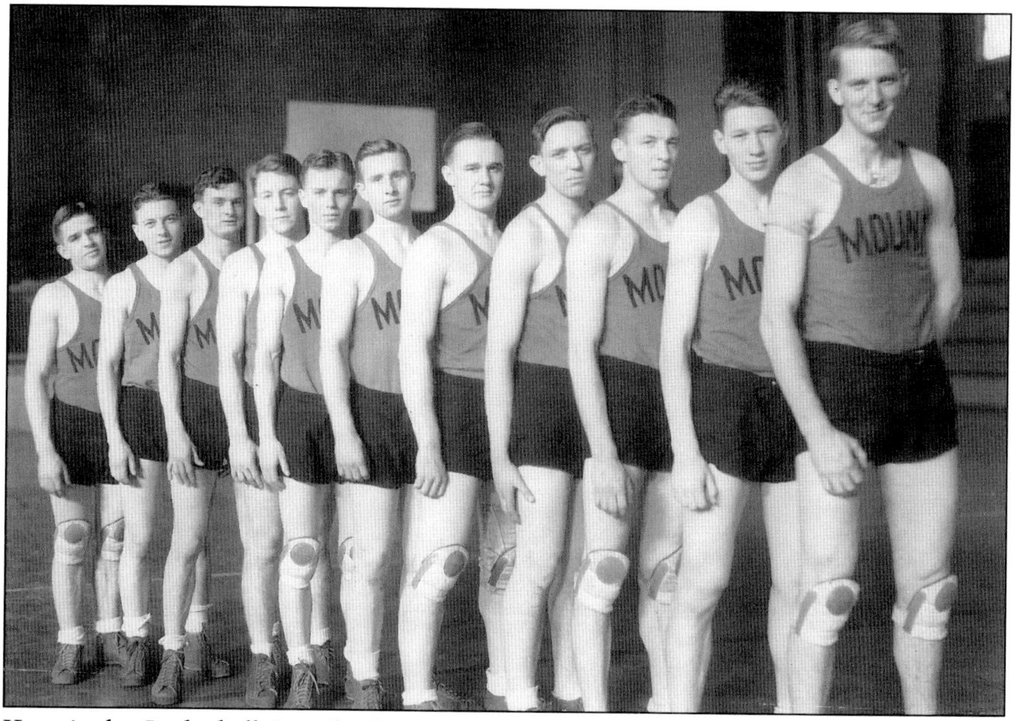

Here is the Basketball Squad of 1929-1930. From left to right, the players are Heim, Atahley, Leyda, Moore, Devore, Beach, Grimes, Raber, Glenwright, Wiand, Lindamood.

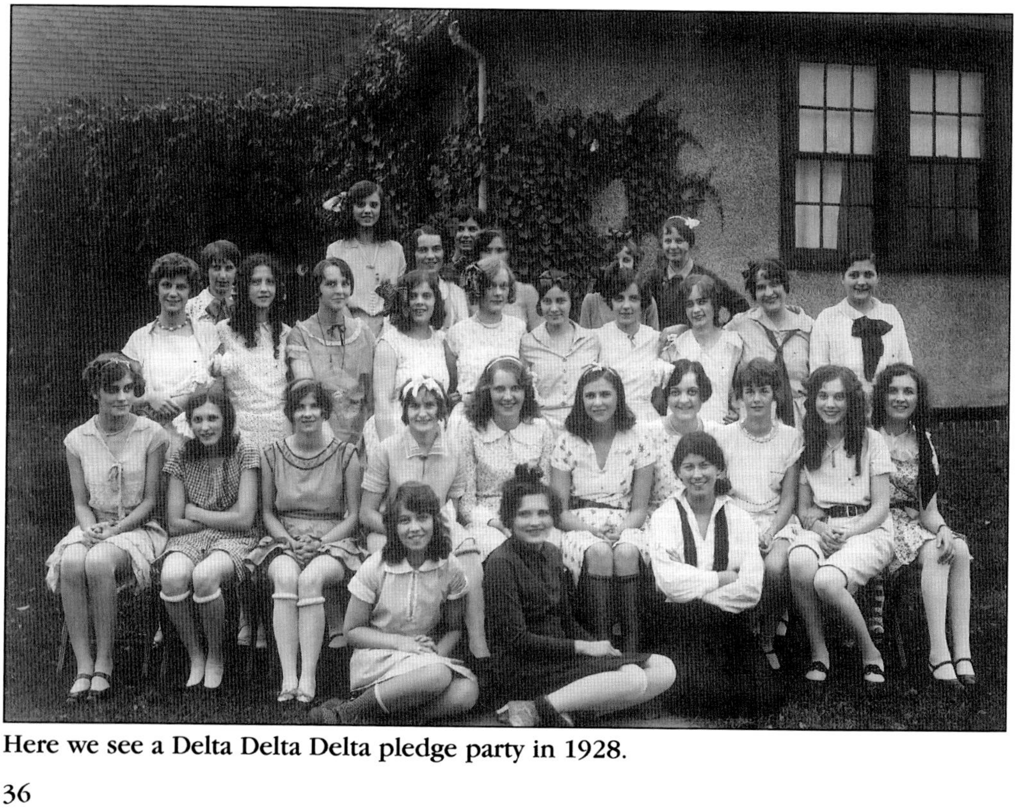

Here we see a Delta Delta Delta pledge party in 1928.

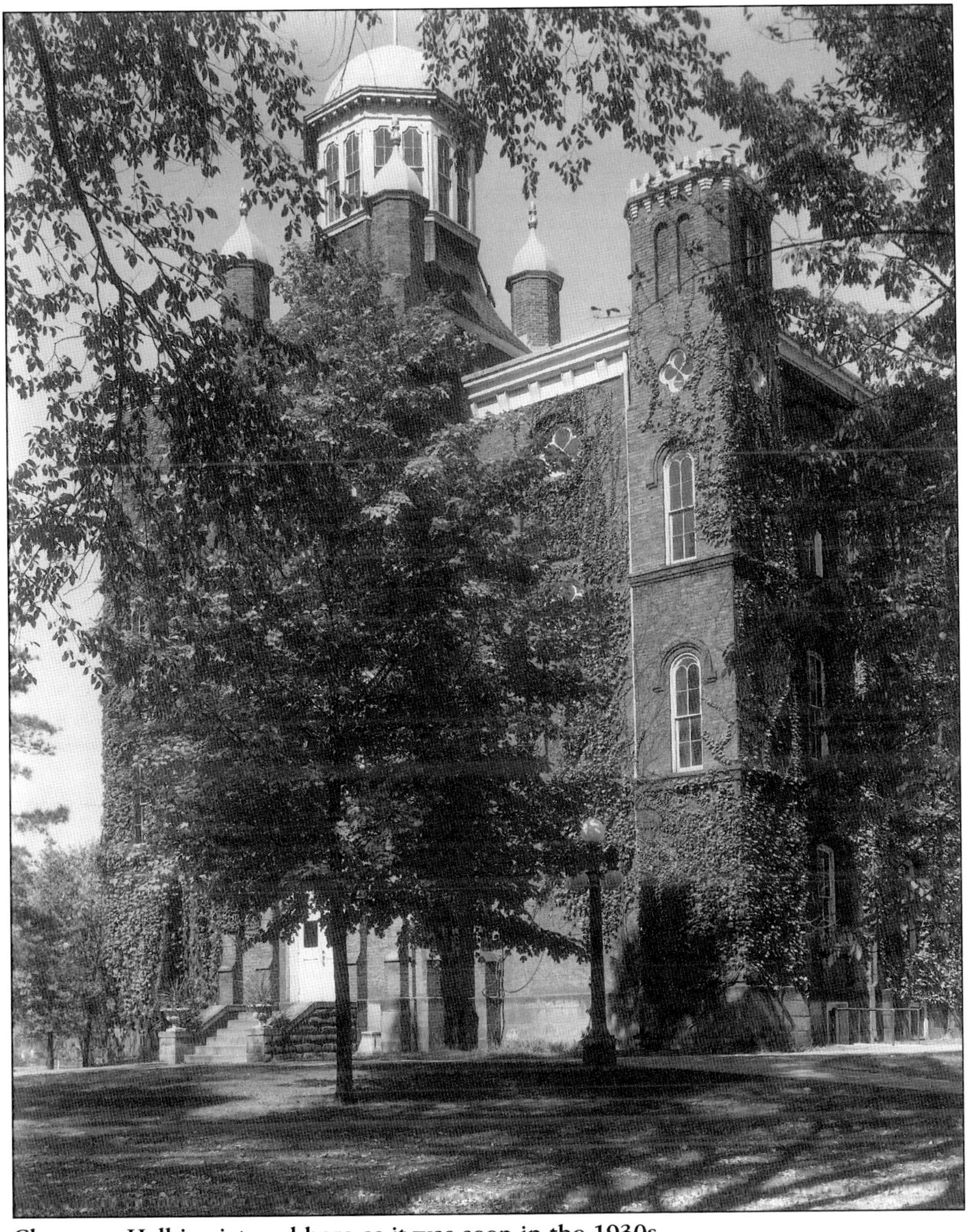

Chapman Hall is pictured here as it was seen in the 1930s.

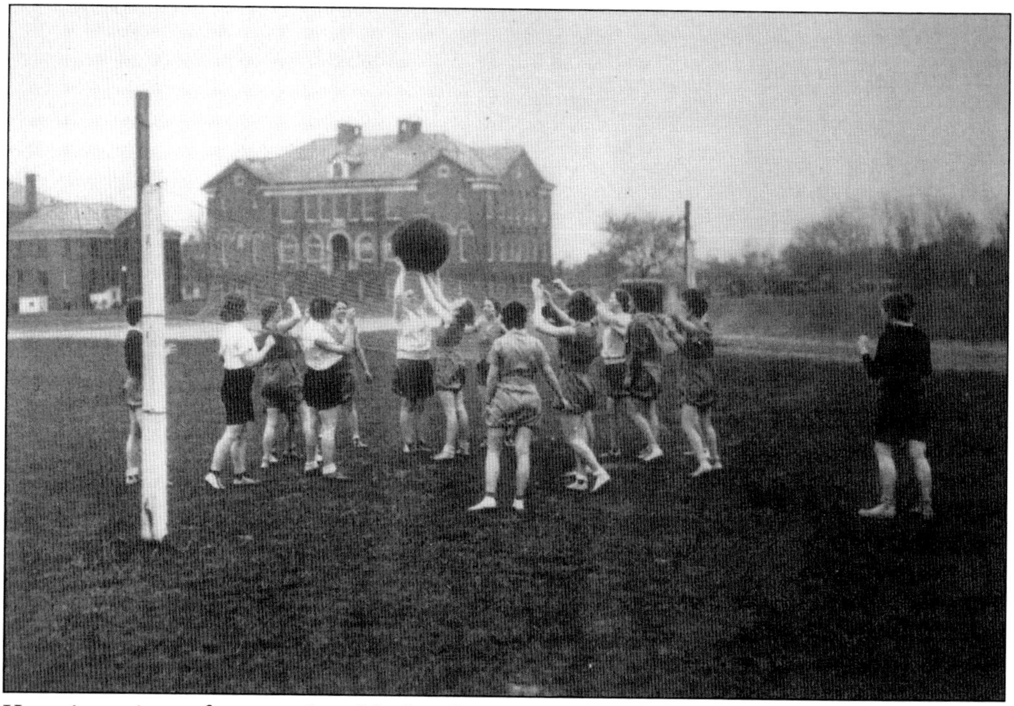

Here is a view of women's athletics. It was a part of the Intramural League games in 1933.

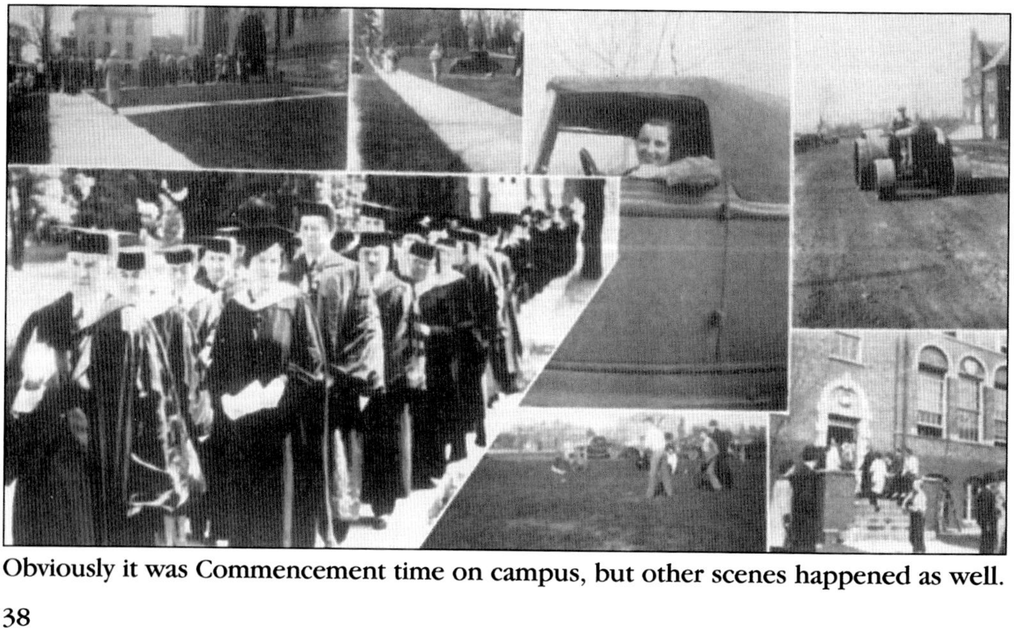

Obviously it was Commencement time on campus, but other scenes happened as well.

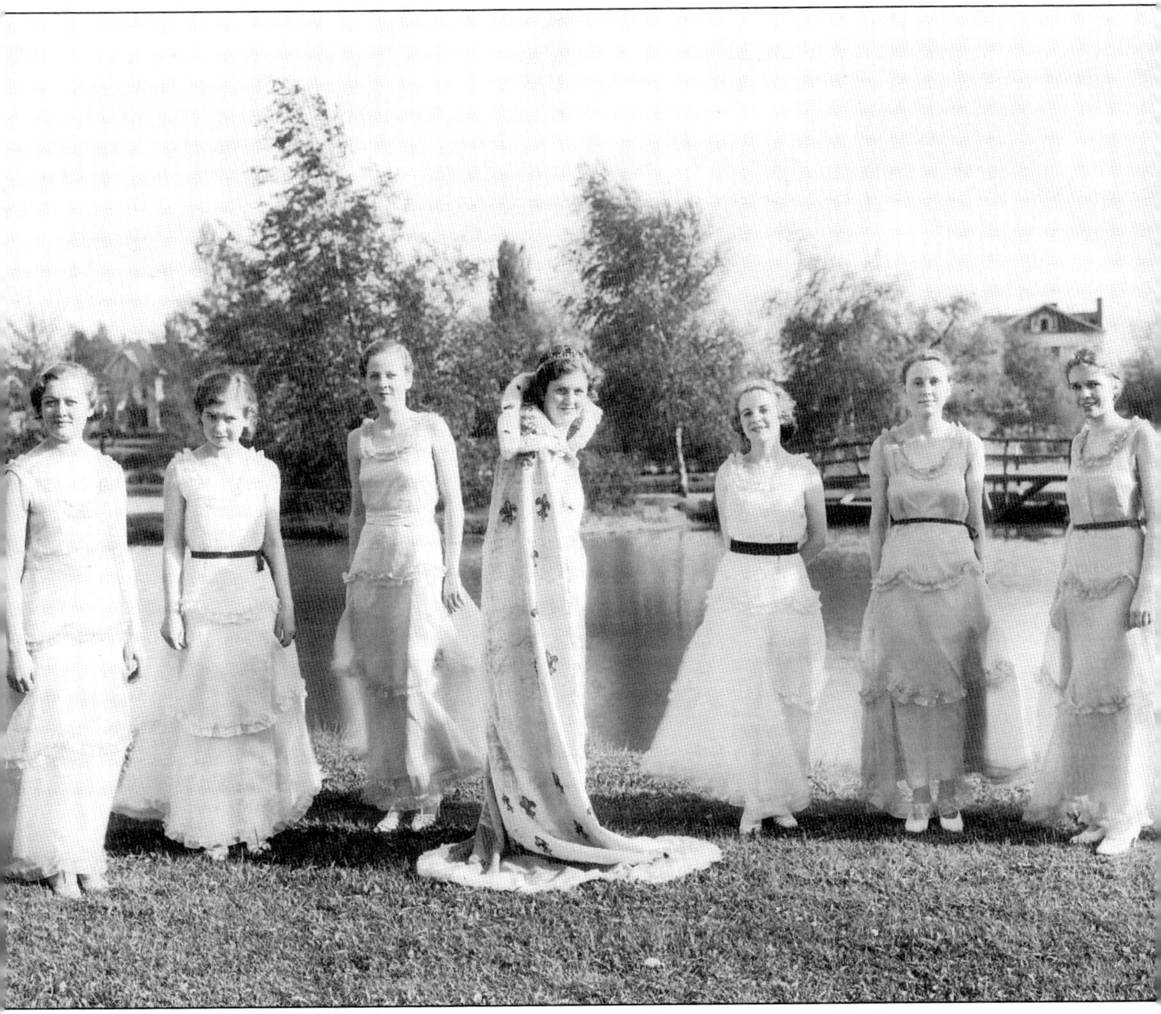

Here is view of the classic participants on campus for May Day in 1932.

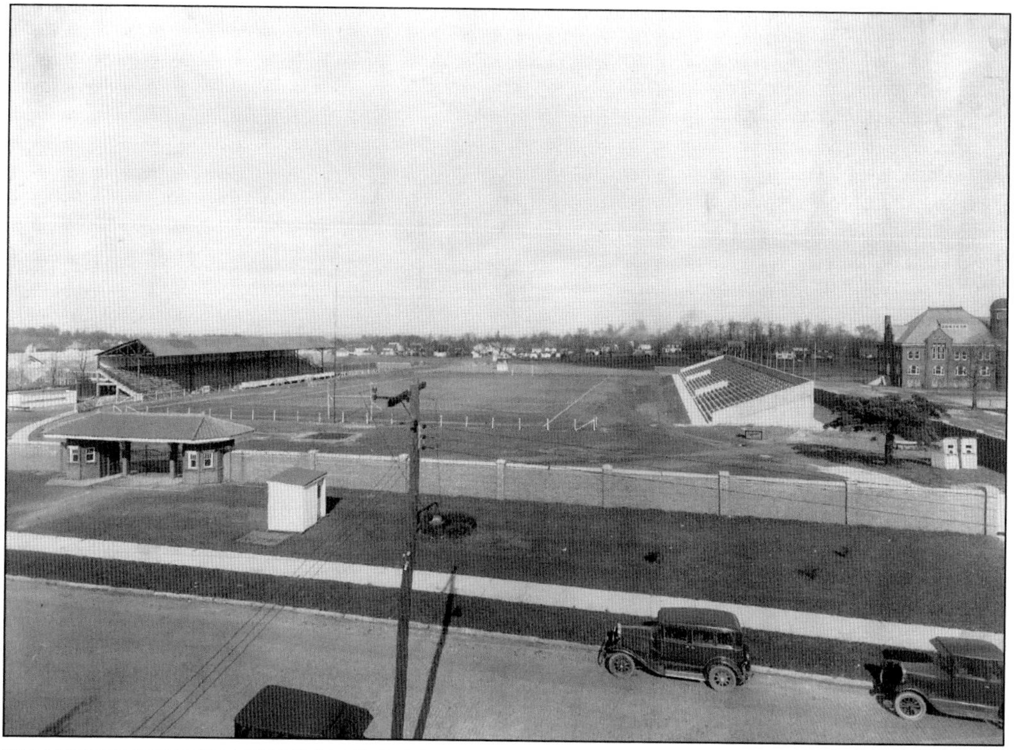

Above is a view of the athletic field, the stadium, and Morgan gymnasium years ago. Notice the age of the automobiles.

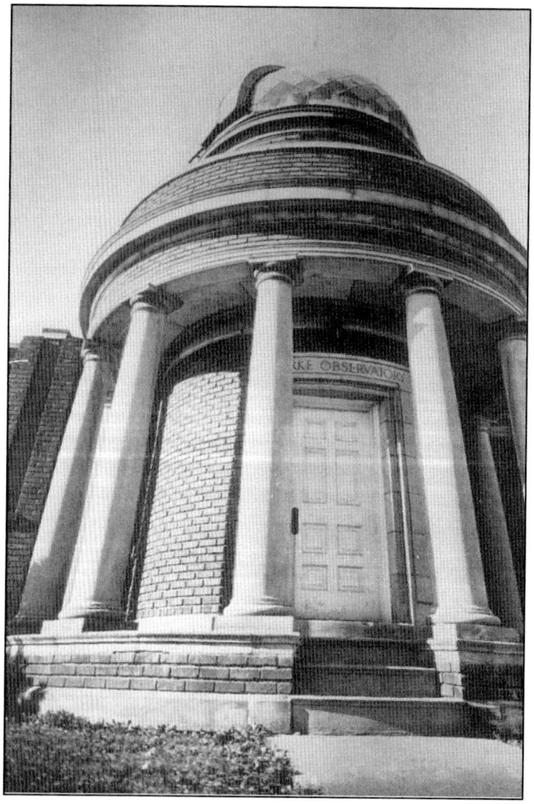

This image shows a close-up of the Clarke Observatory in 1933.

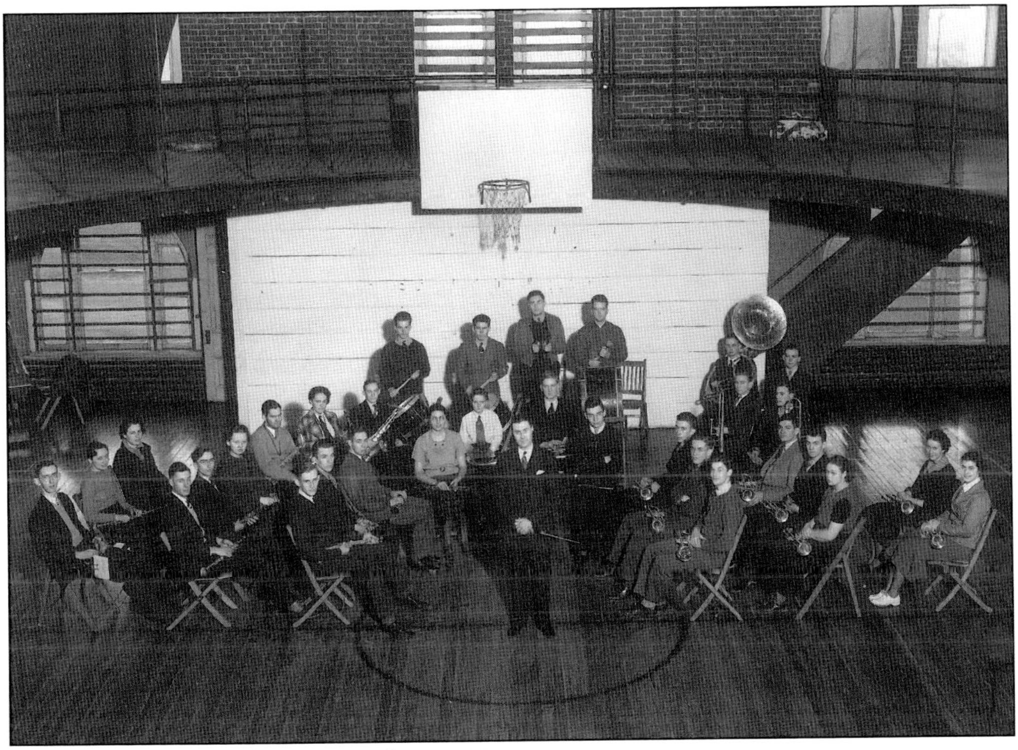

There they are, the campus band in 1935.

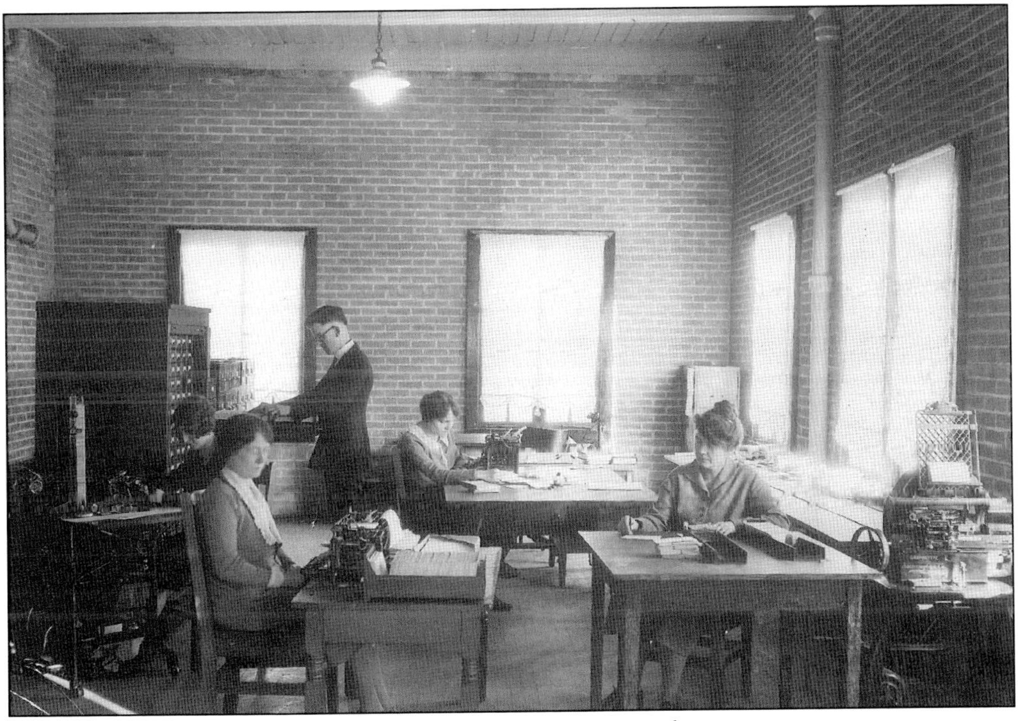

Pictured is the Alumni Office with good activities in 1926.

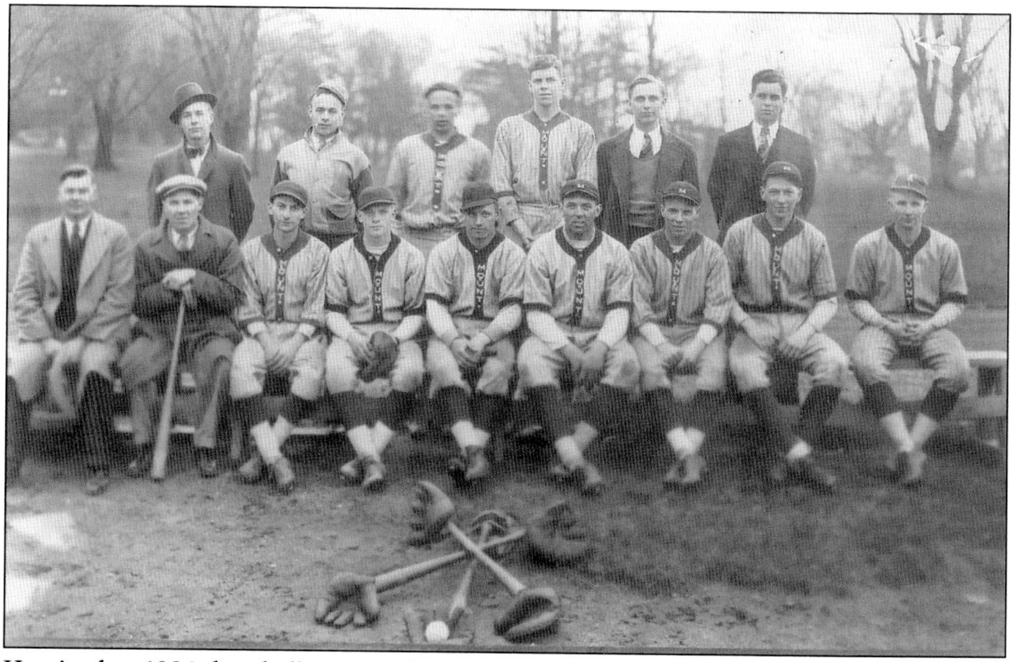

Here's the 1931 baseball team of the Raiders. Notice that "Mount" is spelled on their uniforms.

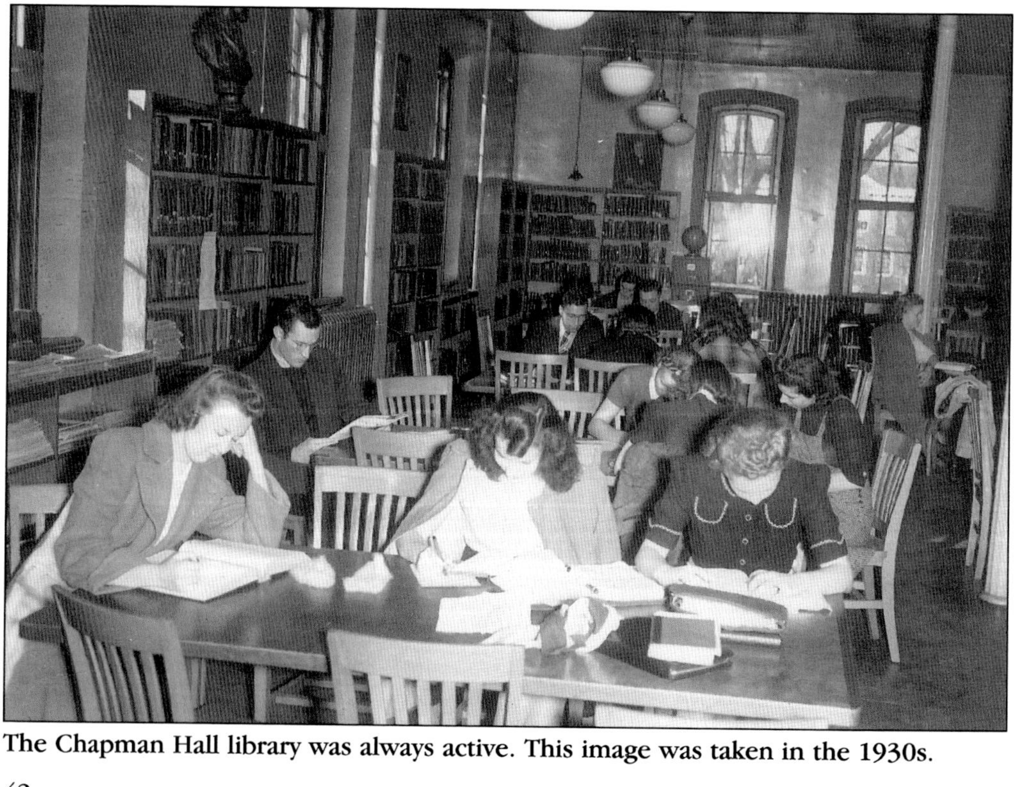

The Chapman Hall library was always active. This image was taken in the 1930s.

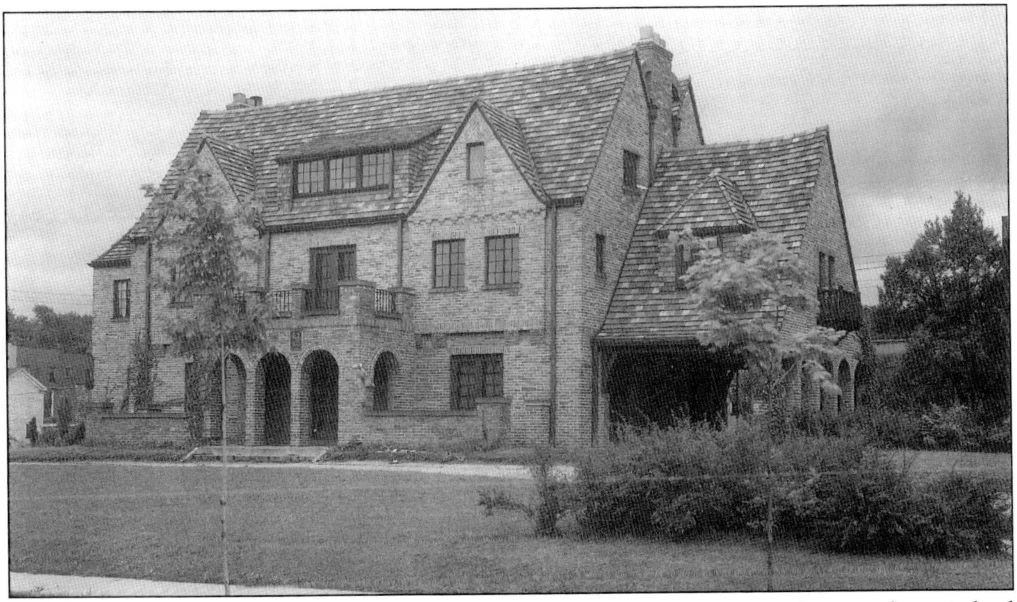

In 1942 the College acquired this building from Phi Kappa Tau, and a year later it had been refurnished and it opened as the Student Union for the campus.

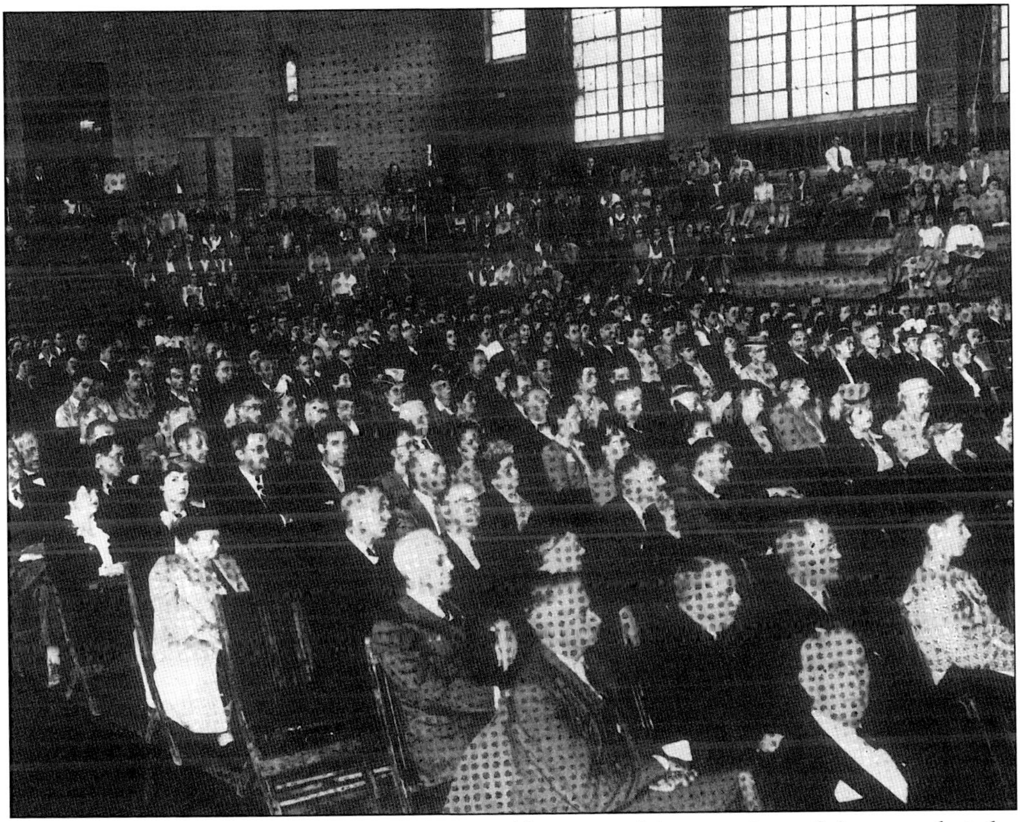

The College celebrated a Centennial in 1946; pictured is a portion of the crowd at the celebration meeting in Memorial Hall, where the basketball court was located.

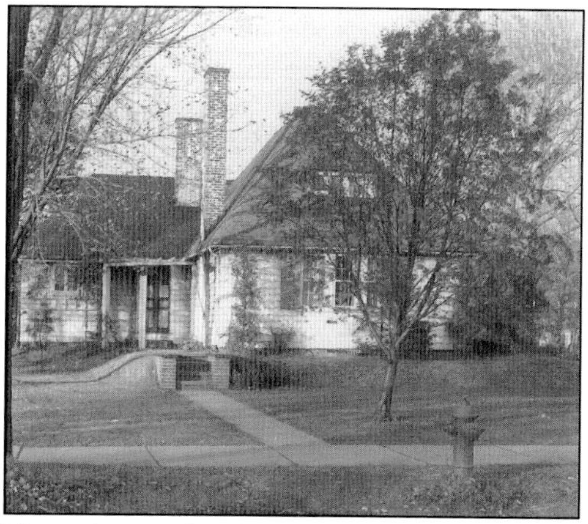

This photo of Delta Delta Delta was taken in 1948.

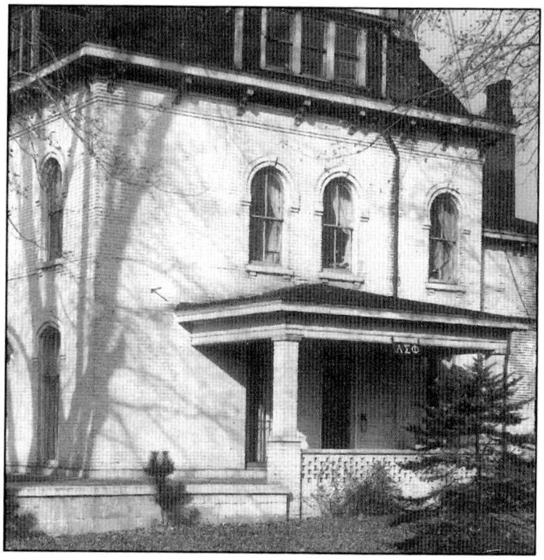

This is a photo of Alpha Sigma Phi.

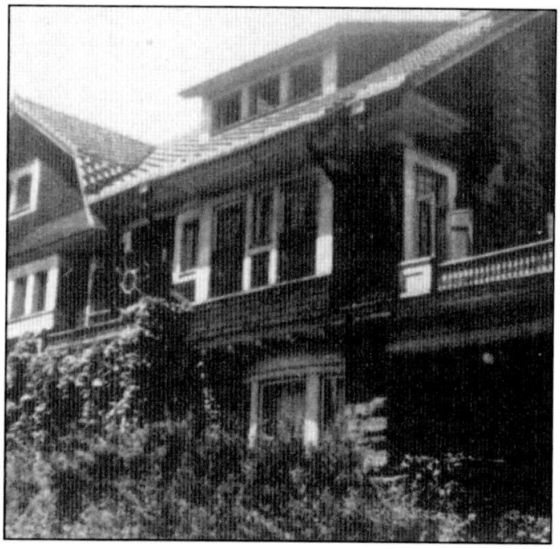

This photo of Sigma Nu was taken 1946.

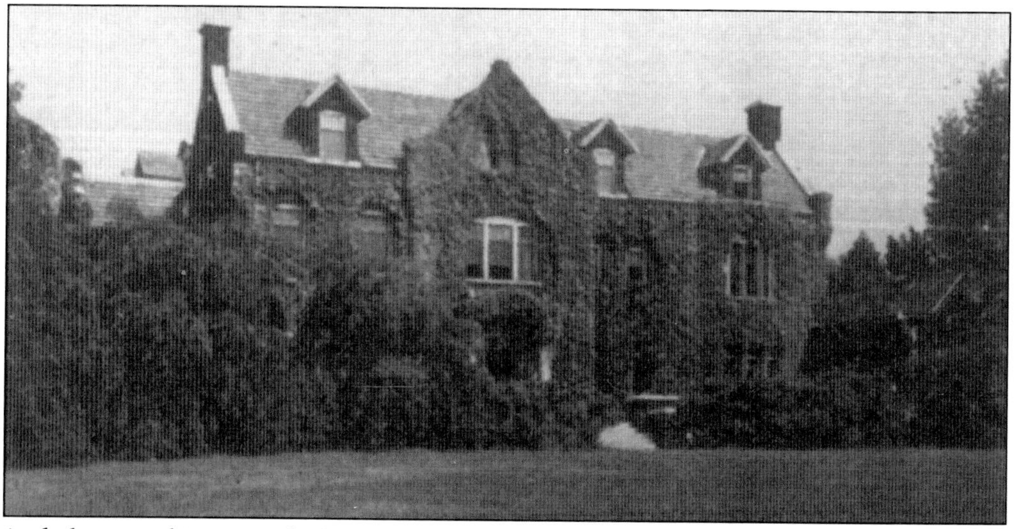

And also was this one, which is of Phi Kappa Tau.

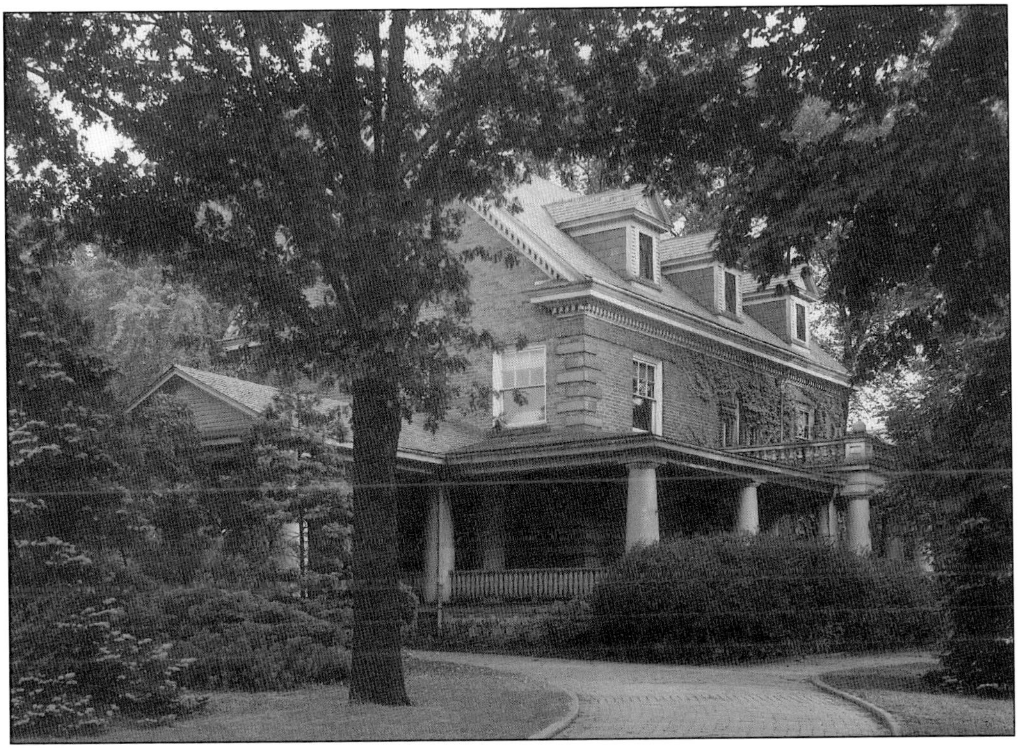

This lovely home of Mrs. Catherine Dussell was donated to the College in 1940 to be used as a women's dormitory. It was located next to the president's residence. Mr. Dussell, who had died, had been on the college board of trustees for many years.

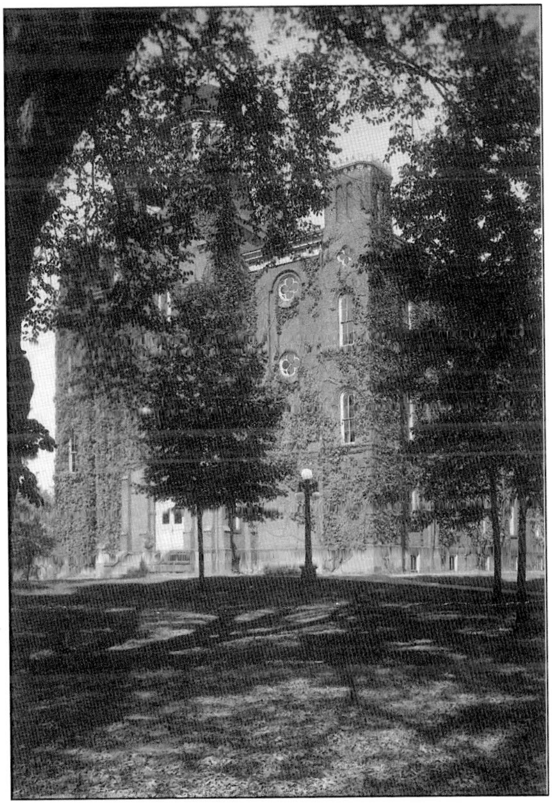

Yet another view of Chapman Hall, this time displaying its circular windows. The year is 1941.

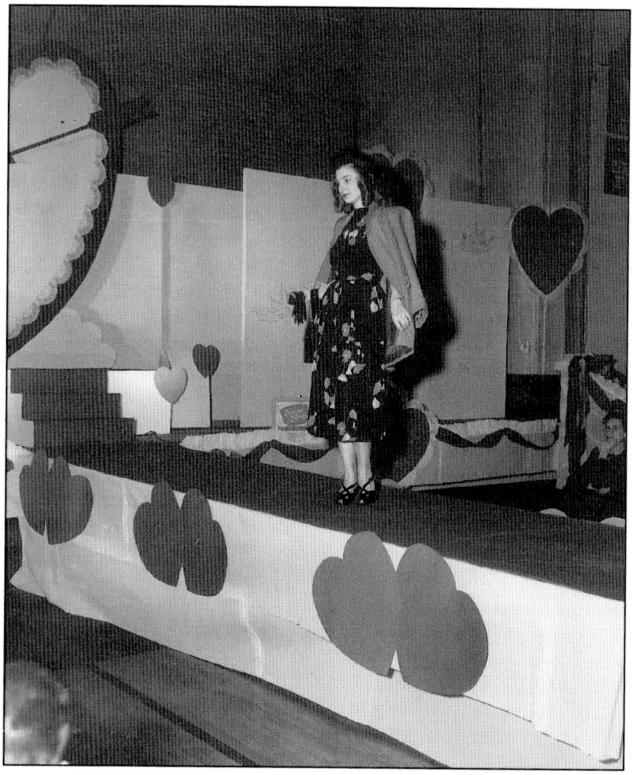

From the Style Show of February 14, 1948, Norma Mumow performs.

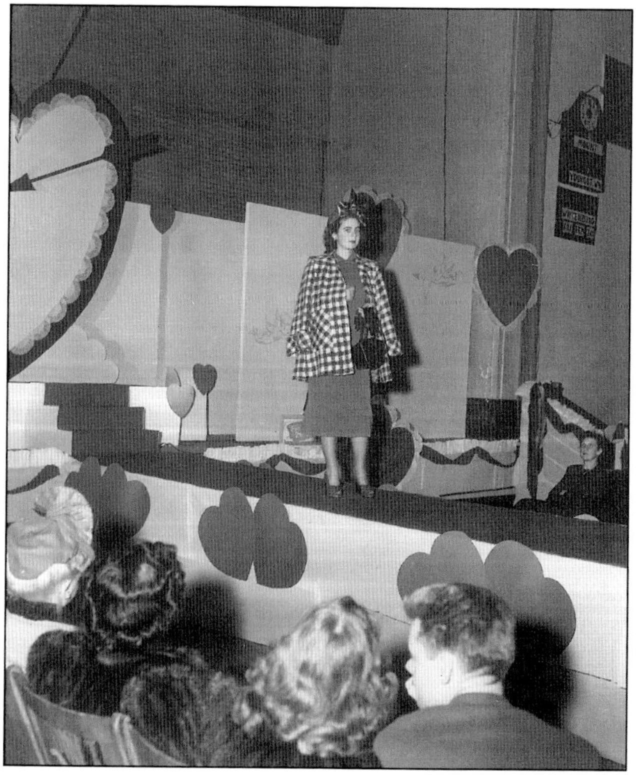

Another one on stage was Alice Trader, pictured here.

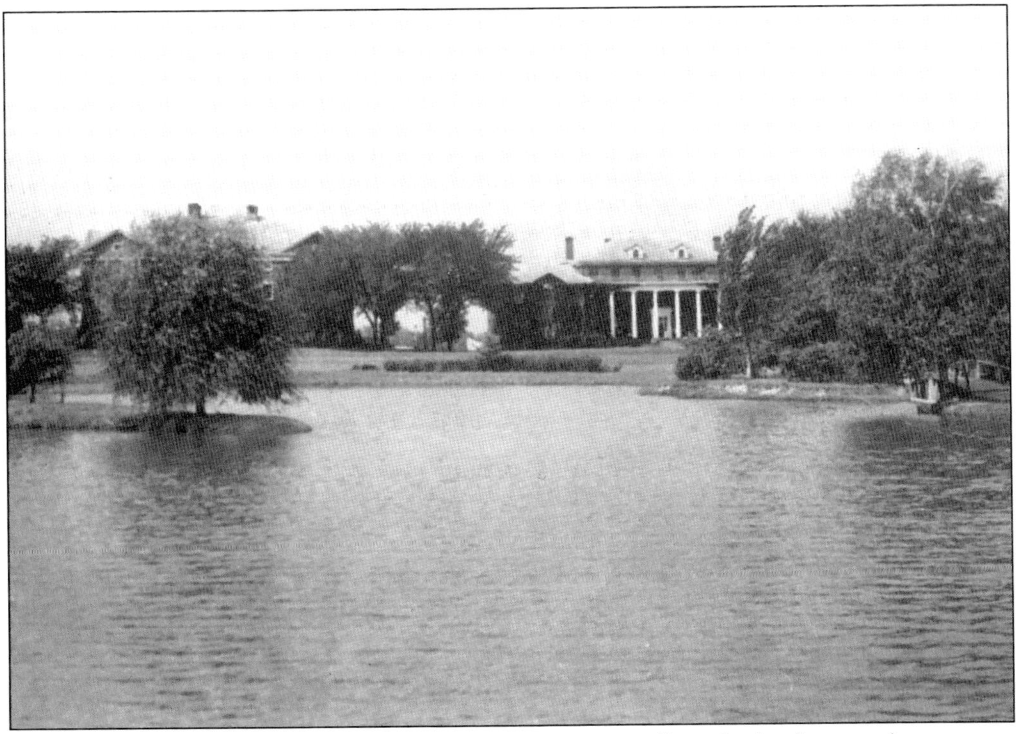

Here is a 1946 campus scene of the lake with Elliott Hall in the background.

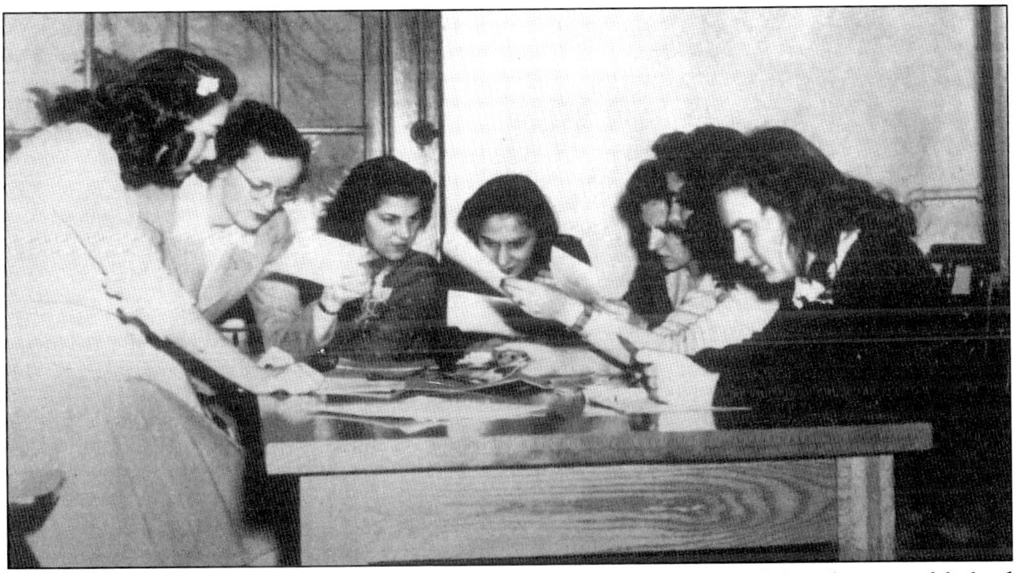

The yearly *Unonian* staff is from the student body. The annual has been published since the time of the very first graduation from Mount Union College. In this 1946 picture are, from left to right, Betty Evans, Joy Lawrence, Elizabeth Benedict, Stella Pastis, Lora Hurst, Norma Archibald, and Beverly Hanley.

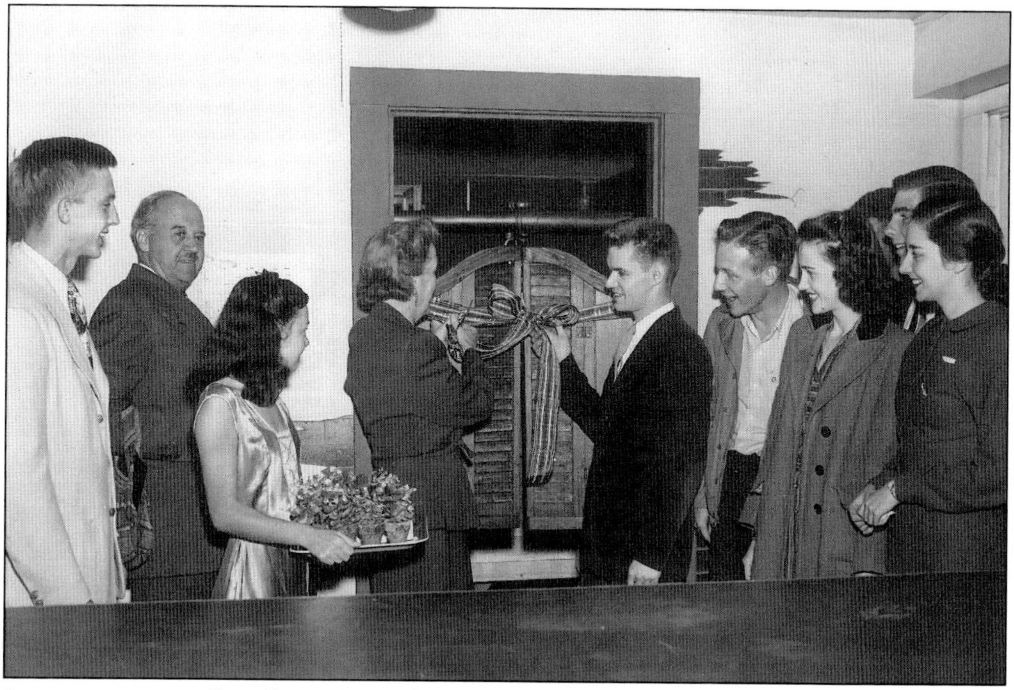

A great moment for all awaiting the opening of "The Gay Nineties Snack Bar" on campus in 1948.

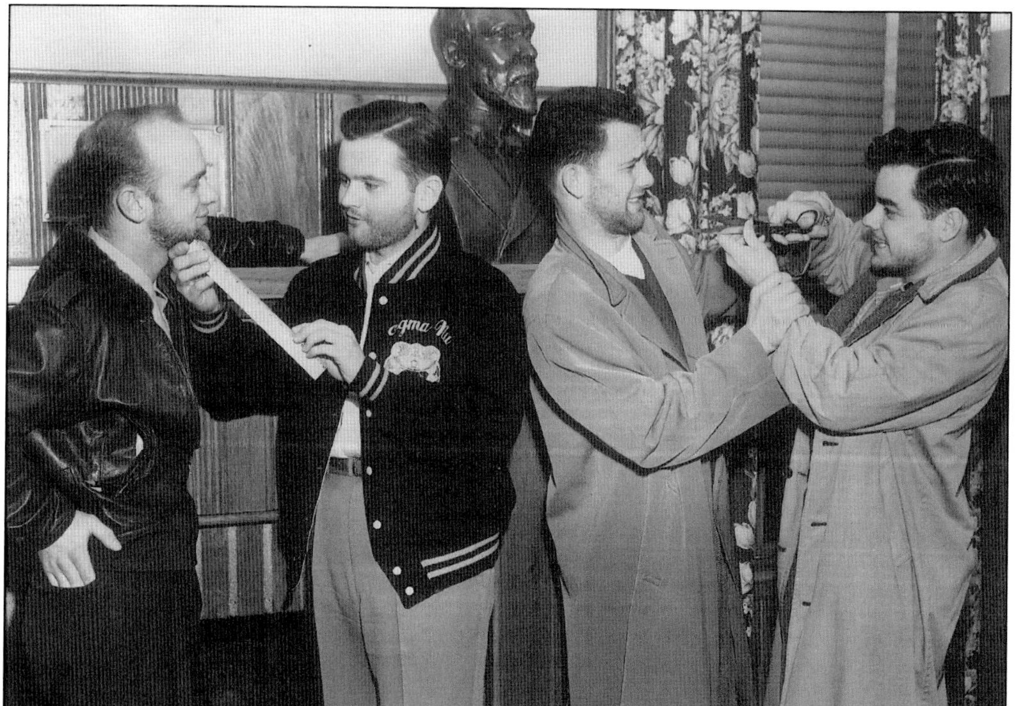

Above is a view of candidates running for the campus activity leading to "Beard Awards," 1949.

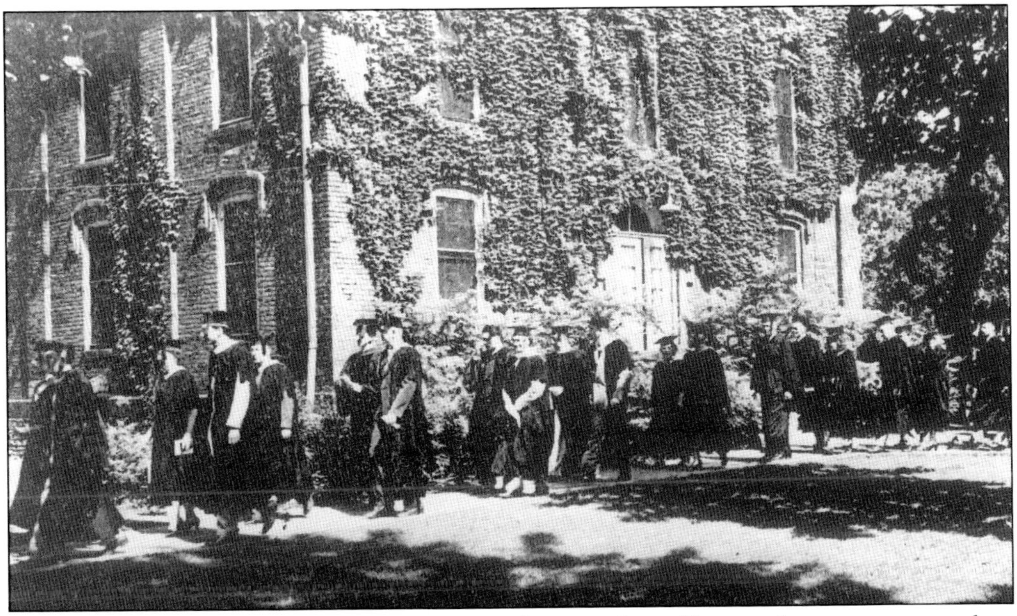

A yearly event, but this was in the 1950 graduation time. No march was proper unless it moved close to Chapman Hall, as this one did.

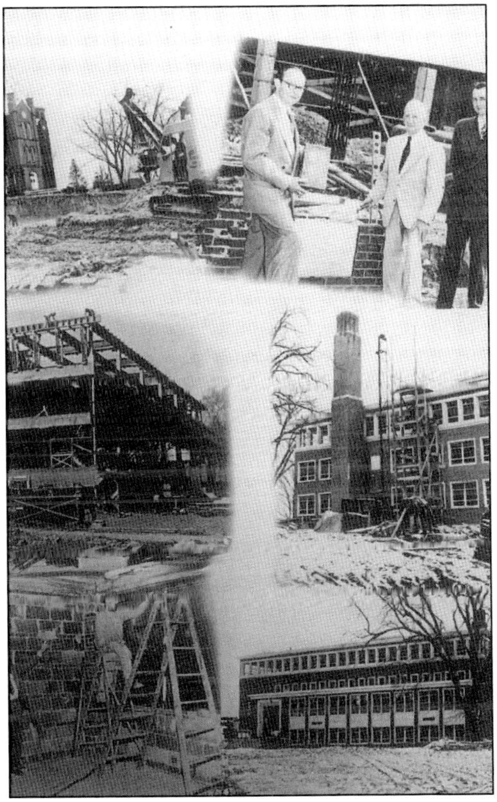

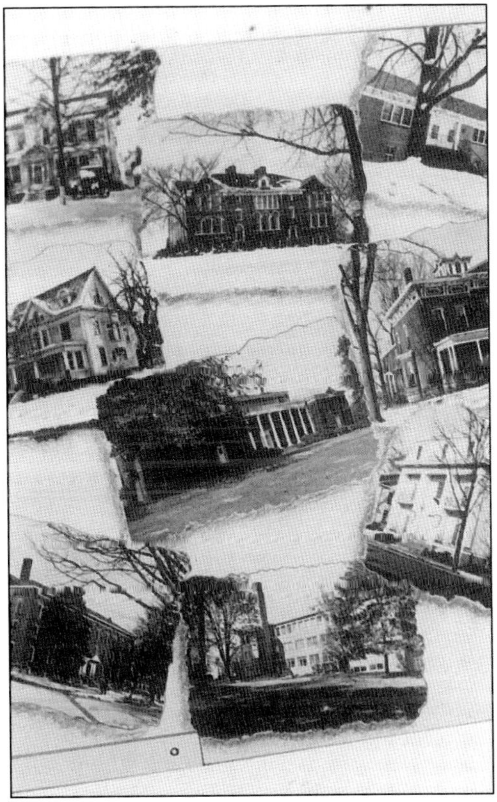

The two pictures above combine with campus buildings, both old and new.

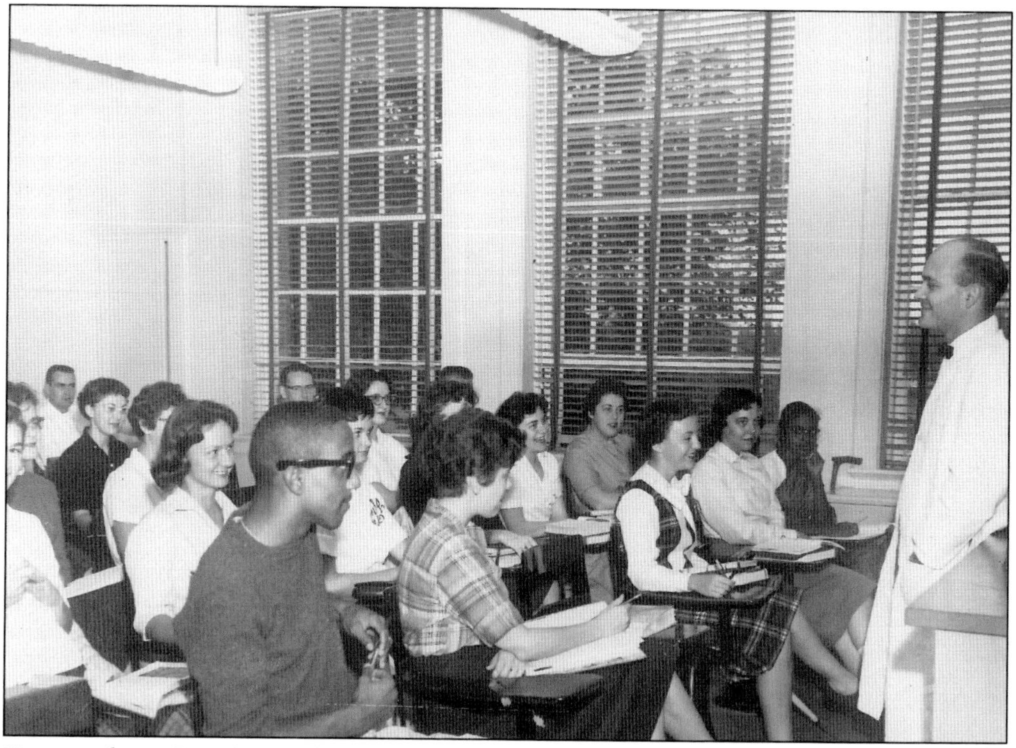

Here we have Dr. Blount chatting with graduates who, with others, have returned for this homecoming in the 1960s.

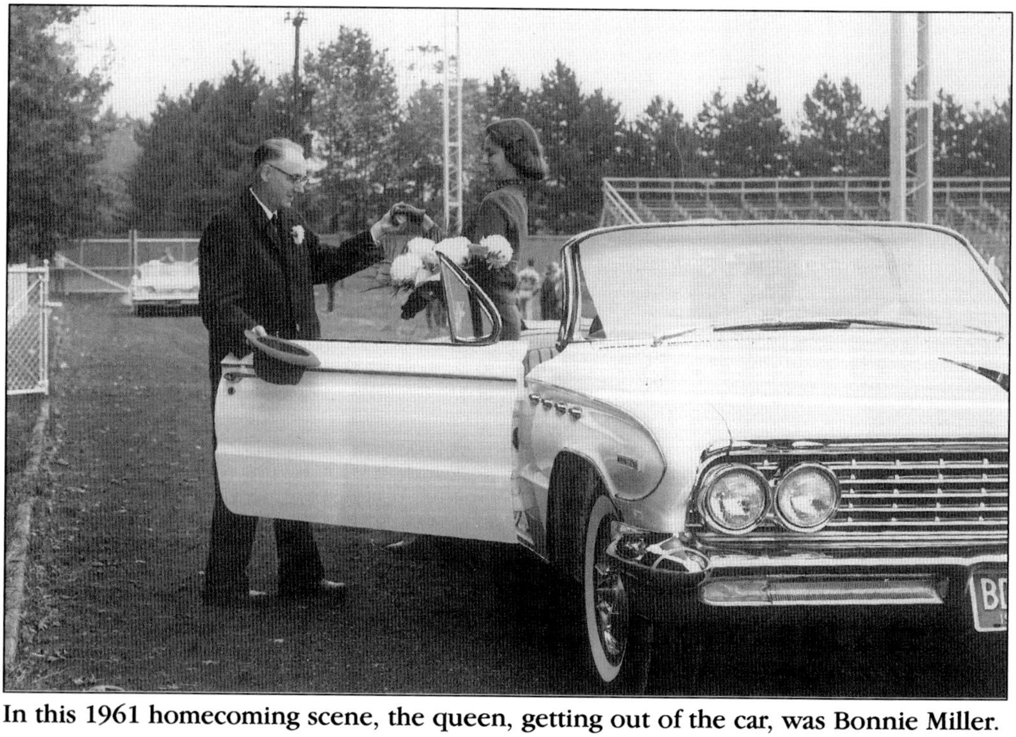

In this 1961 homecoming scene, the queen, getting out of the car, was Bonnie Miller.

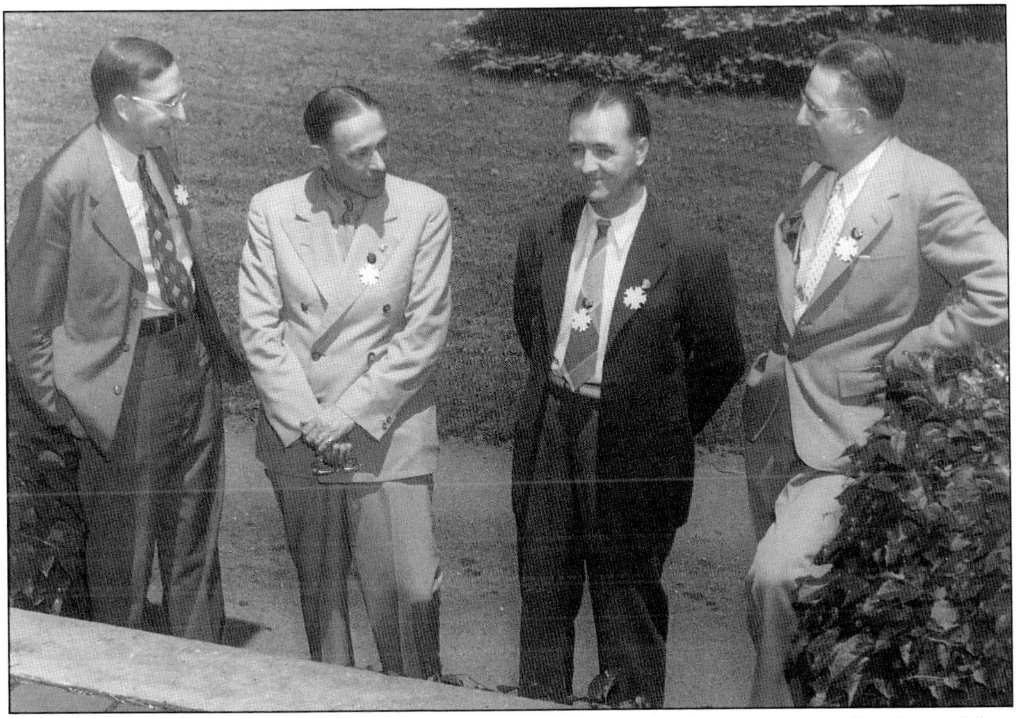

A.B. Kitmiller, J.M.Scott, W. James, and E. Figgron were back on campus for the golden anniversary of Sigma Nu.

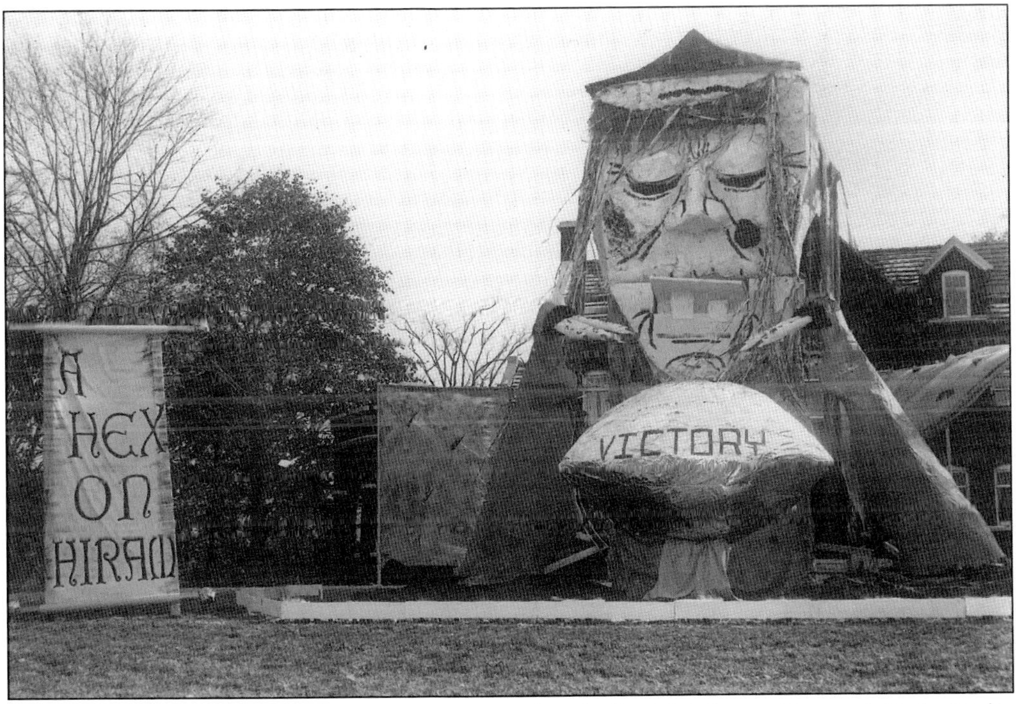

Look at the homecoming decoration winner for 1962—Phi Kappa Tau and Alpha Delta Pi combined.

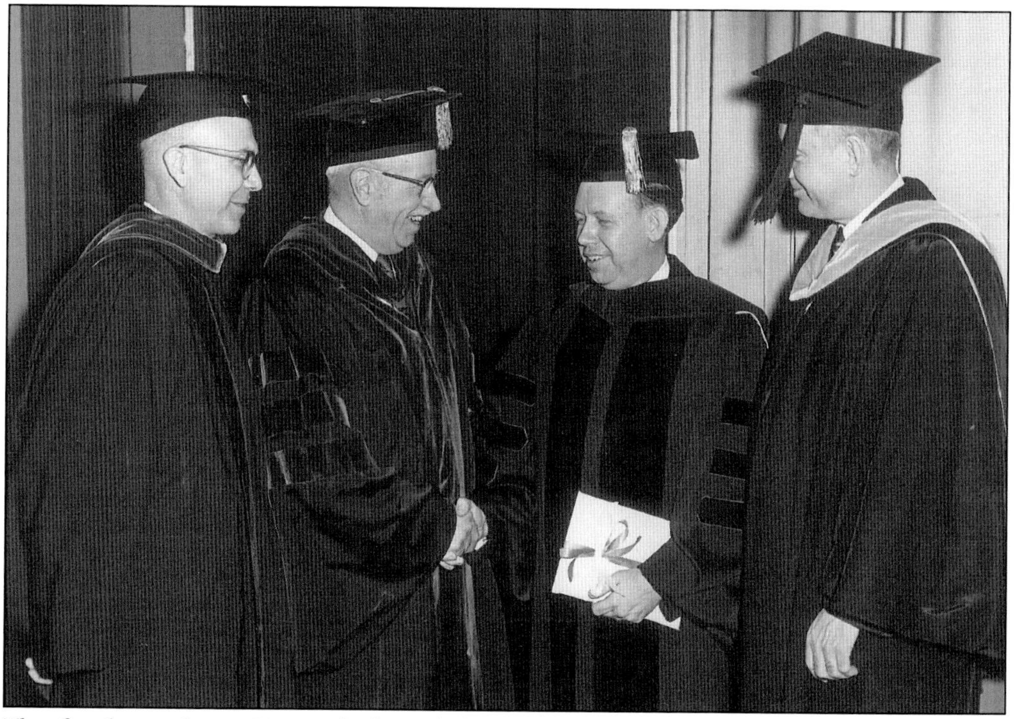

The faculty gathers. Pictured, from left to right, are Dr. Bimey Gross; Dr. William Morgan, Rev. Norman Crewson, and Dr. Ronald Weber, acting president.

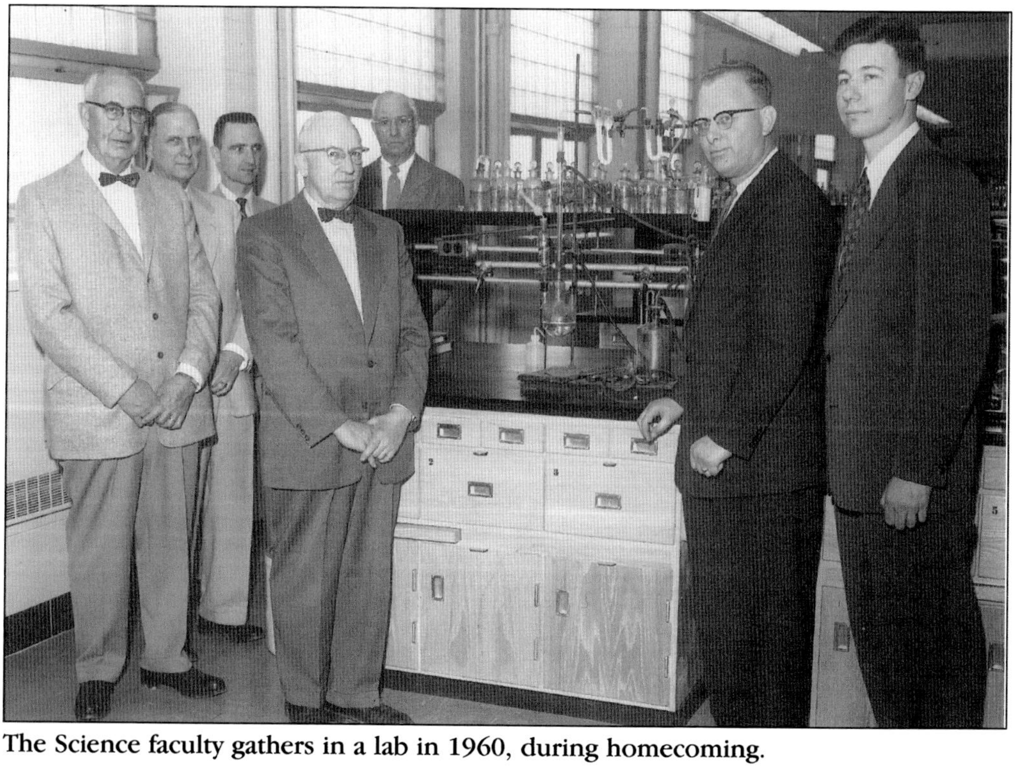

The Science faculty gathers in a lab in 1960, during homecoming.

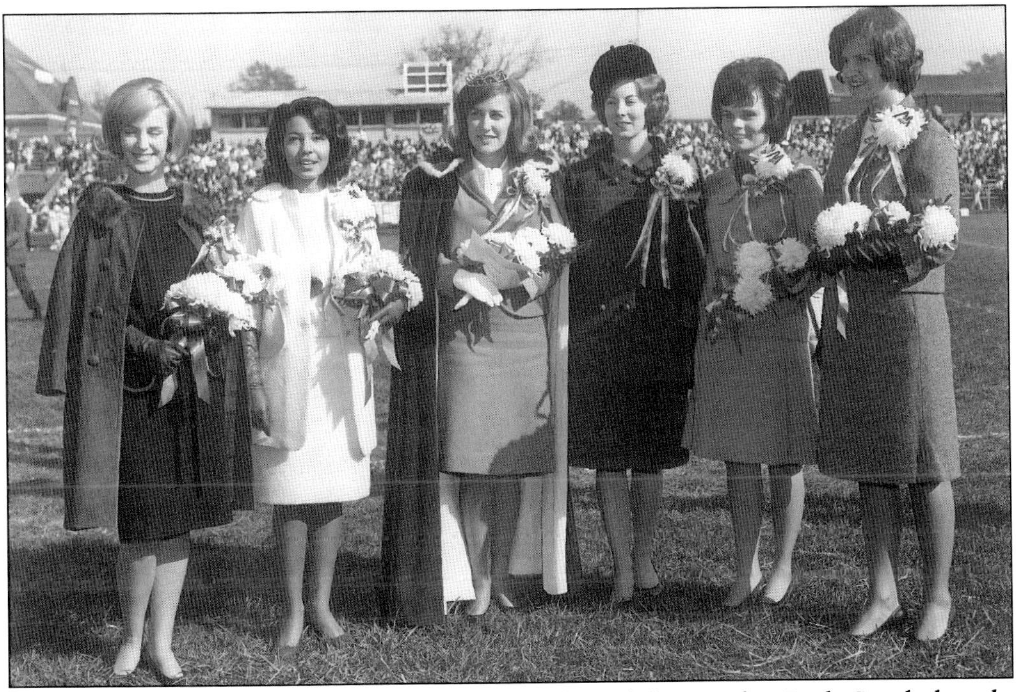

It's the 1965 homecoming and gathered are, from left to right, Paula Lauderbaugh, Anita Richmond, 1965 Queen Tari Travis, 1964 Queen Michelle Marstrell Catalano, Joan Thomas, and Barbara Weaver.

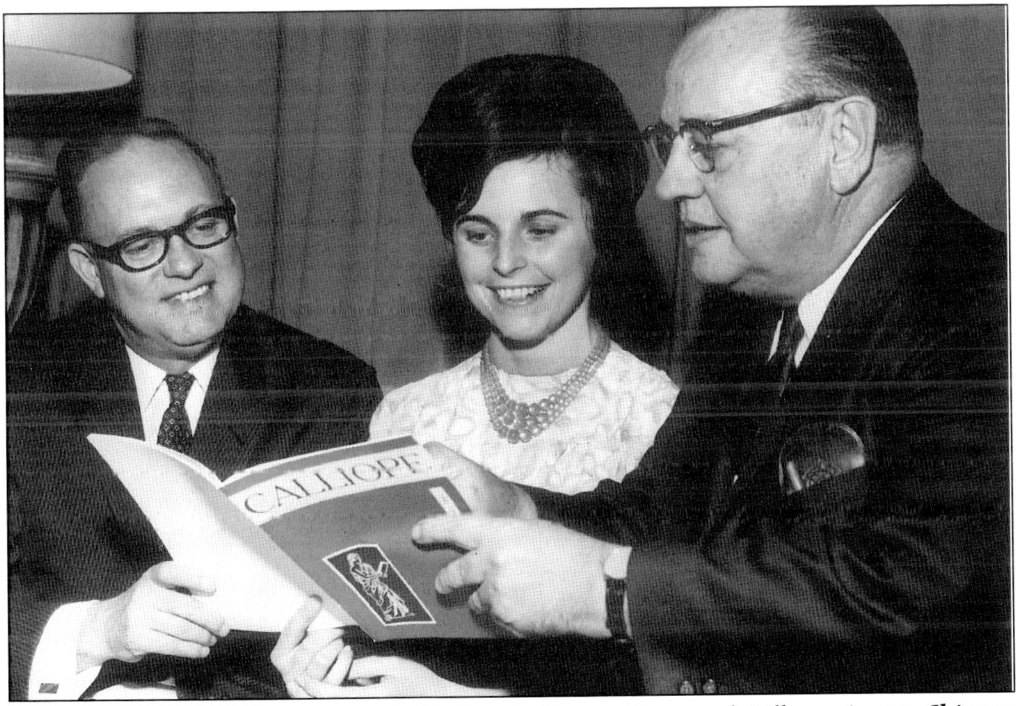

Here are Dr. Paul Chapman, Heidi Muller, Calliope editor, and Milburn Auers, *Chicago Sun-Times* editor. They were at the 1965 publications banquet on campus.

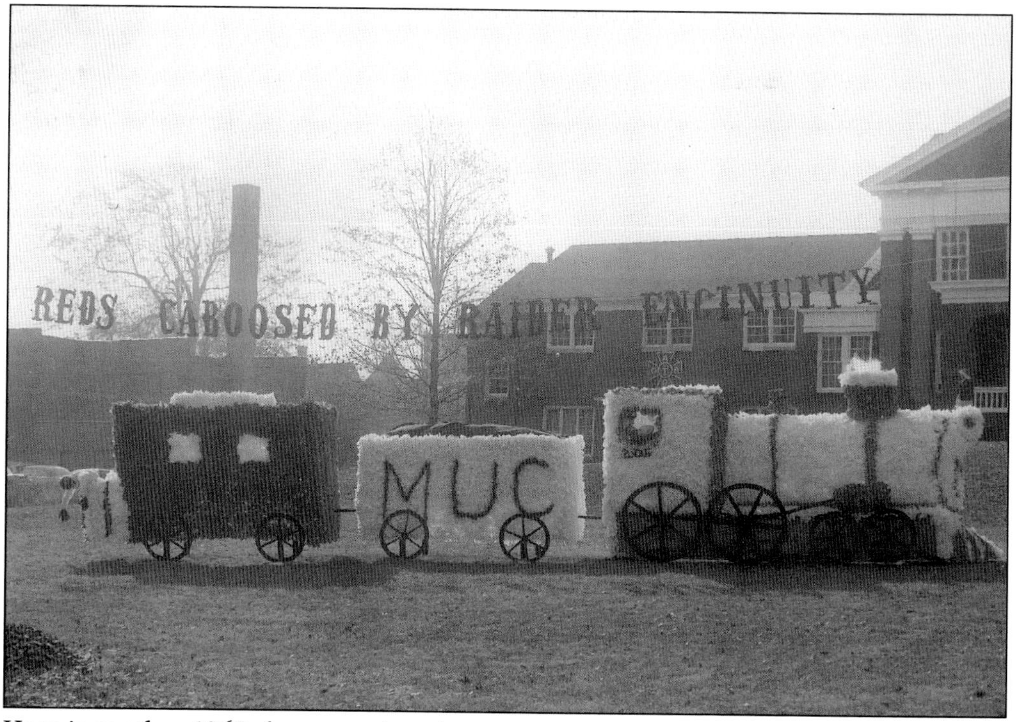

Here is another 1960s homecoming view.

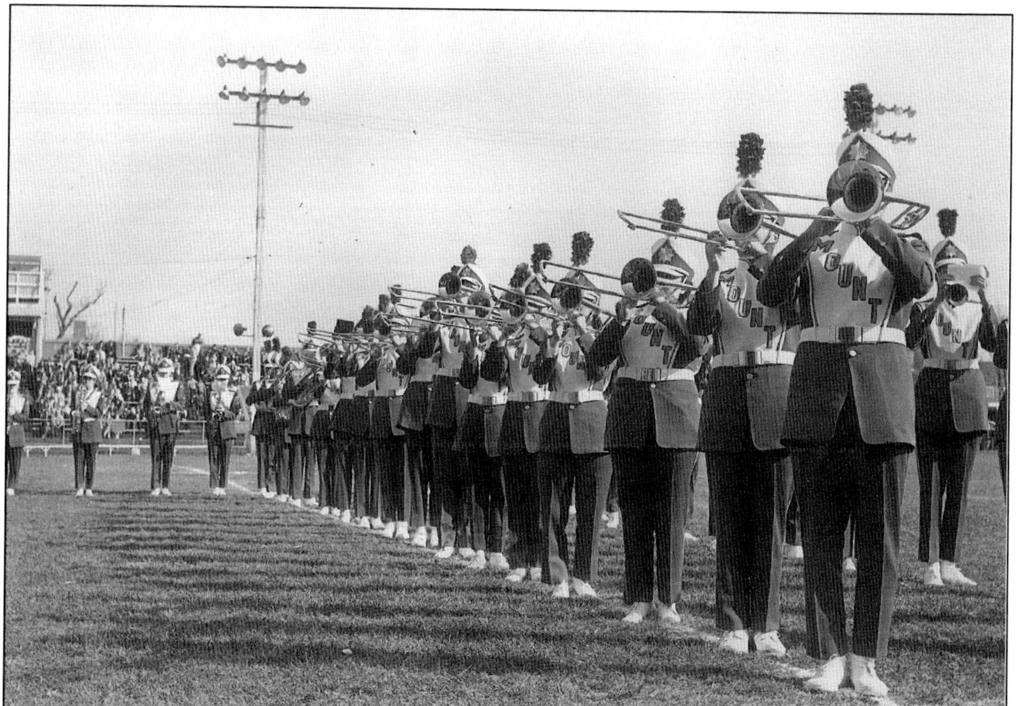

The Mount Marchers are here sporting their new purple and white uniforms during another 1960s homecoming.

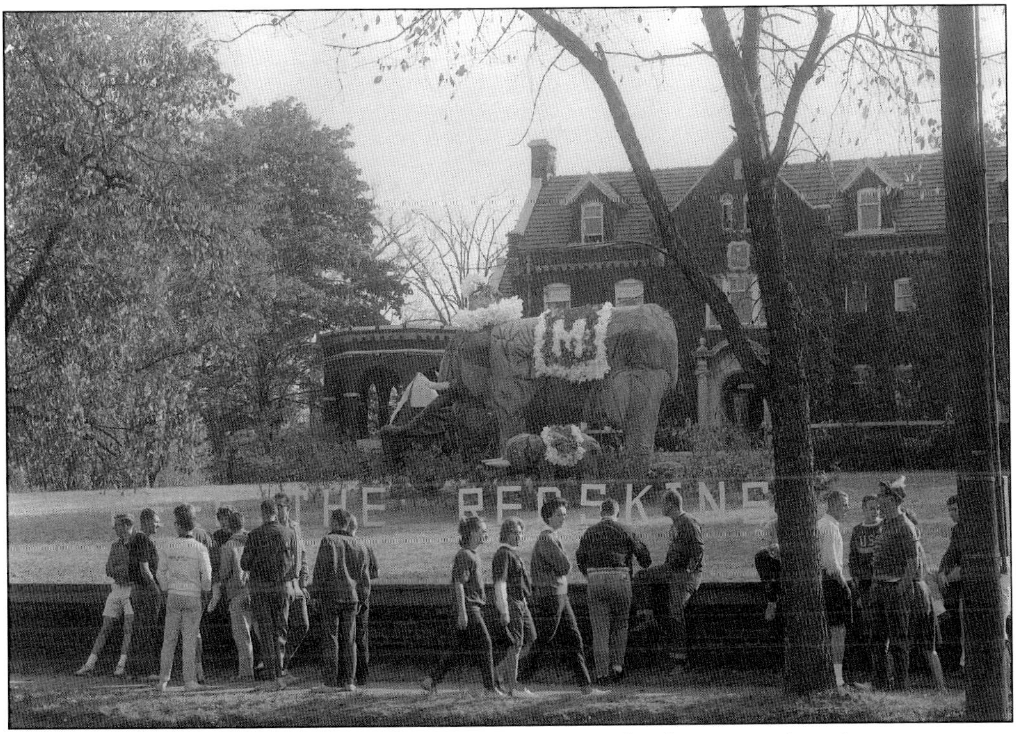

Lots of autos slowed down on Union avenue to see this homecoming view.

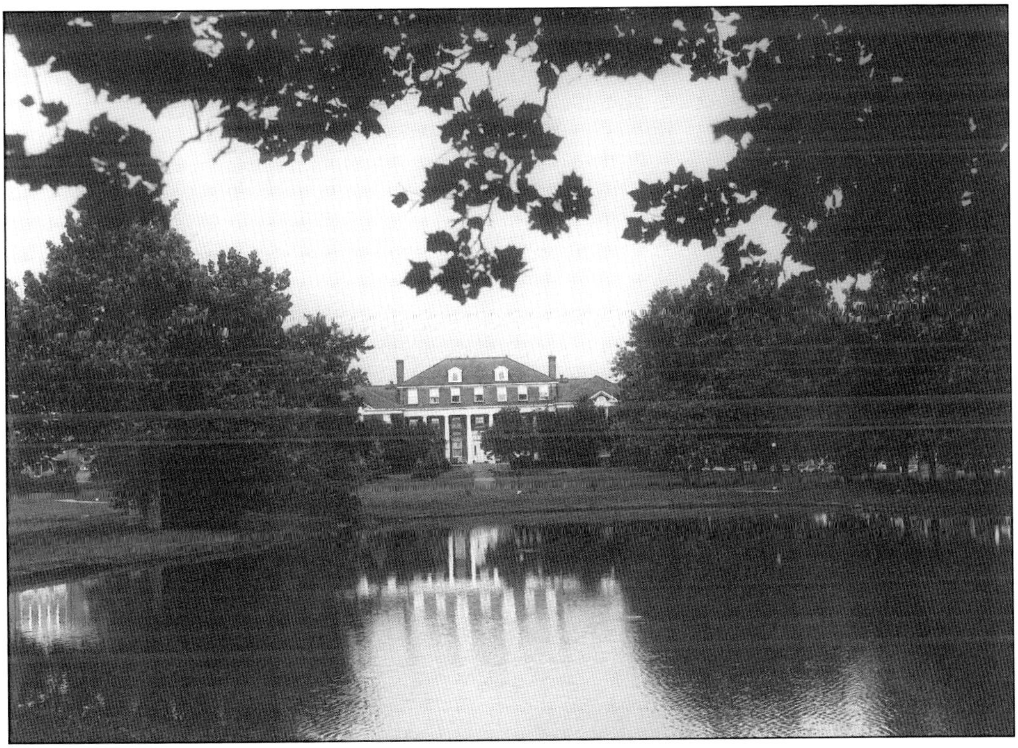

Here is a photo of Elliott Hall, and, as always, with the lake in front.

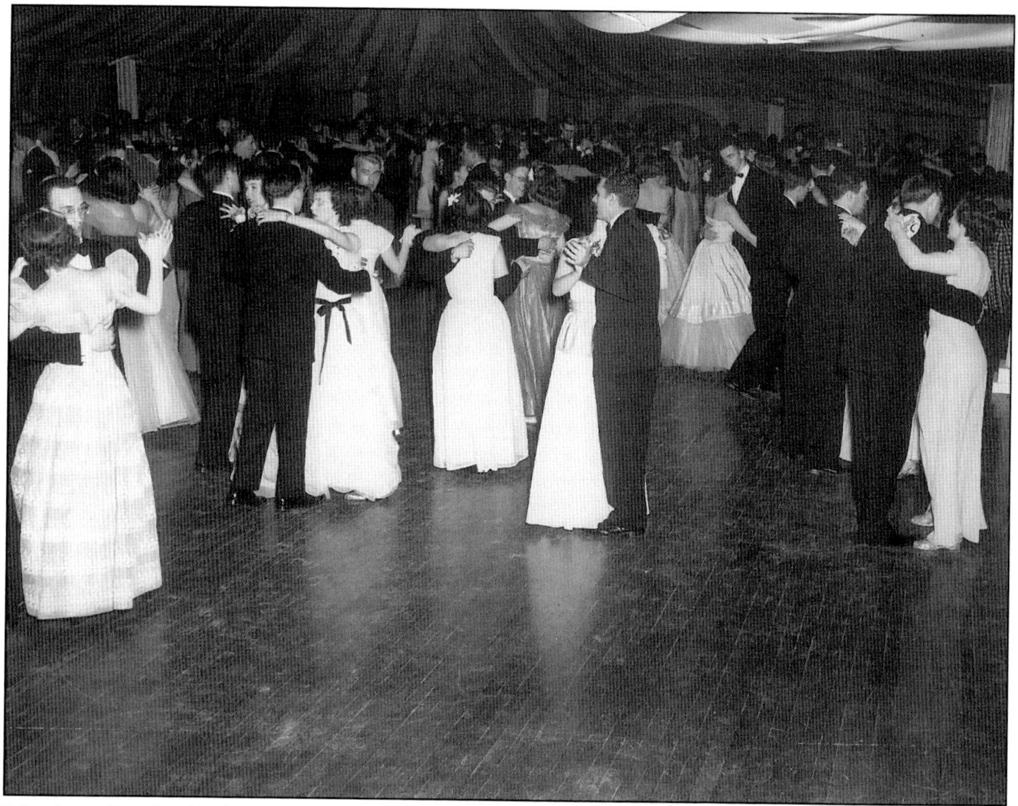

It's time for the Jr-Sr prom in the 1950s!

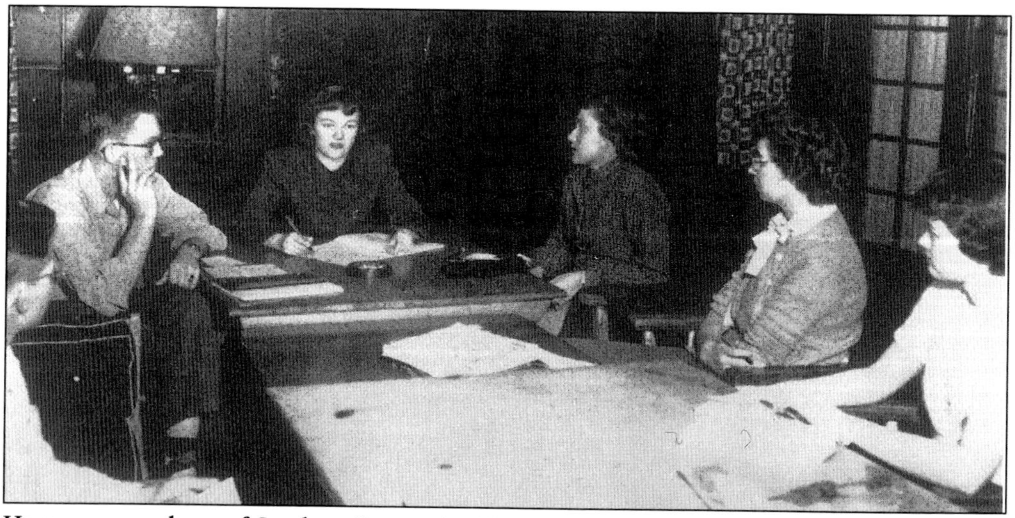

Here are members of Student Senate in 1950. Pictured, from left to right, are G. Rays, R. Ramsey, K. McFadden, I. Parker, W. Pentecost, and D. Ritter.

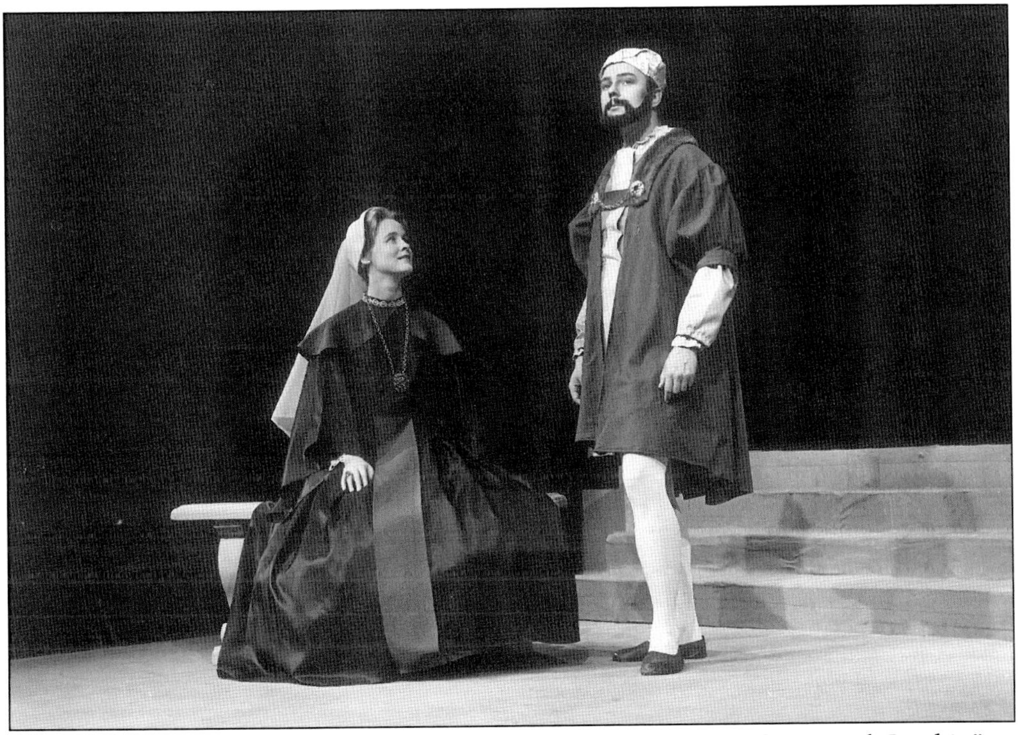

This 1964 image shows Rachael Shaffer and Philip Fox on stage for "Royal Gambit."

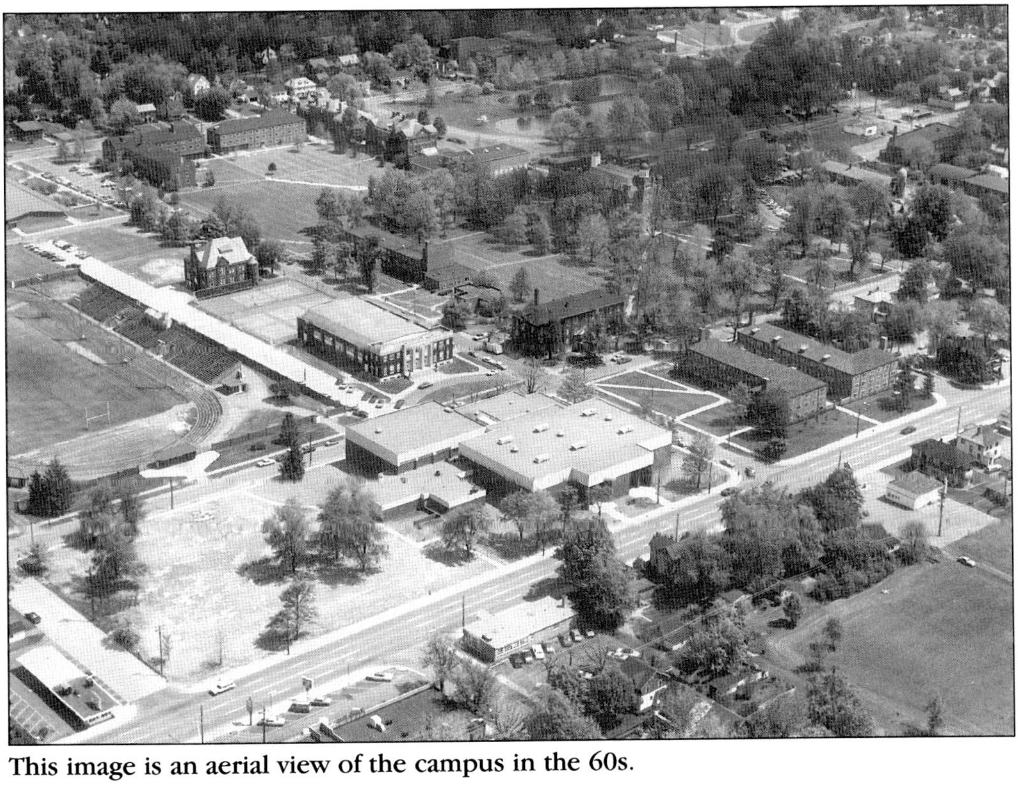

This image is an aerial view of the campus in the 60s.

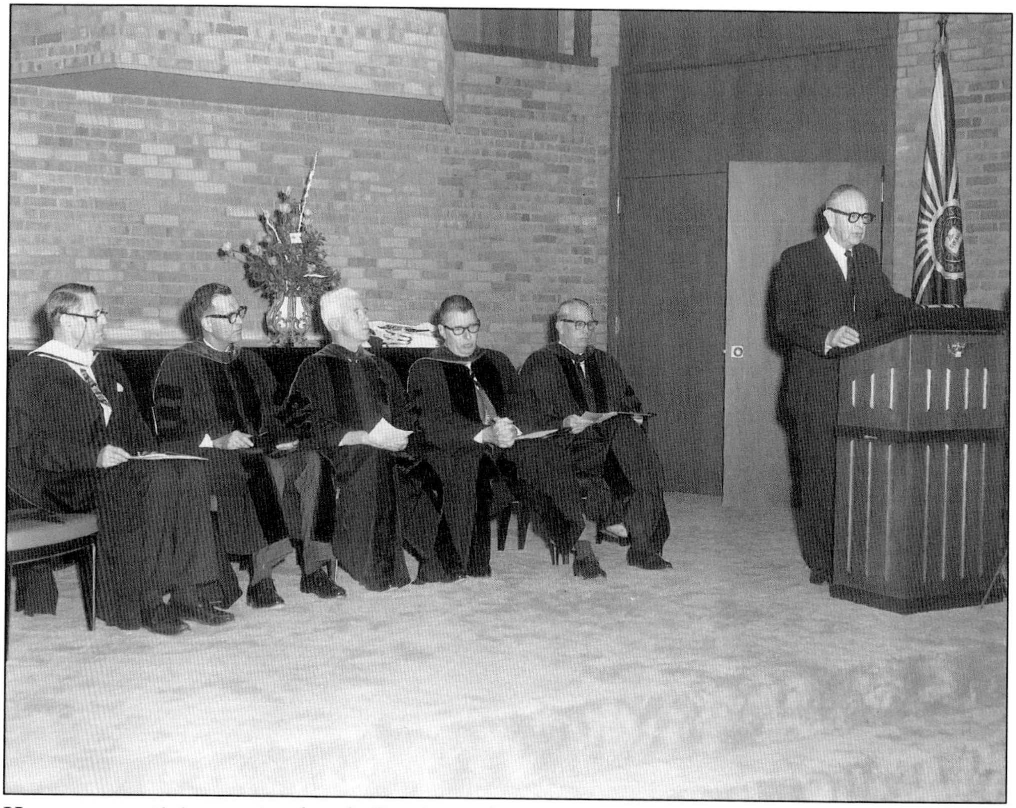

Here are participants in the dedication of Cope Hall. Pictured, from left to right, are Prof. Stewart, Chaplain Sales, Bishop Kearns, Dean Christie, President Bracy, and Dr. King. The year is 1964.

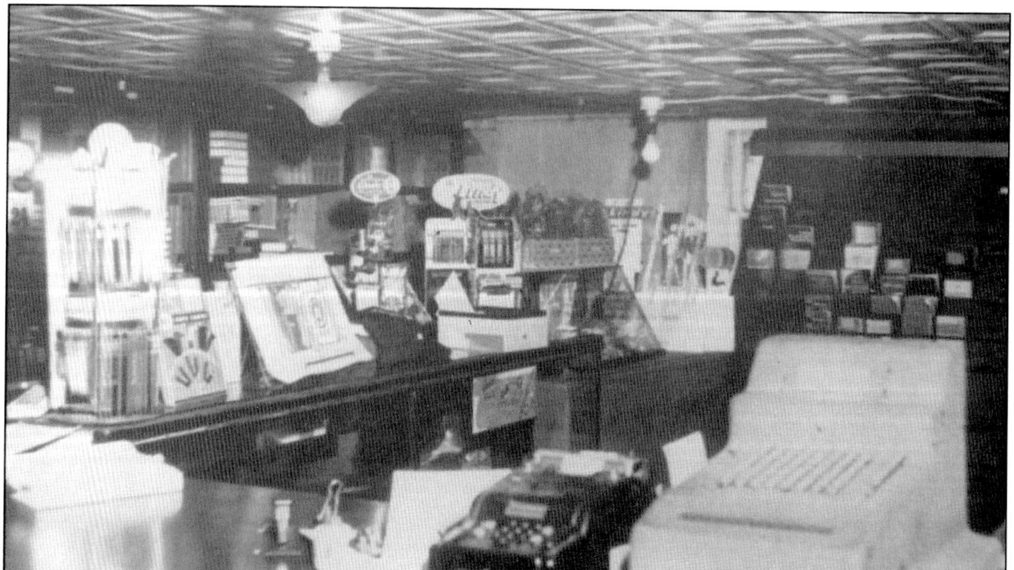

This 1966 photo shows a brief trip to the campus bookstore in the basement of the Admin building.

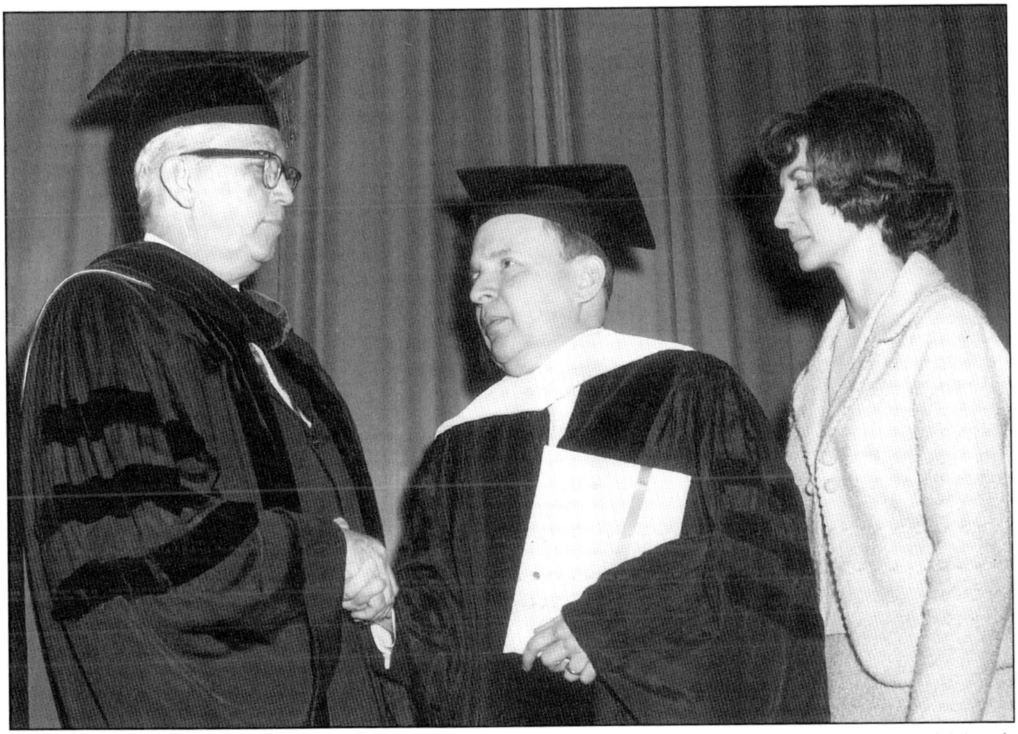

In 1954, Richard Kinney becomes the third person in the world, totally deaf and blind, to become a college graduate.

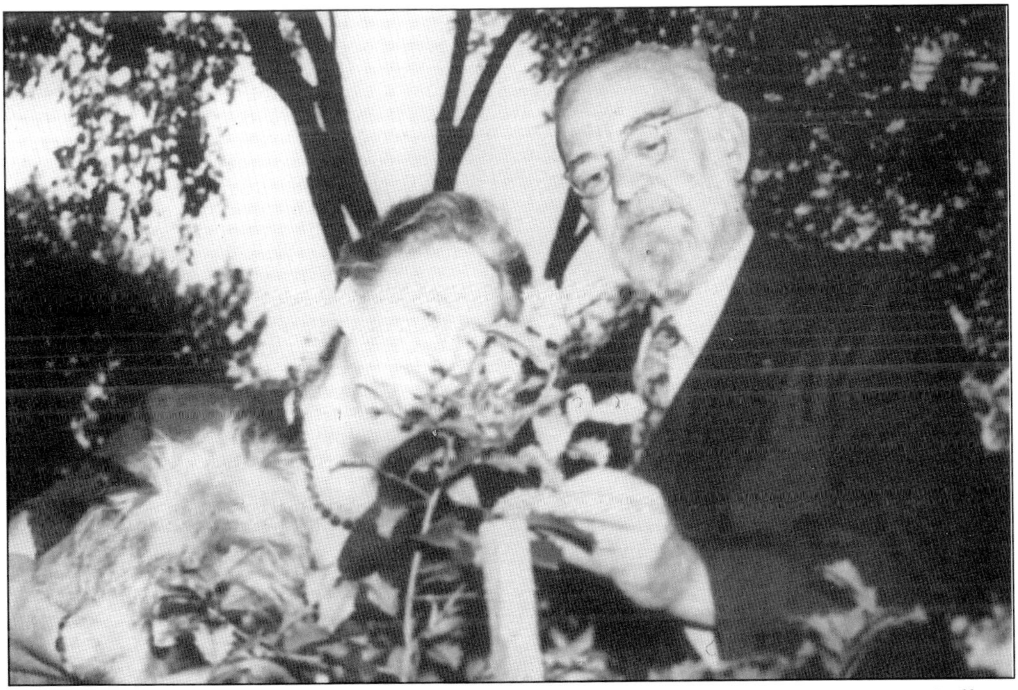

Here we see Mr. and Mrs. Eckler. Both served many years on the Mount Union College faculty. This photo was taken of them in 1952.

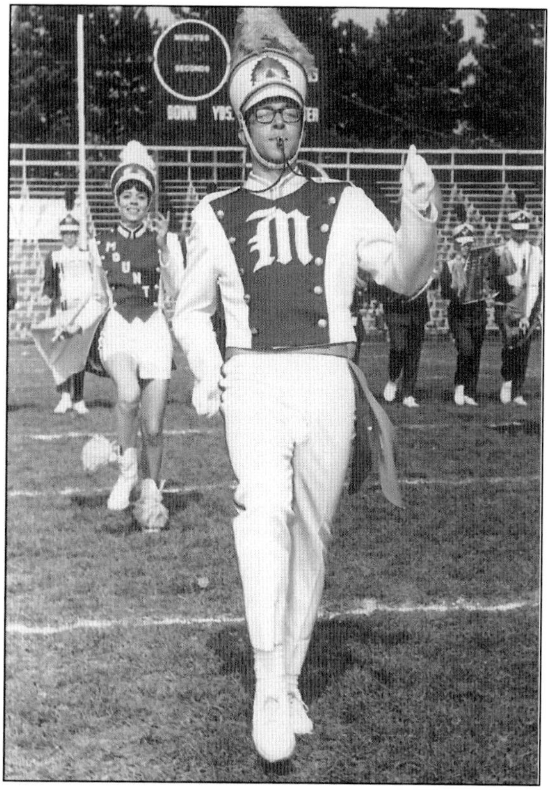

It's homecoming again. And here are Drum Major Richard Shields, with Lesley Ferris next in the great parade.

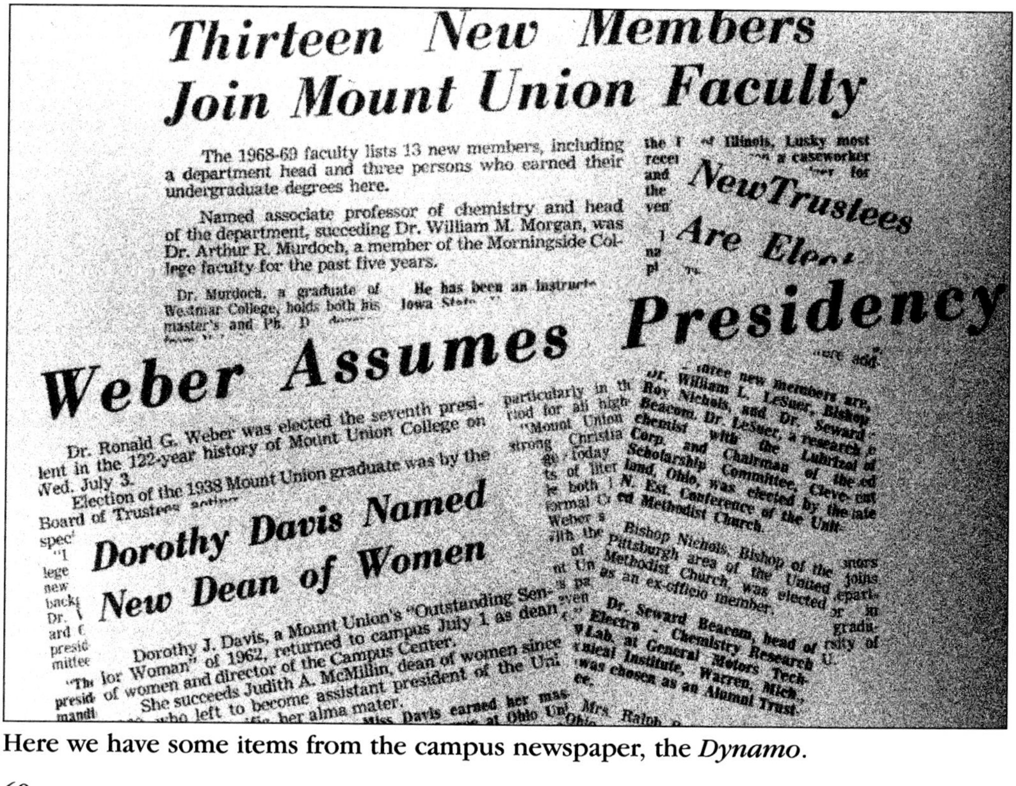

Thirteen New Members Join Mount Union Faculty

The 1968-69 faculty lists 13 new members, including a department head and three persons who earned their undergraduate degrees here.

Named associate professor of chemistry and head of the department, succeding Dr. William M. Morgan, was Dr. Arthur R. Murdoch, a member of the Morningside College faculty for the past five years.

Dr. Murdoch, a graduate of Westmar College, holds both his master's and Ph. D ...

He has been an instruct... Iowa State ...

NewTrustees Are Elect...

Weber Assumes Presidency

Dr. Ronald G. Weber was elected the seventh president in the 122-year history of Mount Union College on Wed. July 3.

Election of the 1938 Mount Union graduate was by the Board of Trustees ...

particularly in th... ried for all high... "Mount Union ... strong Christia...

... three new members are, Dr. William L. LeSuer, Bishop Roy Nichols, and Dr. Seward Beacom. Dr. LeSuer, a research chemist with the Lubrizol Corp. and Chairman of the Scholarship Committee, Cleveland, Ohio, was elected by the N. Est. Conference of the United Methodist Church.

Bishop Nichols, Bishop of the Pittsburgh area of the United Methodist Church, was elected as an ex-officio member.

Dr. Seward Beacom, head of Electro - Chemistry Research Lab, at General Motors Technical Institute, Warren, Mich., was chosen as an Alumni Trust...

Dorothy Davis Named New Dean of Women

Dorothy J. Davis, a Mount Union's "Outstanding Senior Woman" of 1962, returned to campus July 1 as dean of women and director of the Campus Center.

She succeeds Judith A. McMillin, dean of women since ... who left to become assistant president of the Uni... her alma mater.

Miss Davis earned her mas...

Here we have some items from the campus newspaper, the *Dynamo*.

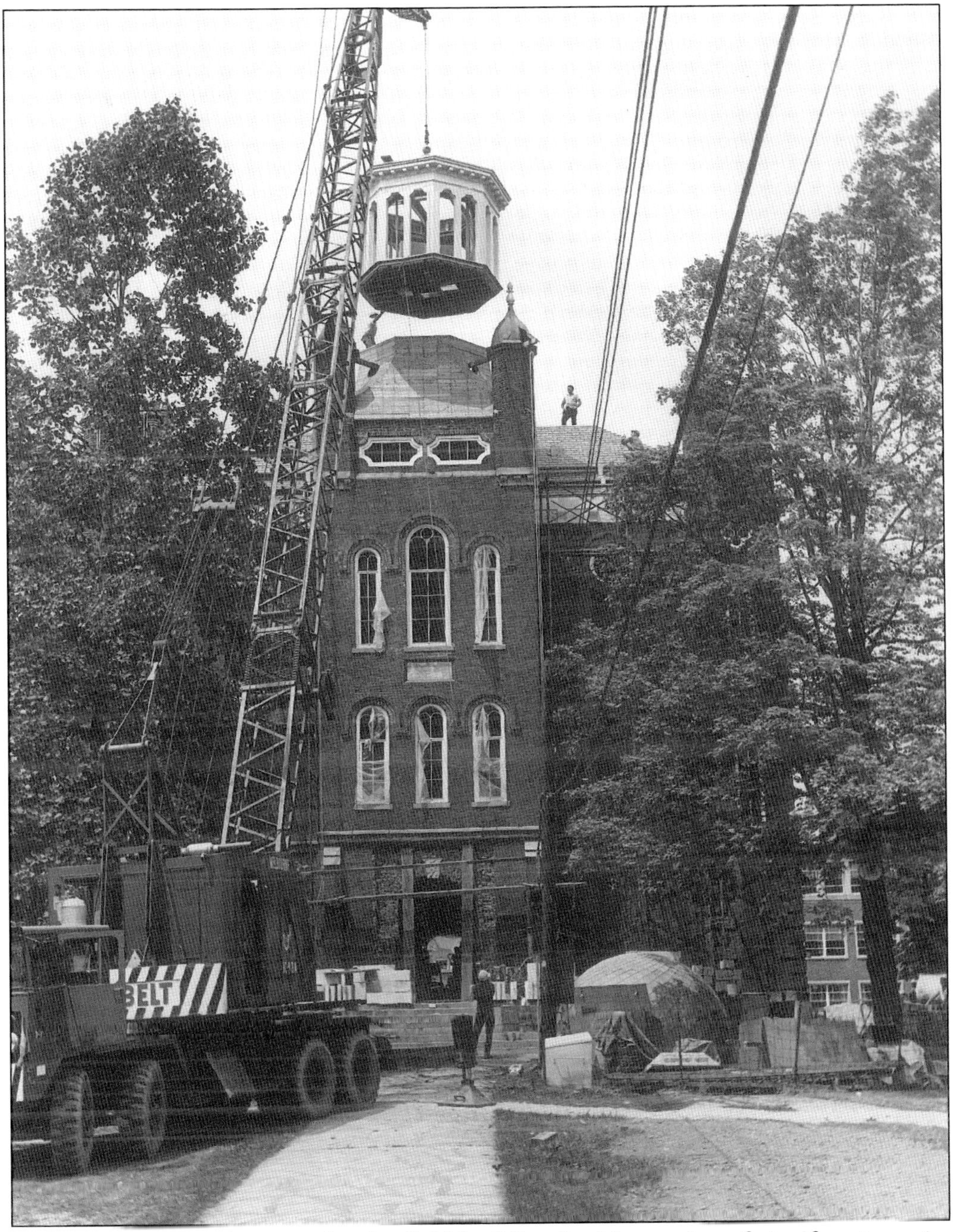

Chapman Hall continues to be the "old building," with a series of significant repairs and remodeling. This view is from the 1960s. The building did not hold classes while it was being renovated.

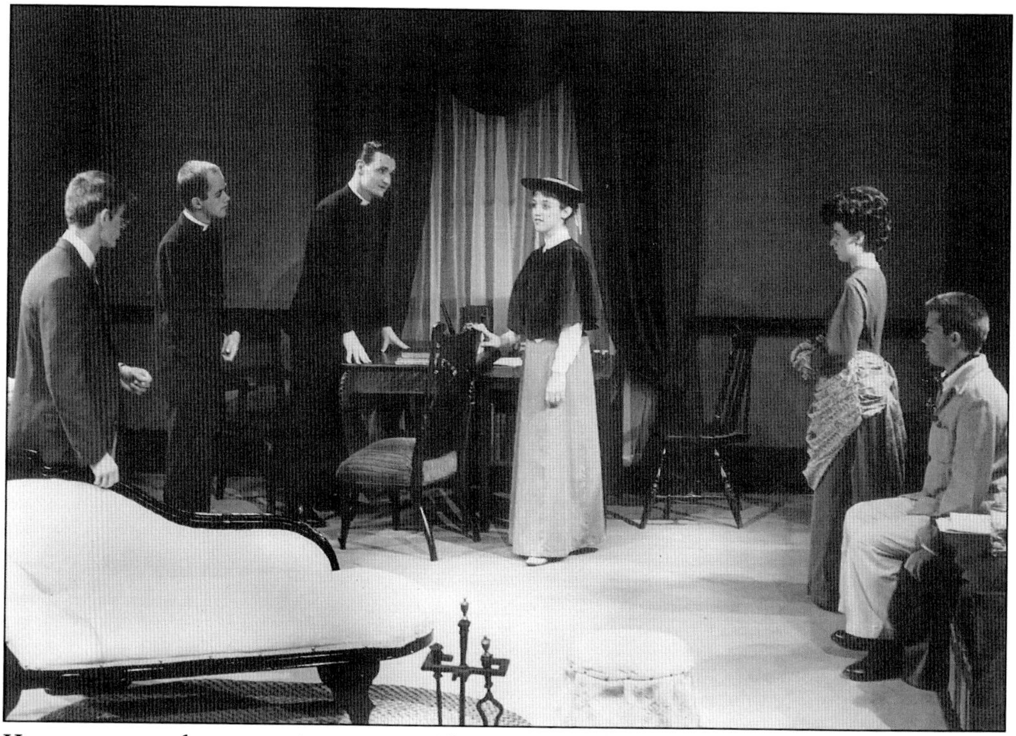

Here are more homecoming scenes! This is a mid-60s scene from *Candida* produced by the campus "Theater 5."

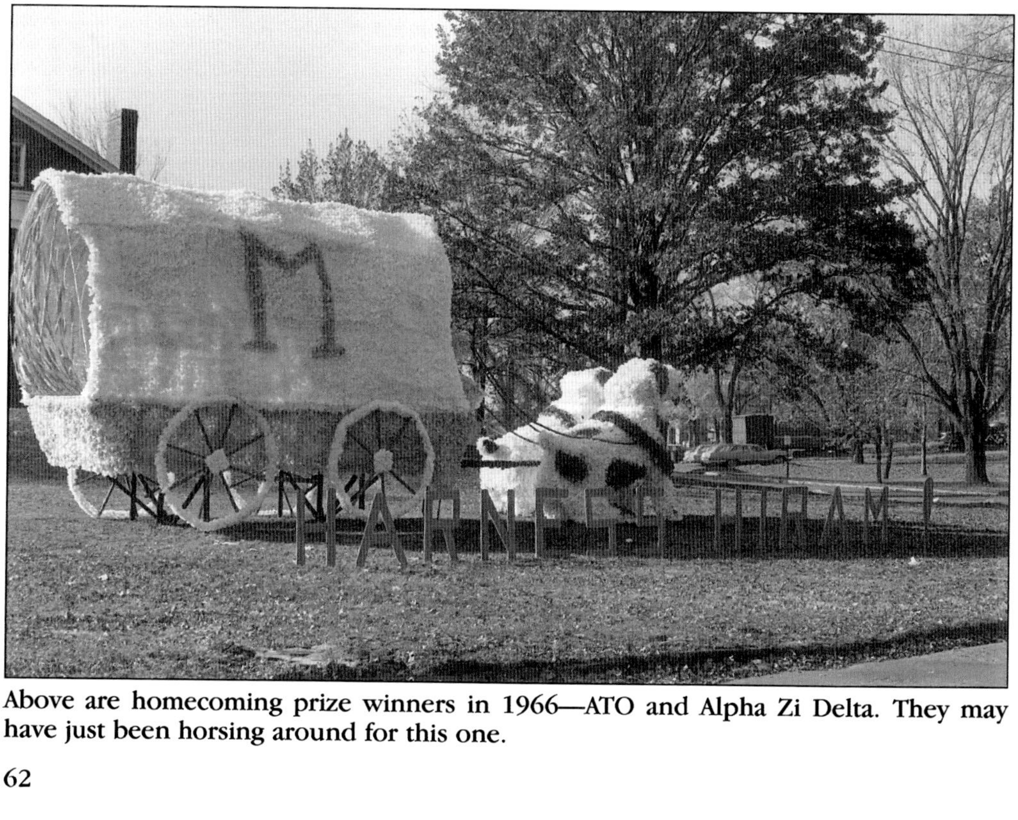

Above are homecoming prize winners in 1966—ATO and Alpha Zi Delta. They may have just been horsing around for this one.

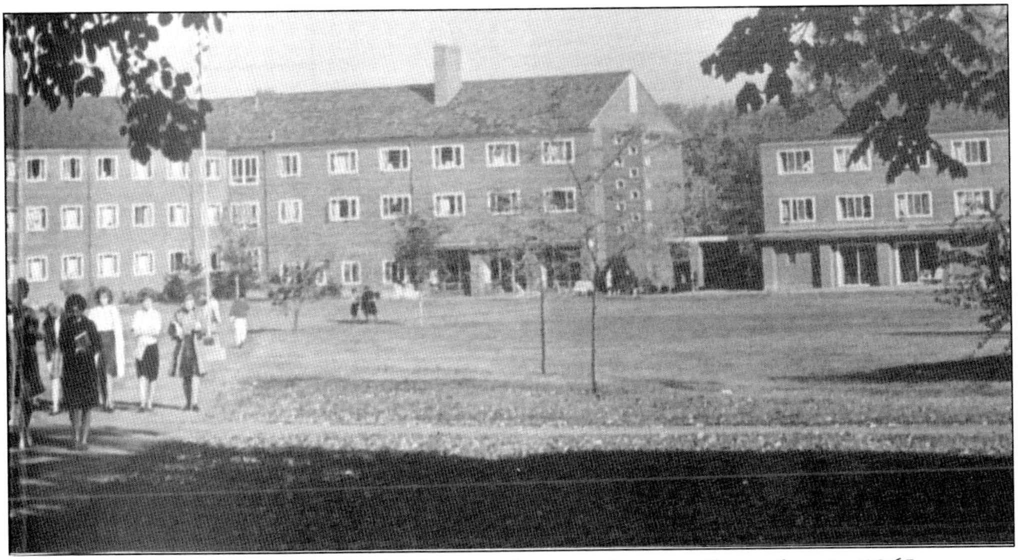

Here we see dormitories in the background, as students walk to class in 1965.

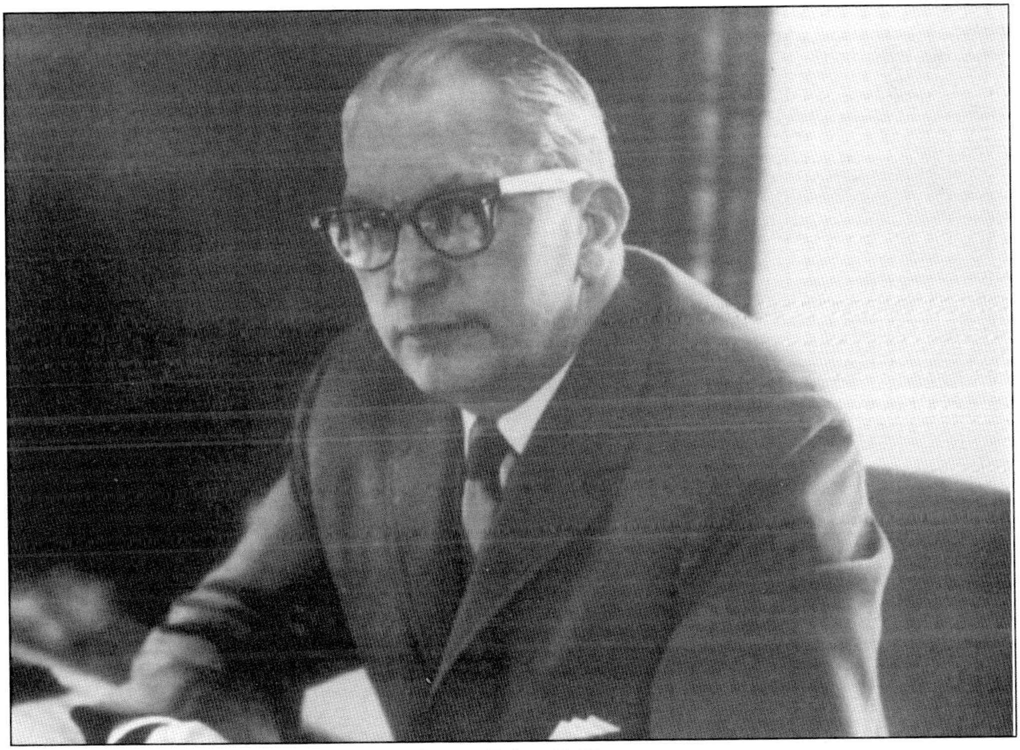

Here is Carl Bracy, serving as President of the College.

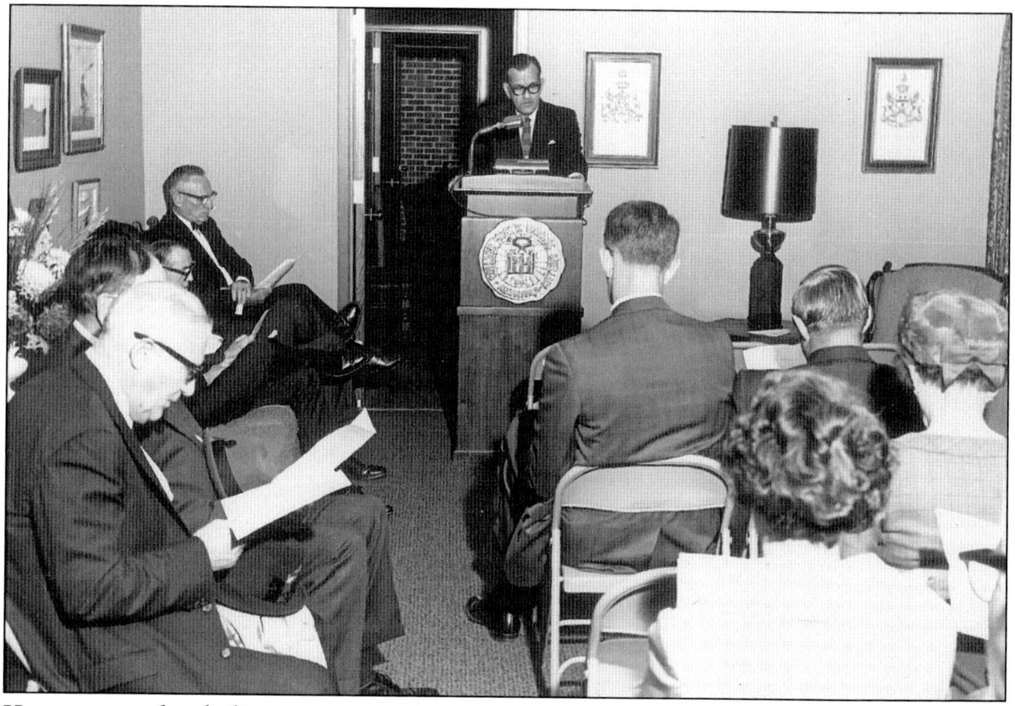

Here we see the dedication service for a new dormitory for the men in 1968. Speaking is Dr. R.H. Sales.

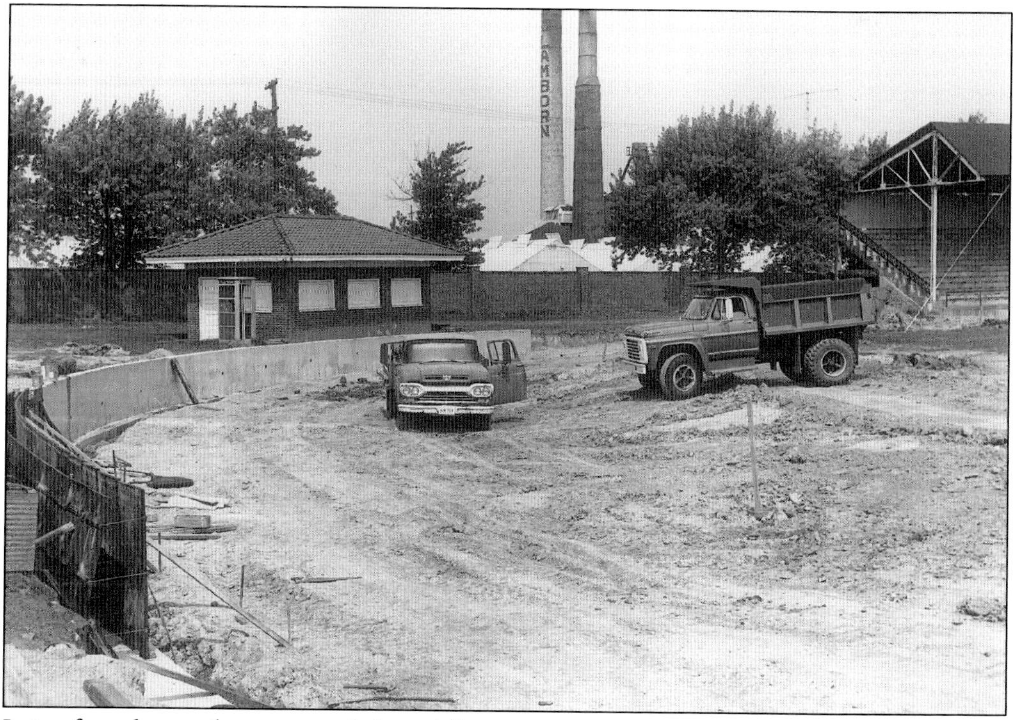

Lots of work was done around the gridiron, as seen in this 1968 image. Updating and enlarging were the focus many of the times.

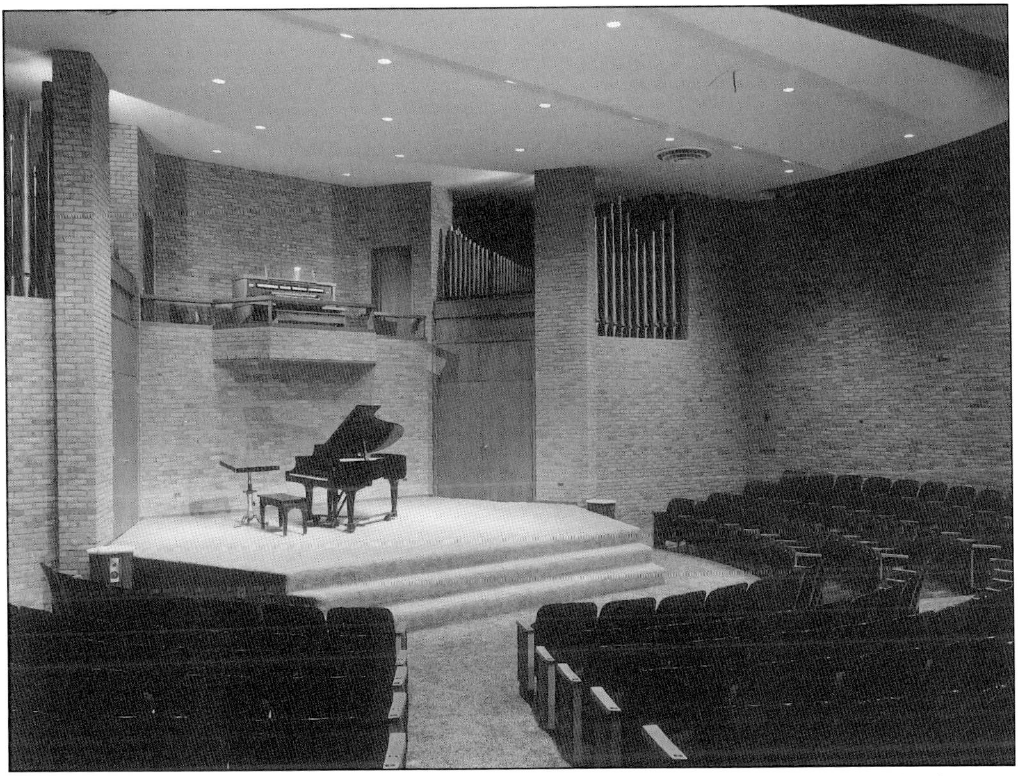

Presser Recital Hall always awaits performers ... and awaits audiences as well. This is a mid-60s photograph.

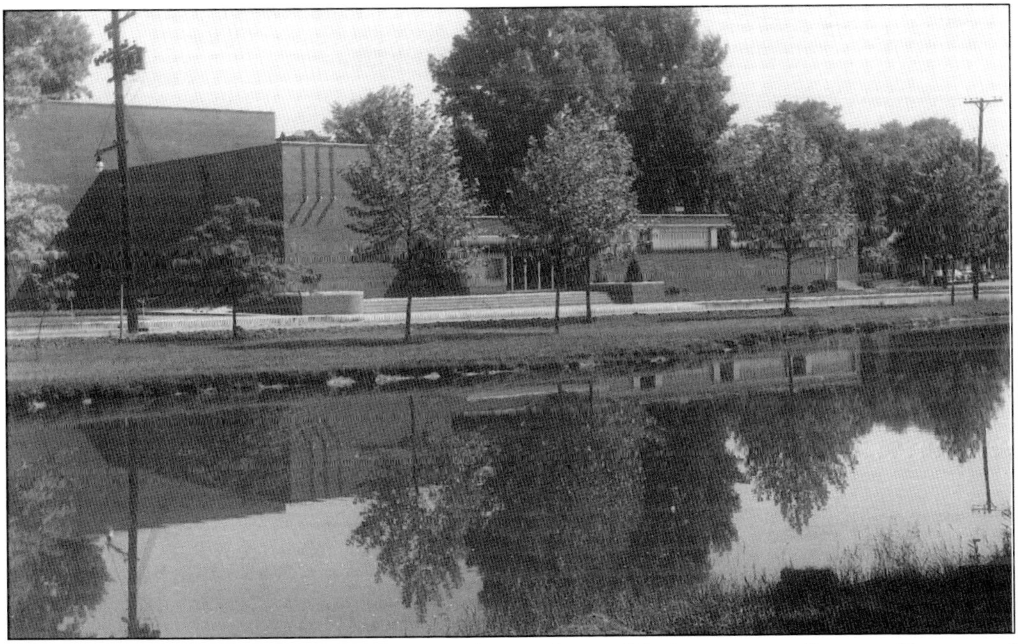

Good campus combinations! Here is the Rodman Playhouse—well, actually two of them, thanks to the reflection which the campus lake provides!

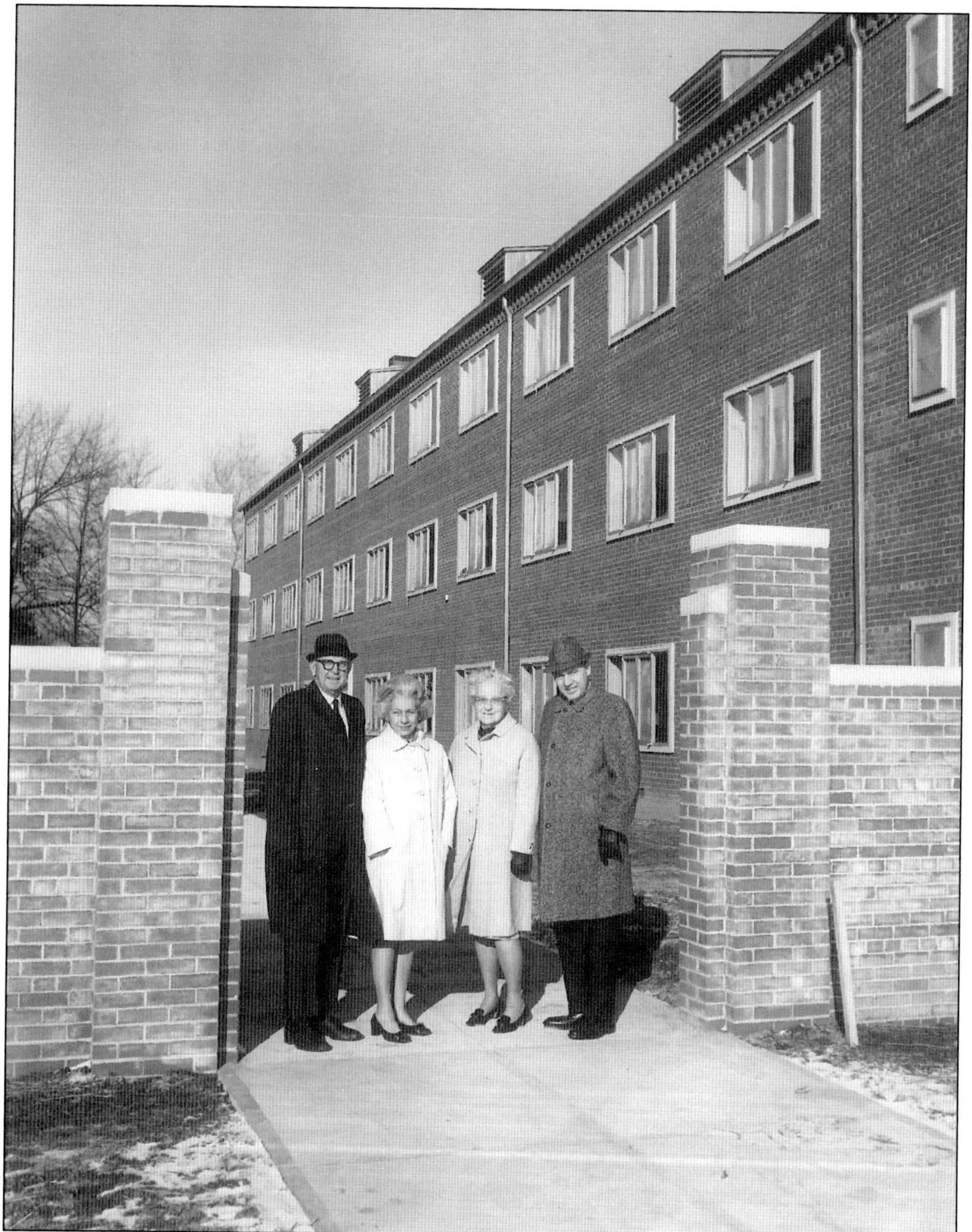

This image shows the Cunningham Hall dedication—1968. Pictured, from left to right, are Mr. and Mrs. N.A. Cunningham, Mrs. B.Y. McCready, and President Ron Weber.

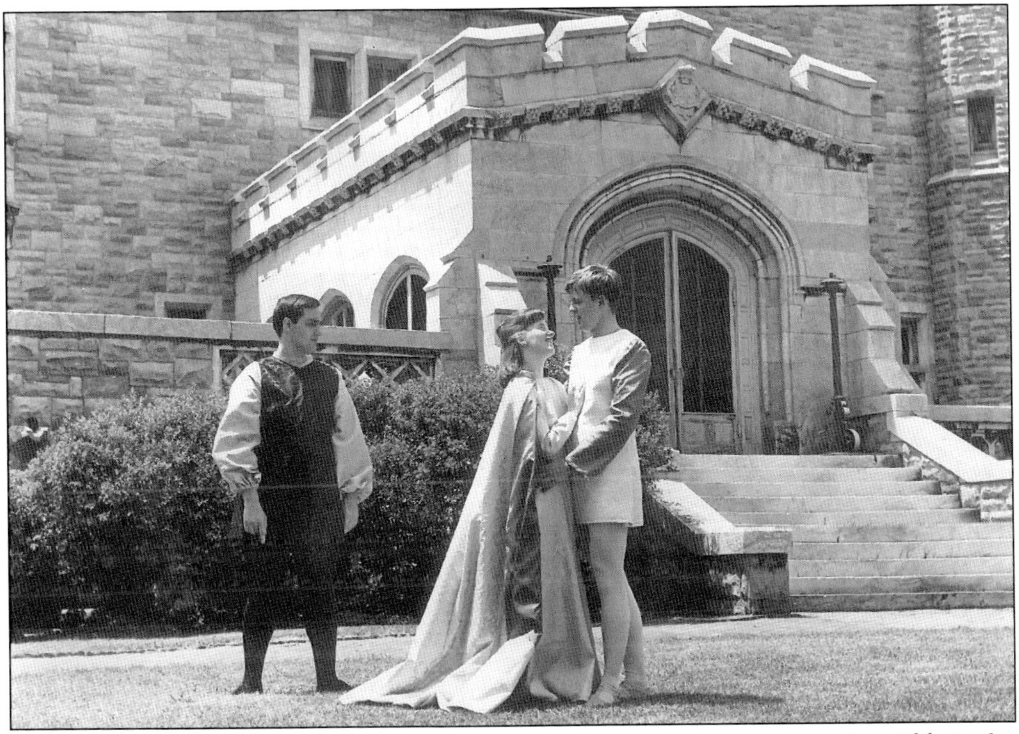

This view is of the drama *Camelot*, produced by Mount Union students in 1966. In the background is the Glamorgan castle in Alliance.

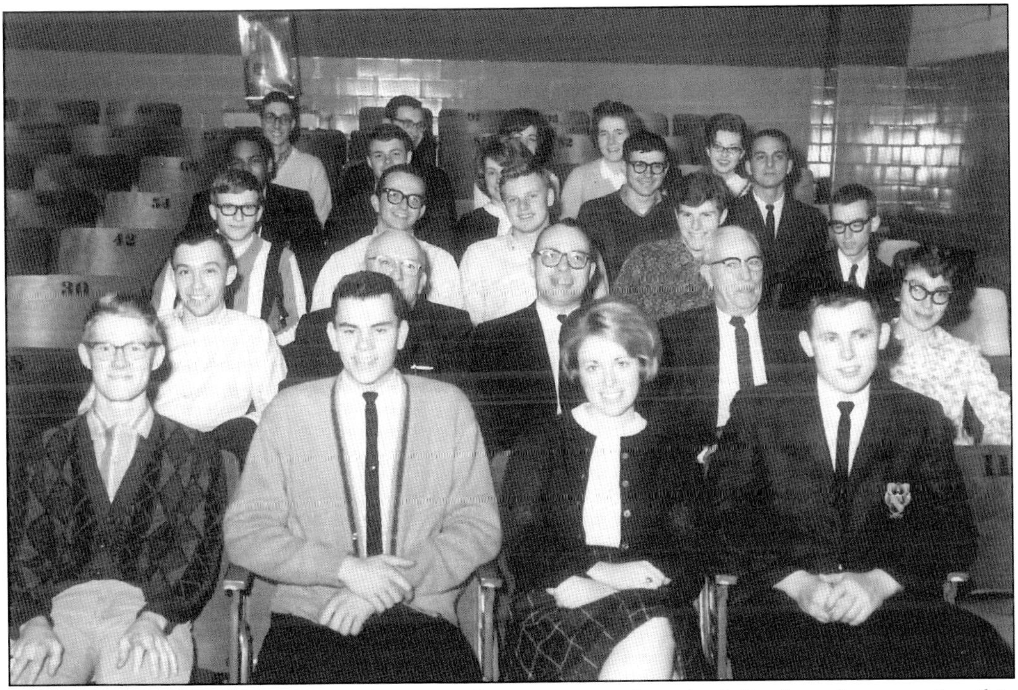

A gathering of the campus chapter of American Chemical Society is seen in this 1965 image.

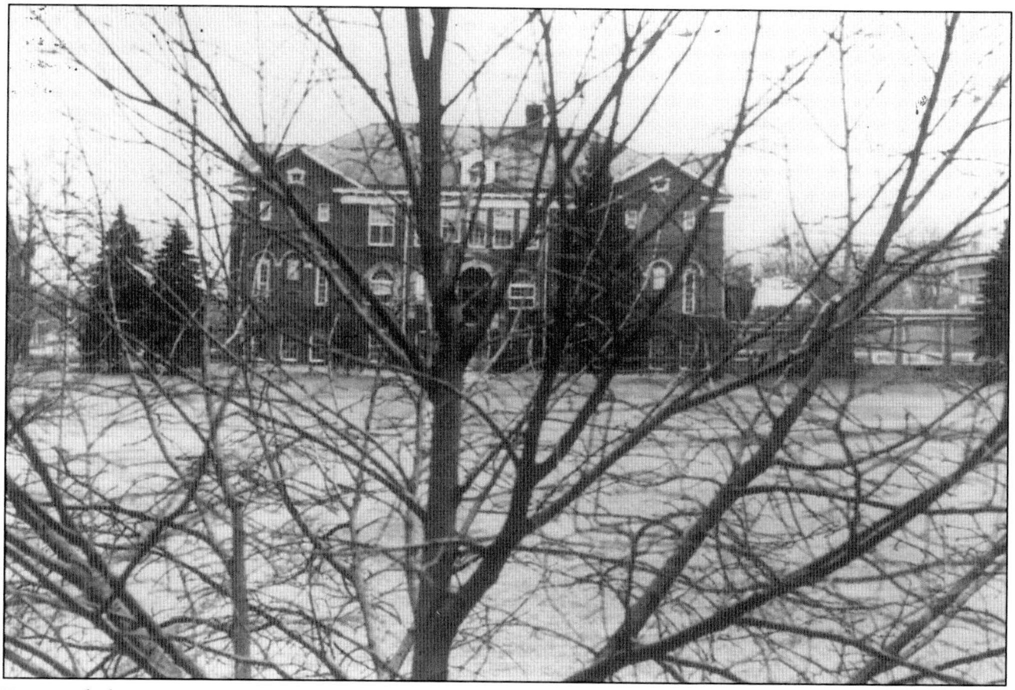

Beyond the wintry trees is an older building.

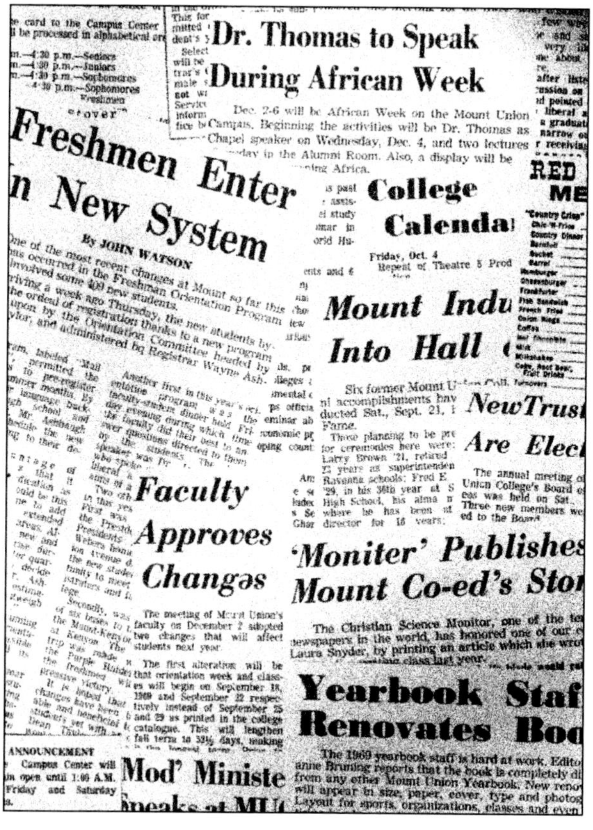

Lots of headline segments here—activity continues always on campus.

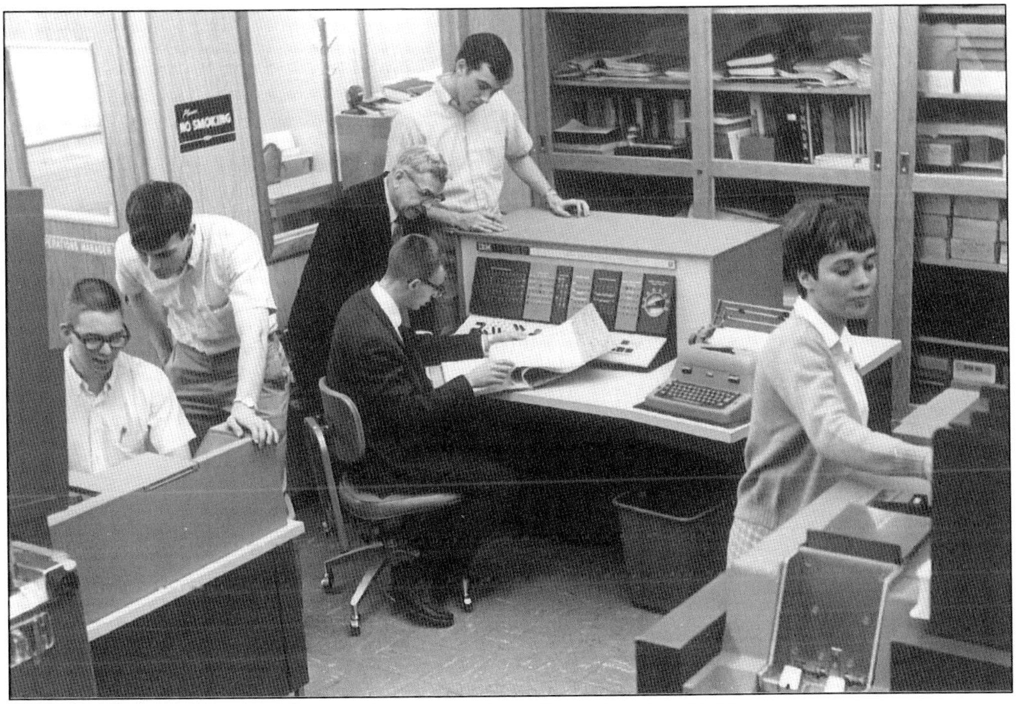

Here is the Computer Center allowing a brief look in the 1960s.

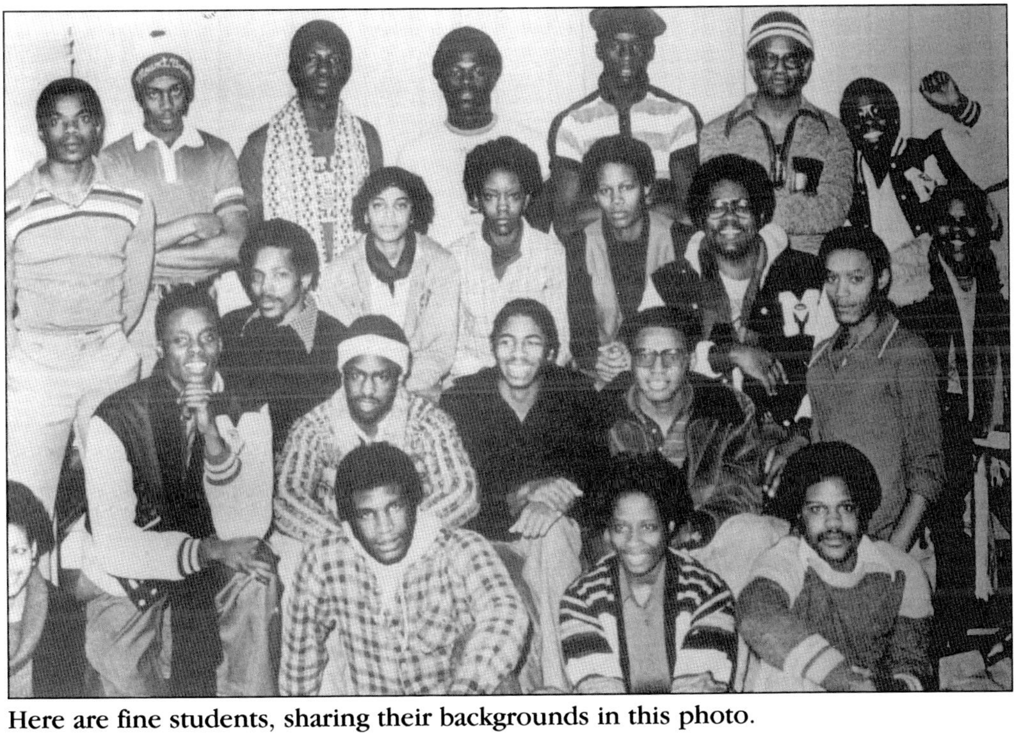

Here are fine students, sharing their backgrounds in this photo.

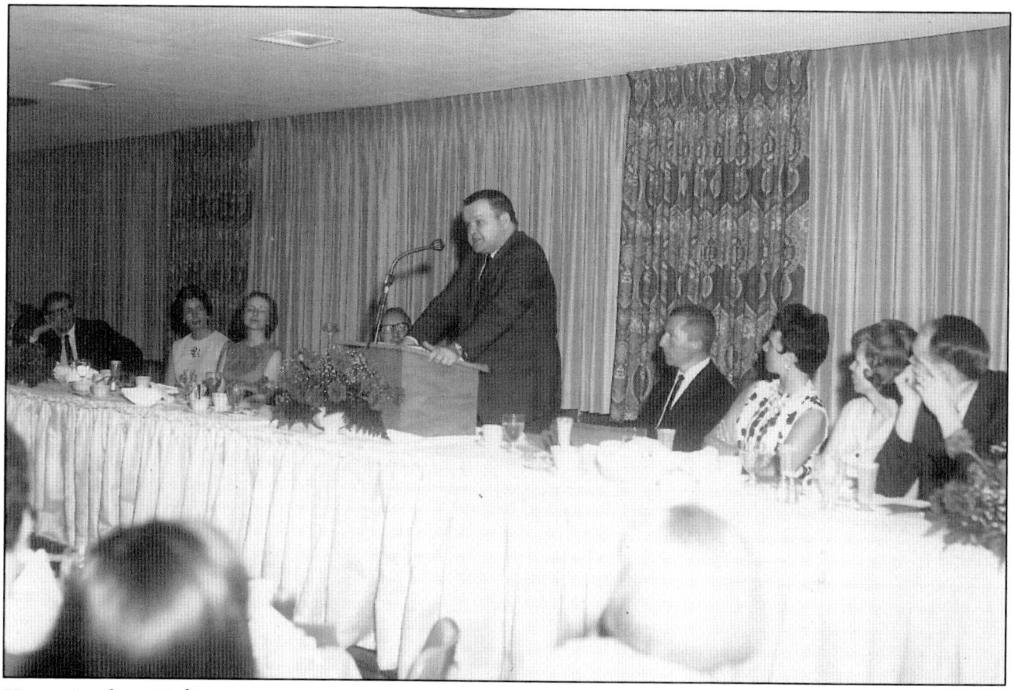

Here is the 1968 communications banquet. Novelist Don Robertson gives the main evening address. Others are members of the Communications Committee.

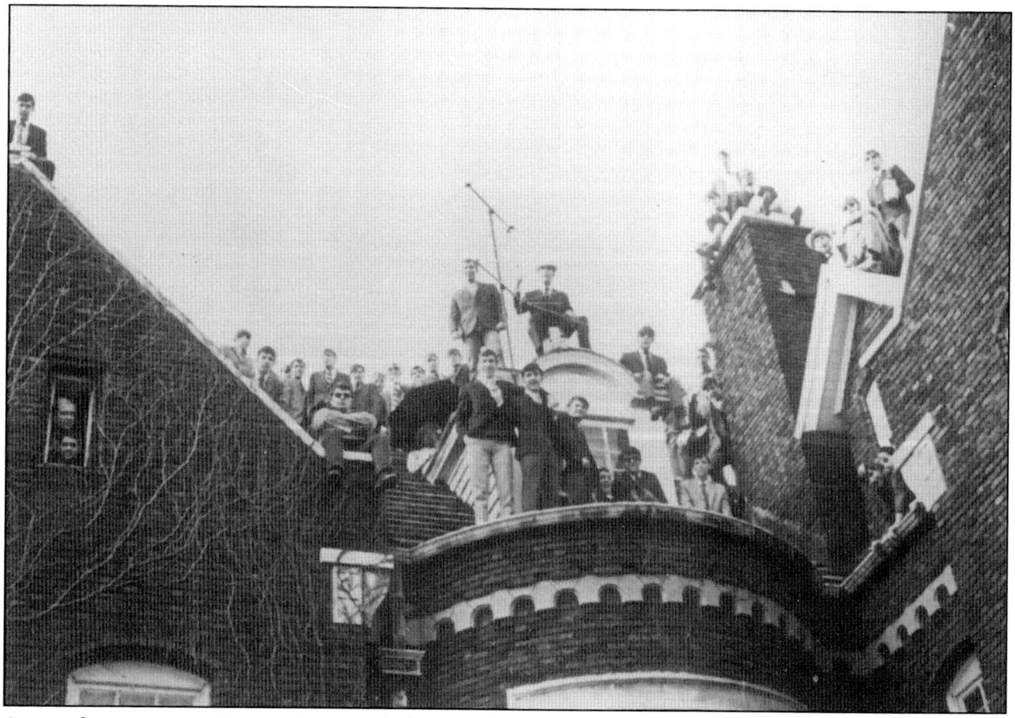

Some fraternities obviously loved the roofs of their building. At least until 1969 when this photo was taken.

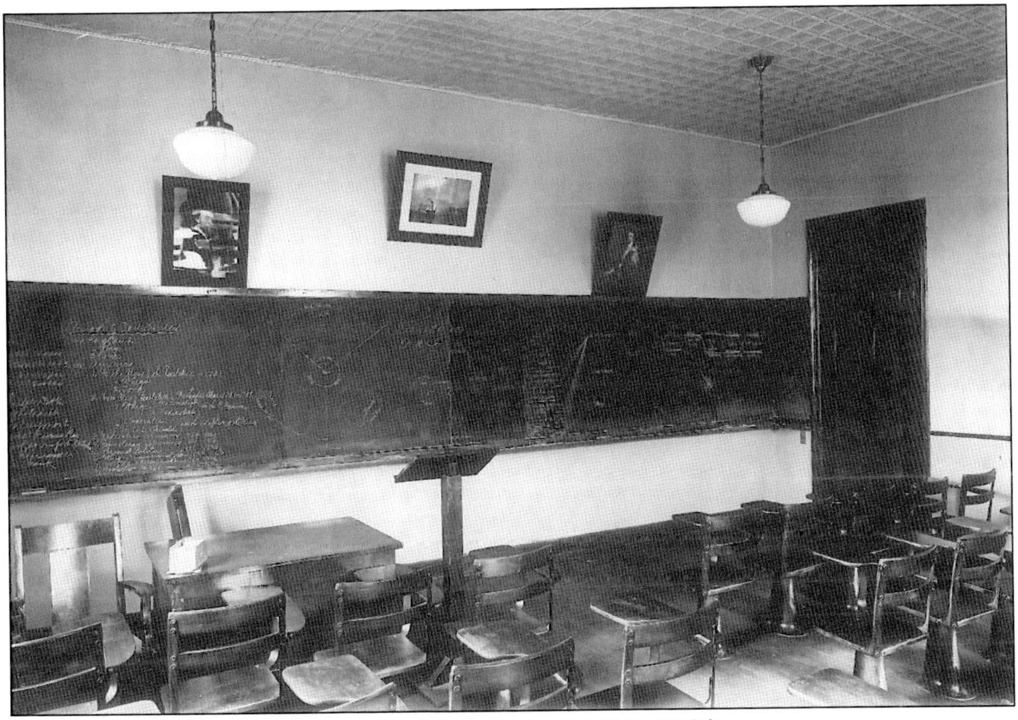

Here is a classroom view from inside Chapman Hall in 1946.

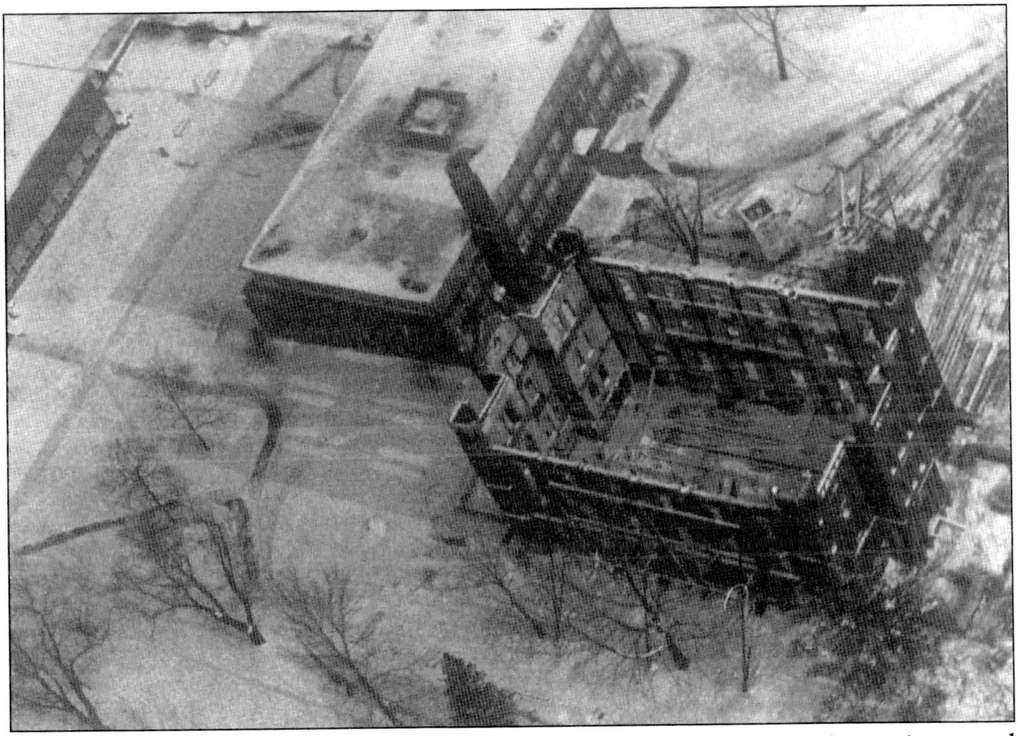

Consider this in line with the other photo which opens our memories just as it opened Chapman Hall. A complete renovation was being done.

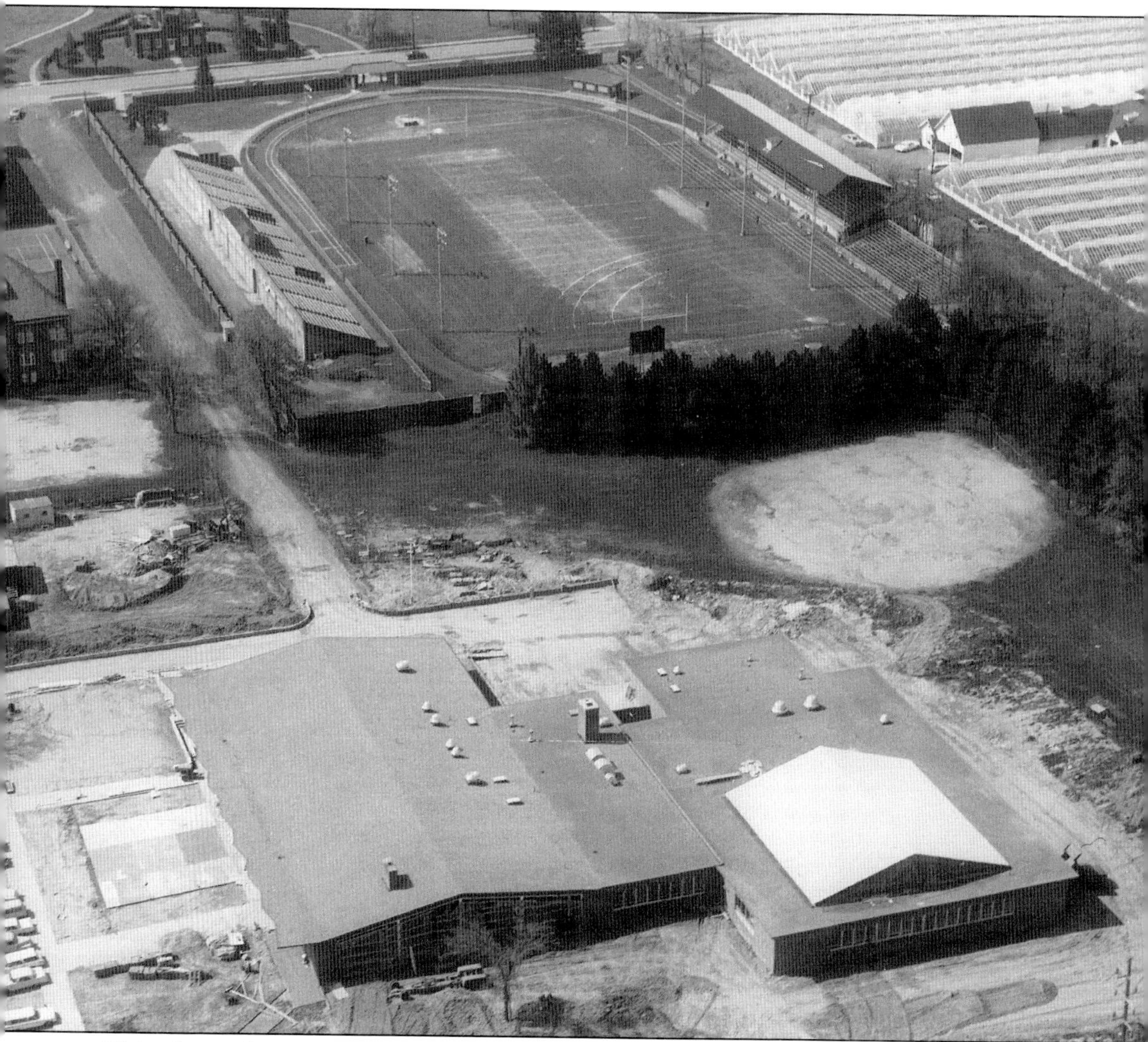

This photo shows an aerial view of the football field and the campus center

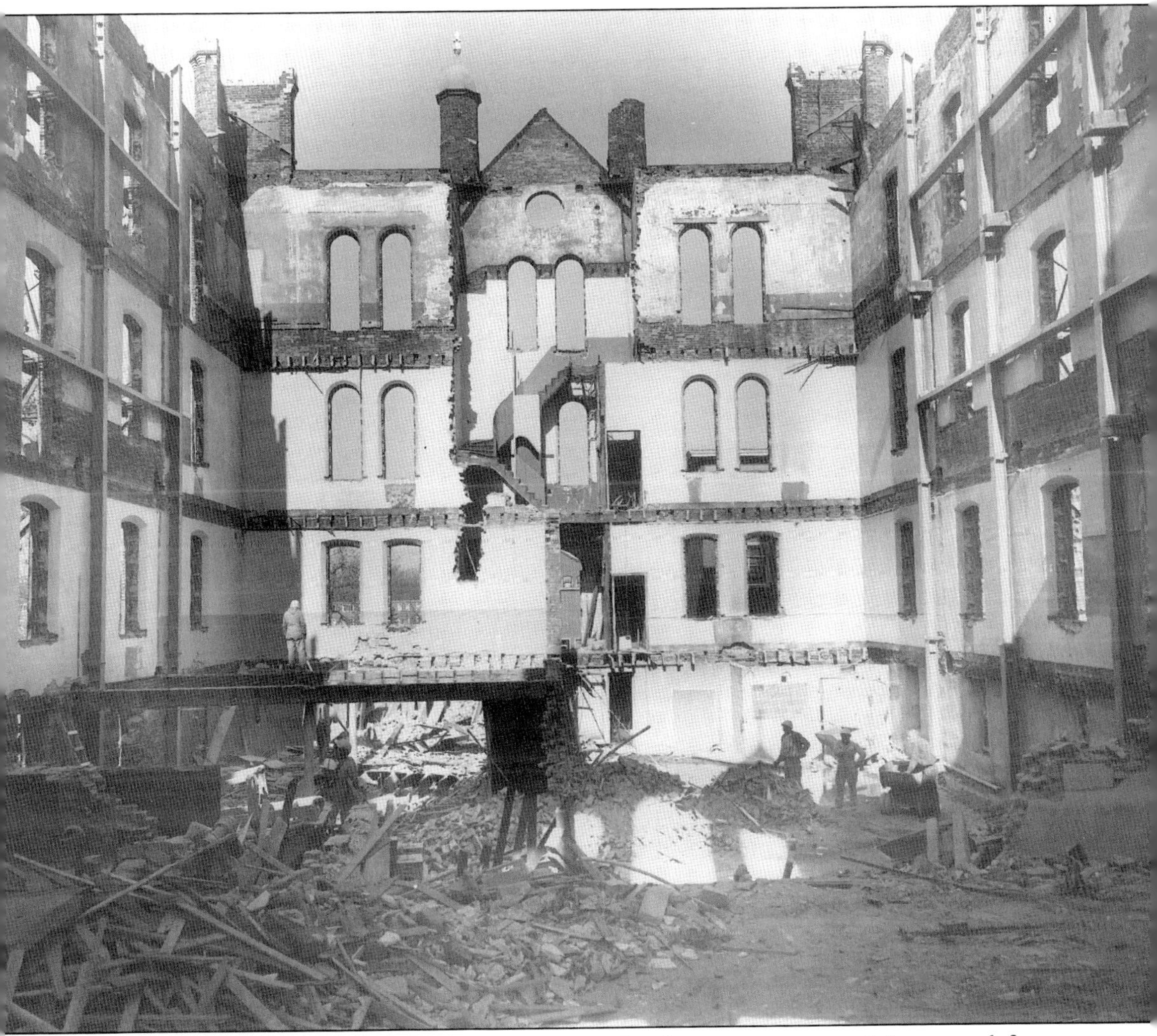

Taking apart is one thing, but this view certainly shares a very special removal from Chapman Hall during the massive restoration of the building in 1966.

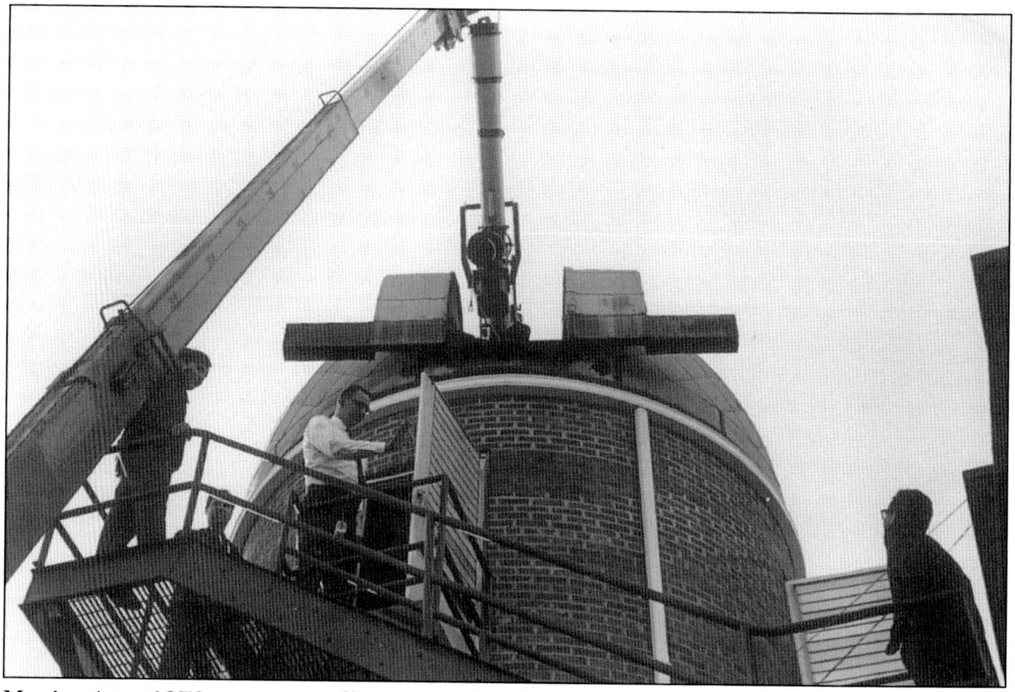

Moving into 1970, we see staff personnel making installation of a telescope.

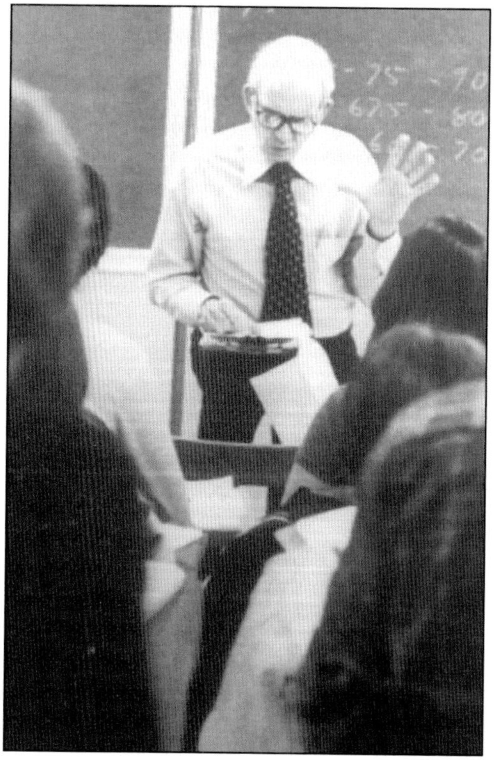

Here we see Prof. Russell sharing information in one of his English classes.

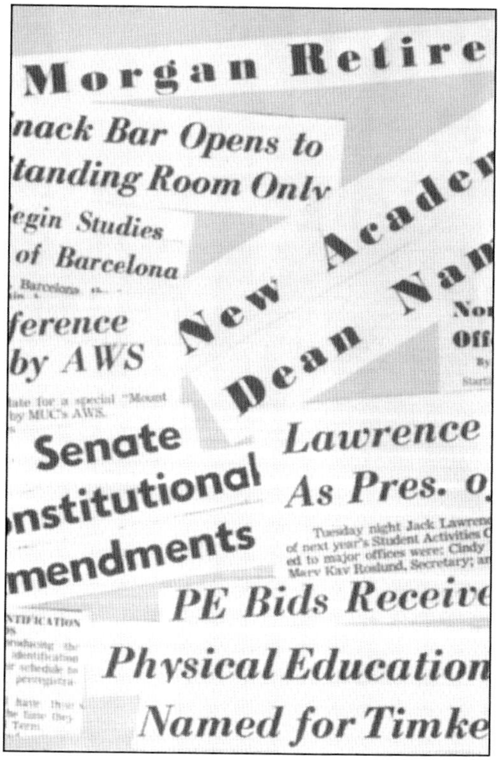

Here are more of those many headlines in the *Dynamo*.

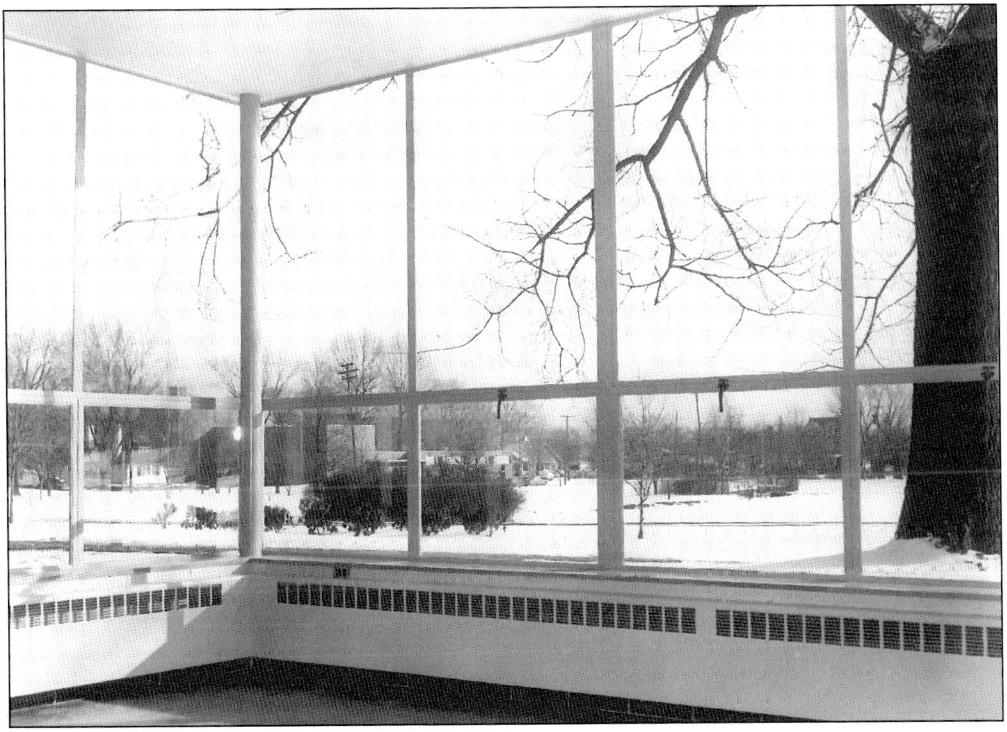

Here is a good campus view from Wilson Hall.

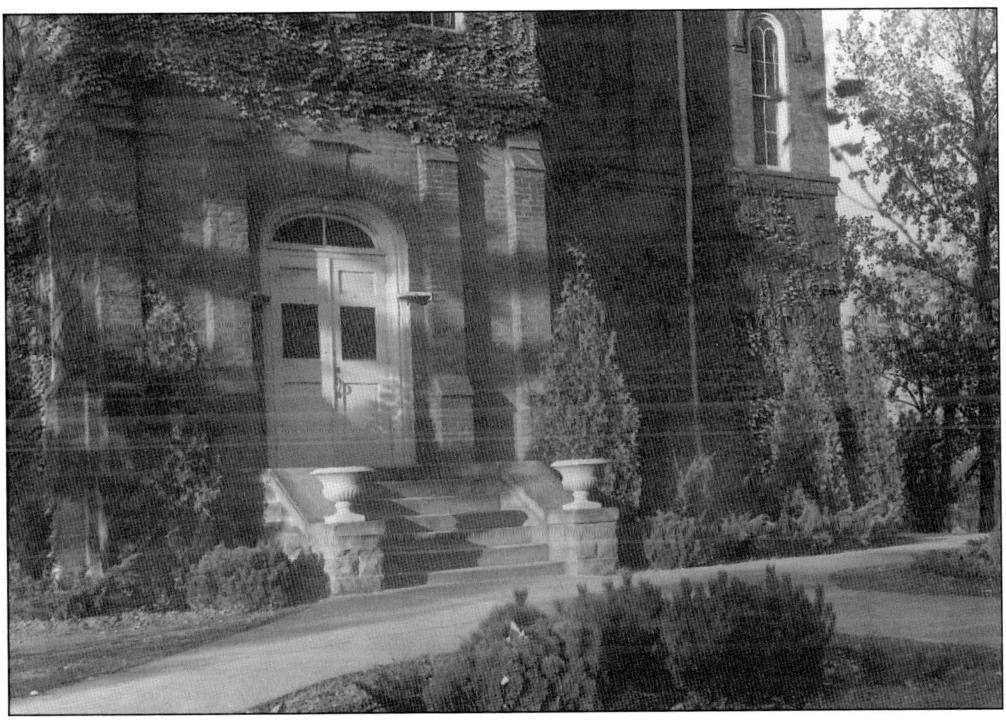

Probably all students have used the doorway—the keynote of Chapman Hall, at least during the old days.

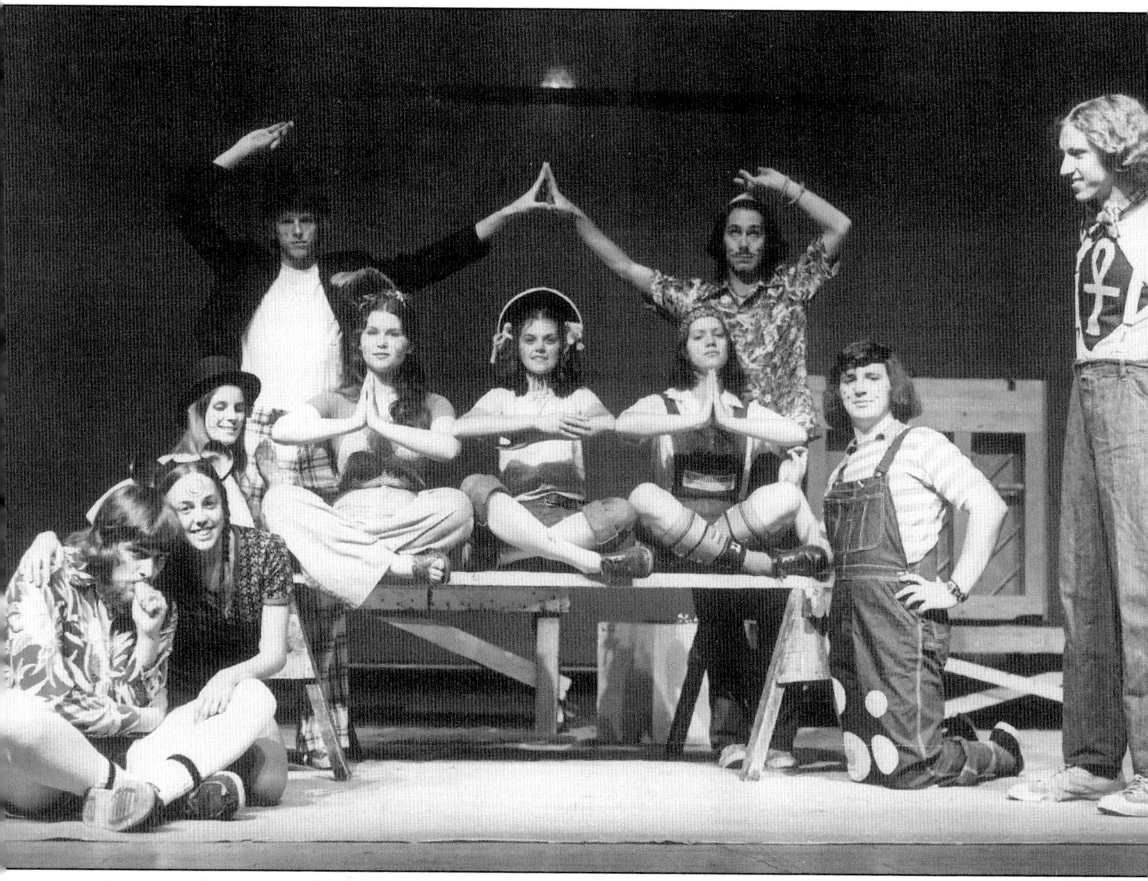

It's another great homecoming, and "Godspell" is the student achievement this time.

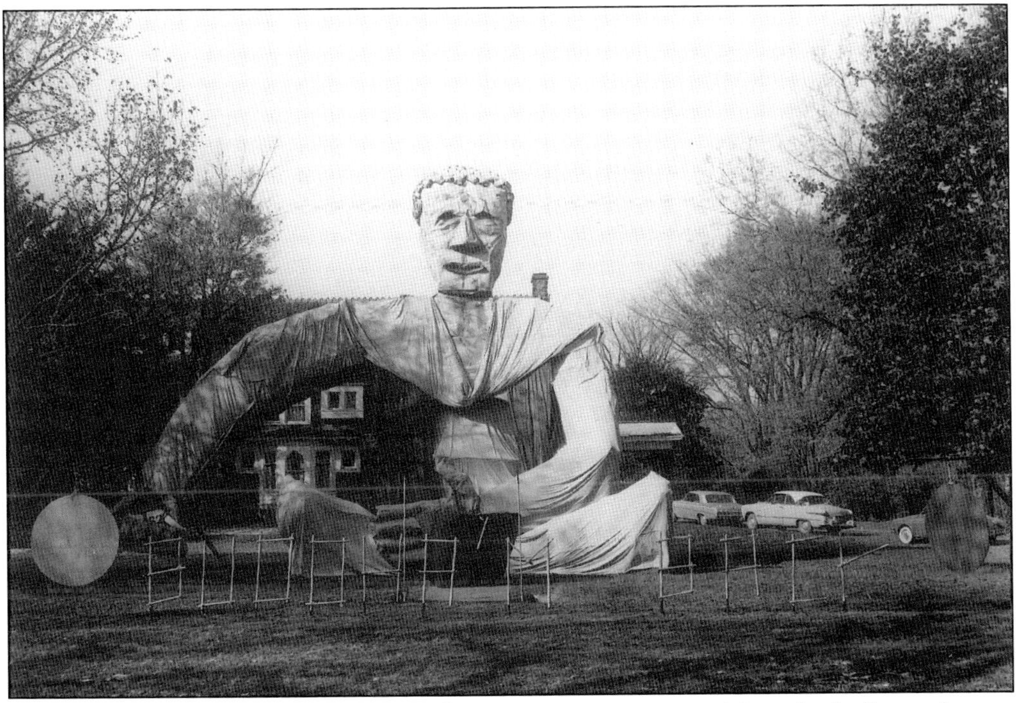

There's no ending to the massive homecoming opportunities—including what to make! This was the 1962 homecoming at Sigma Nu and Tri Delta.

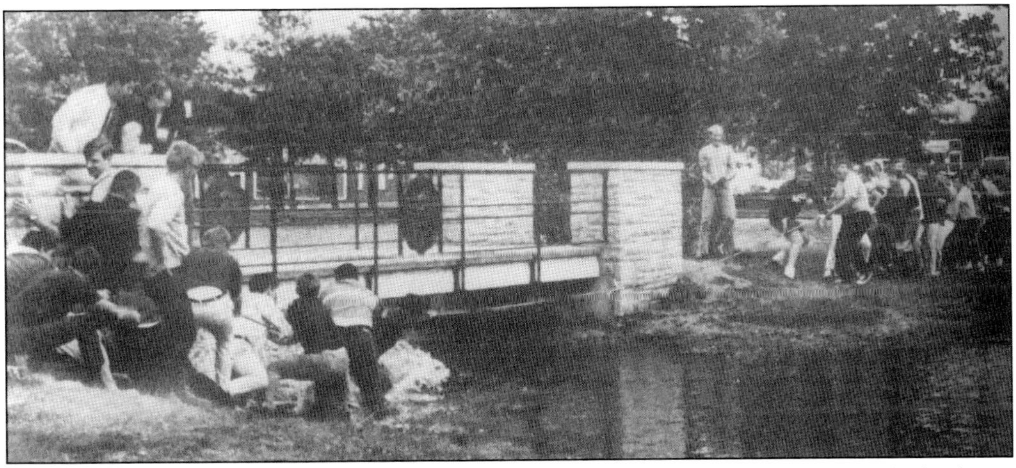

Campus also provided the scene for a freshman-sophomore contest ... with the loser ending up in some water!

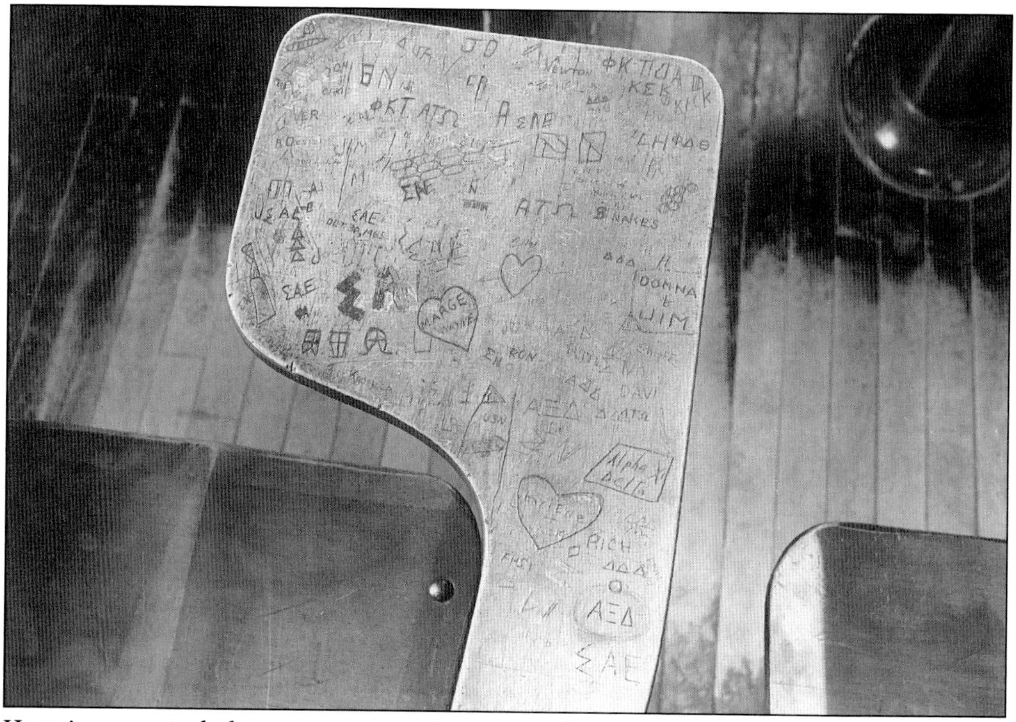

Here is a way to help newcomer students ... well, at least let them learn some names and some junk on a chair desk. Maybe this was in a communications class!

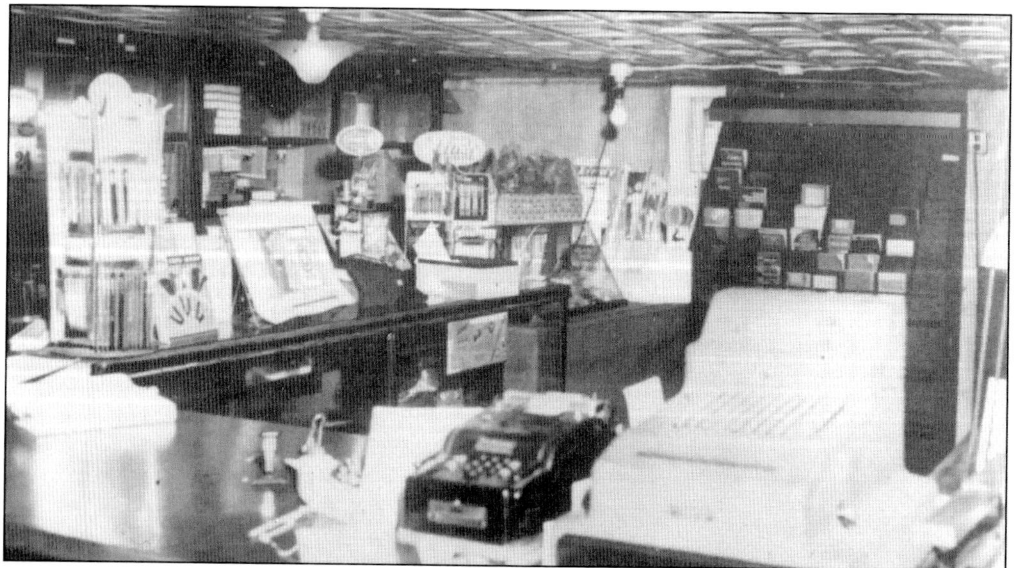

Here we have a quick small view of bookstore materials. An important place for everyone.

Three

Mount Union Today

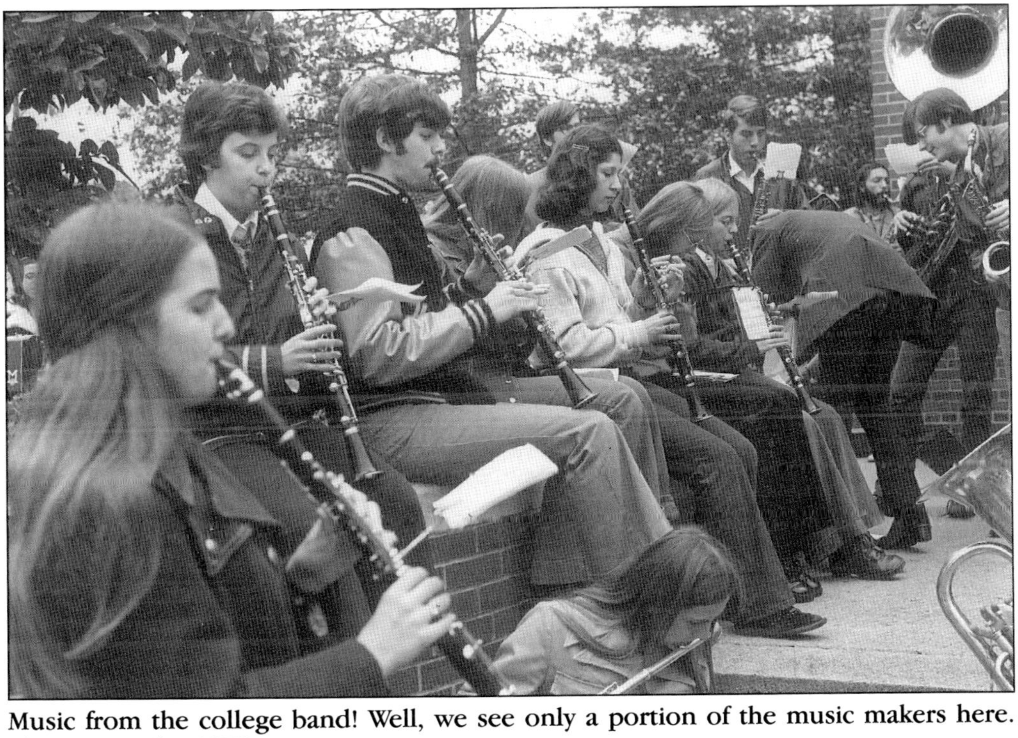

Music from the college band! Well, we see only a portion of the music makers here. This was in the 1970s.

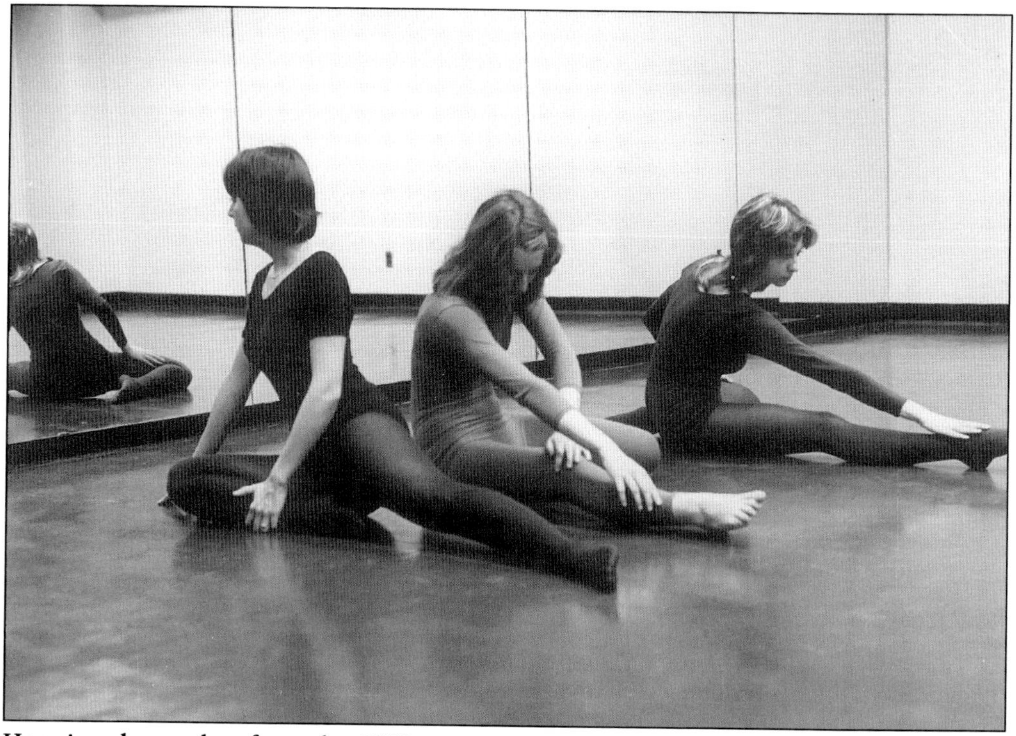

Here is a dance class from the 1970s.

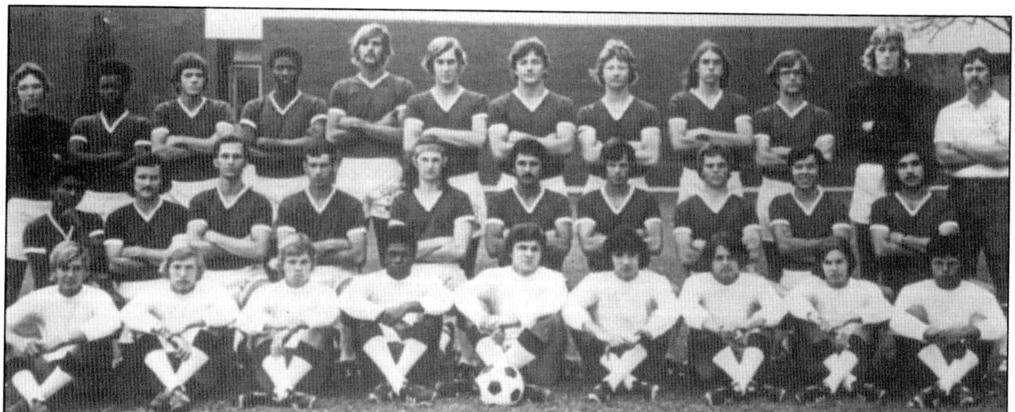

Pictured is a view of the 1975 soccer players. Coach Fisher was named the outstanding coach of the year by the Ohio Collegiate Soccer Association.

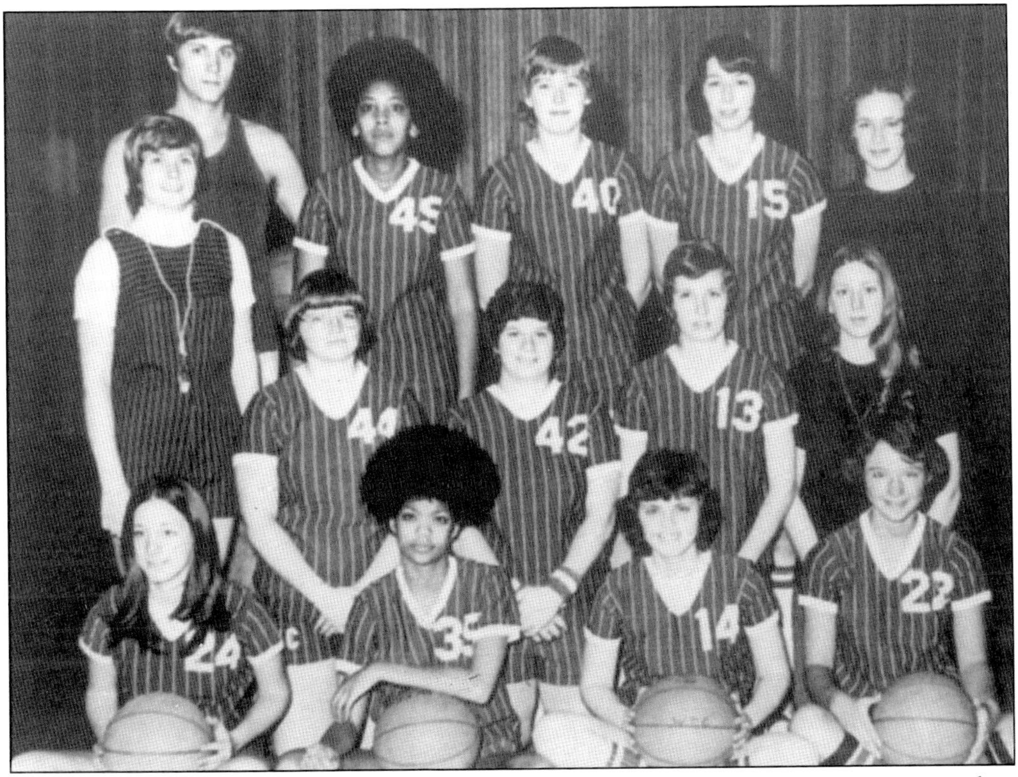

Also from the mid-1970s is this Women's basketball team. (They had many wins, but the toughest score was a 72-70 loss., while the best, perhaps, was a 42-41 victory!)

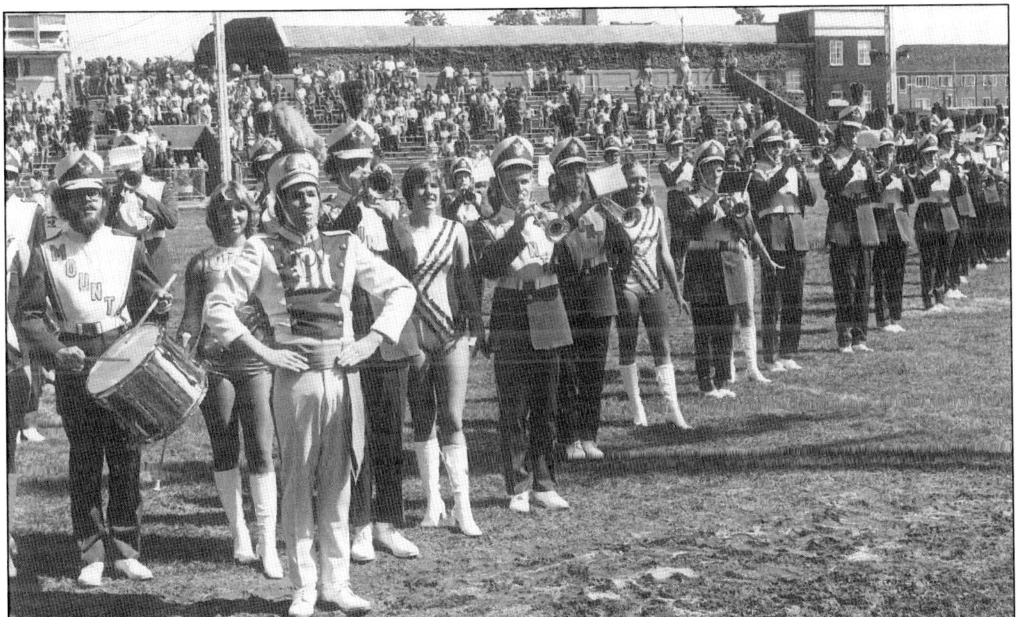

The Mount Union marching band is seen here in 1976 and the music is just what it ought to be.

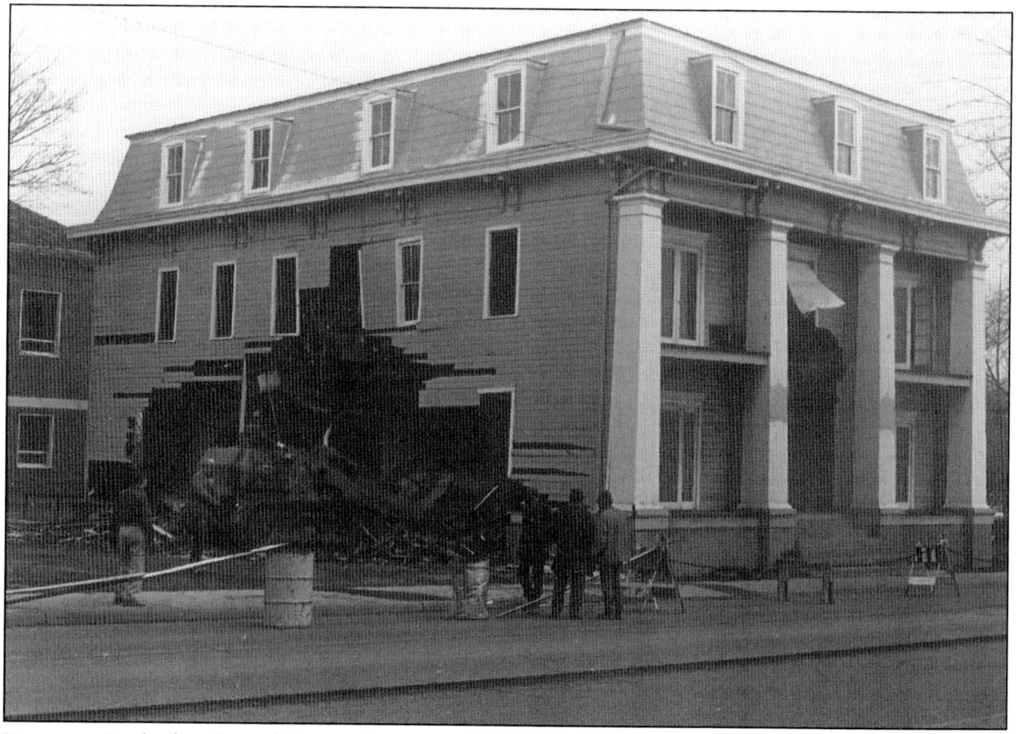

Progress includes demolition of some campus buildings, and, of course, the building of new ones. Here is the way the administration building appeared April 11, 1973.

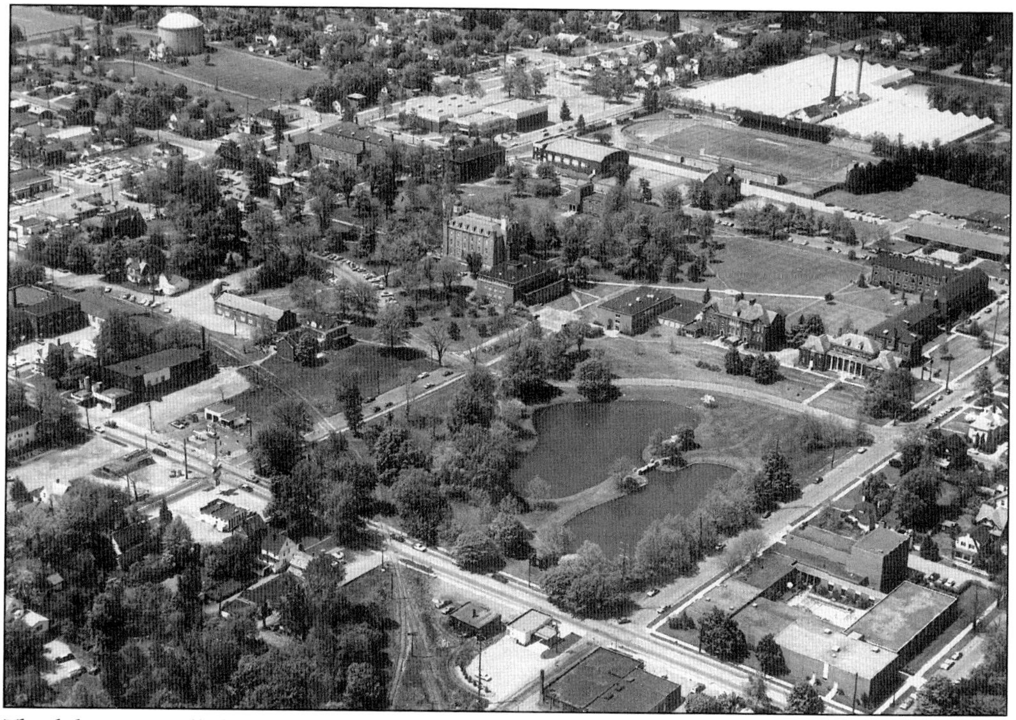

The lakes are still there!

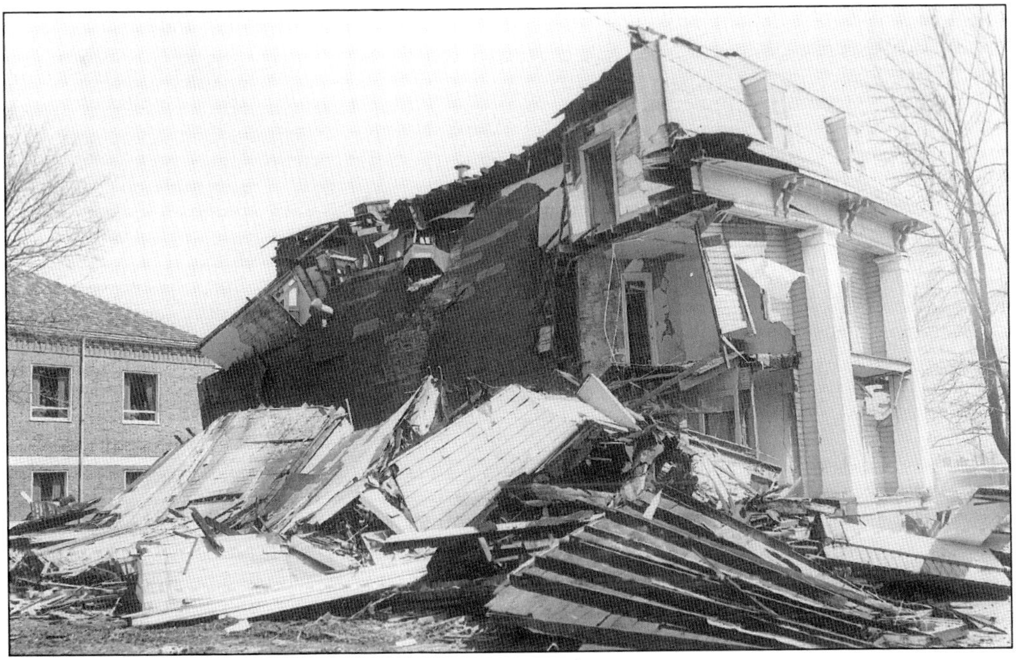

Later that same day, the appearance had changed even more!

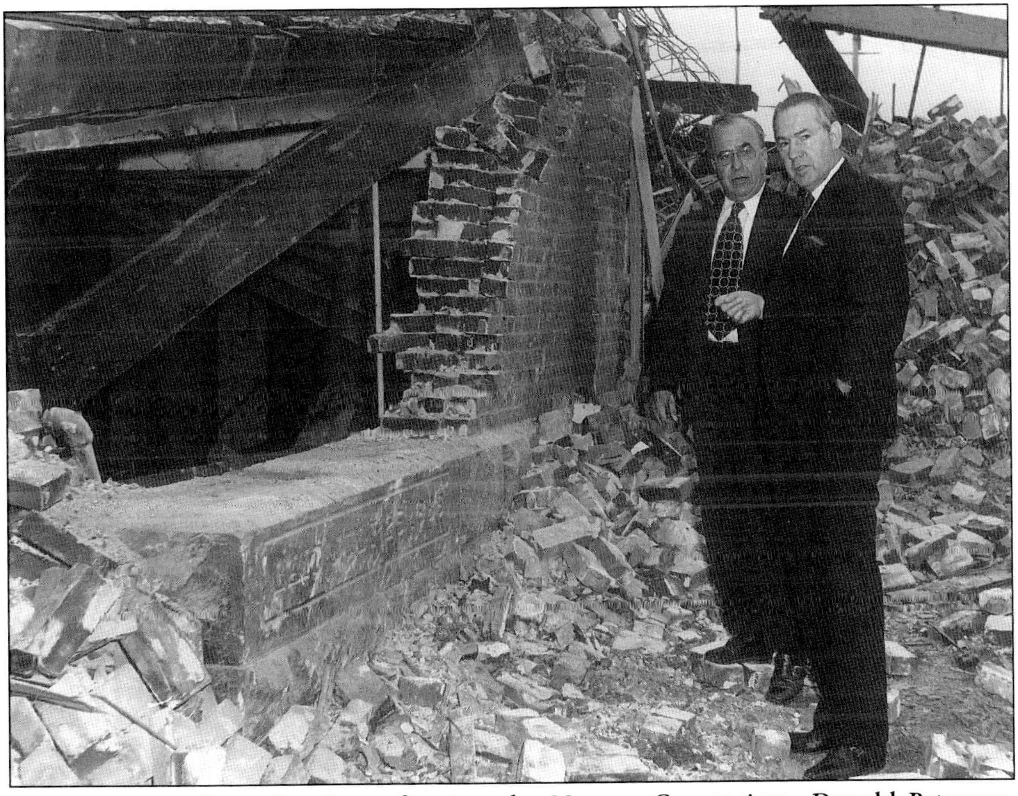

Here's a scene from the time of razing the Morgan Gymnasium. Donald Peterson, Trustee chairman, and Mount's President, Ronald Weber, are checking out remains.

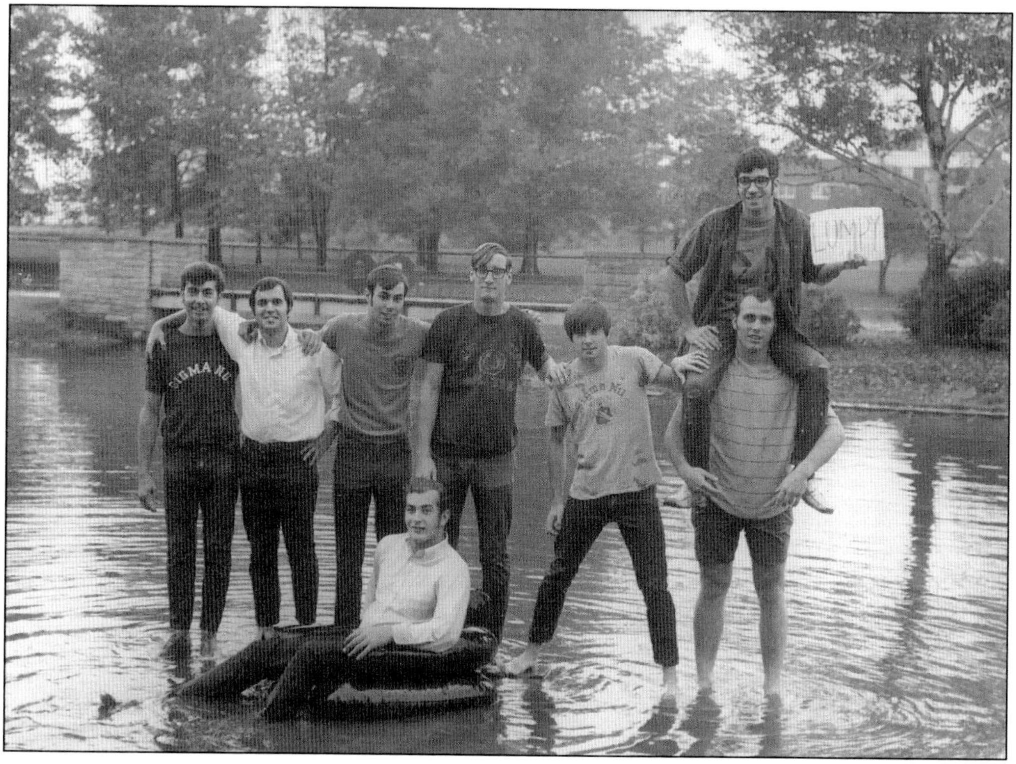

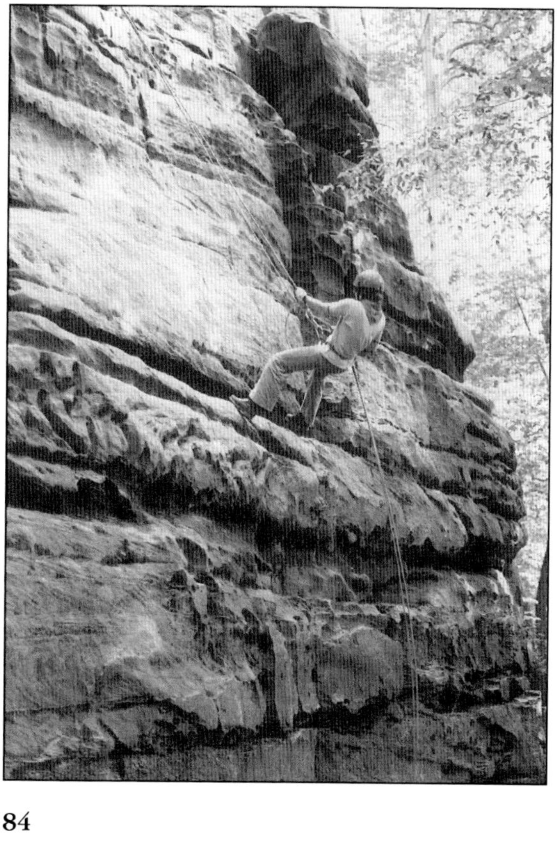

This was a warm day, and we see students on the campus lake.

This image is from a 1977 wilderness trip—just before the autumn classes began.

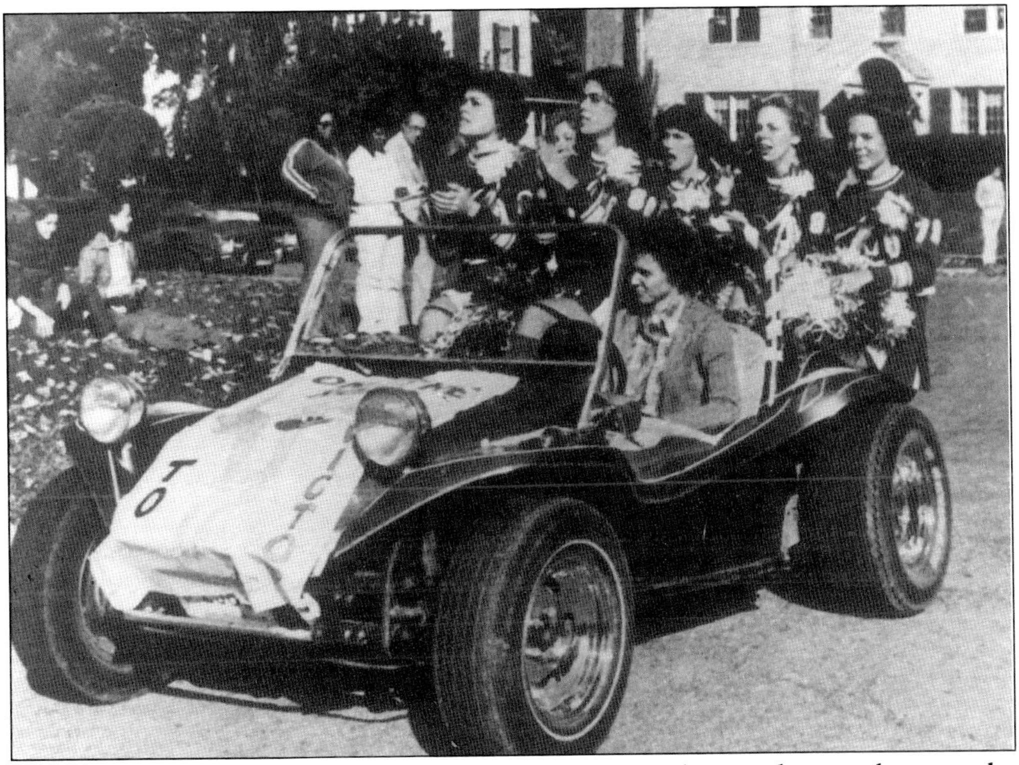

Here are junior-varsity cheerleaders in 1979. They're leading, and in another way, the driver is as well!

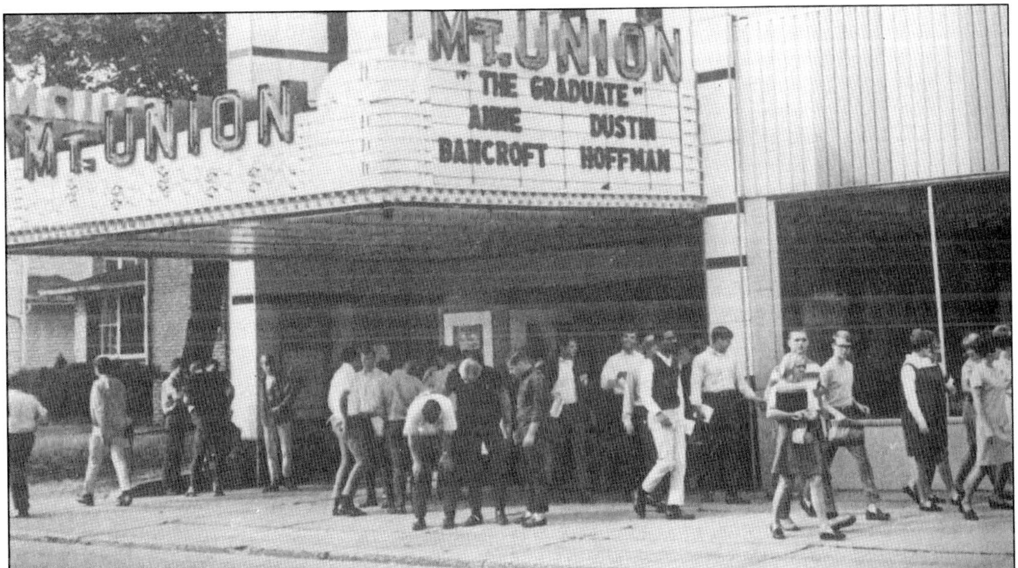

Well, it might be just right for students to frequent the theater, especially when the movies help show them how to get good grades. Meetings also were held in the theater for students.

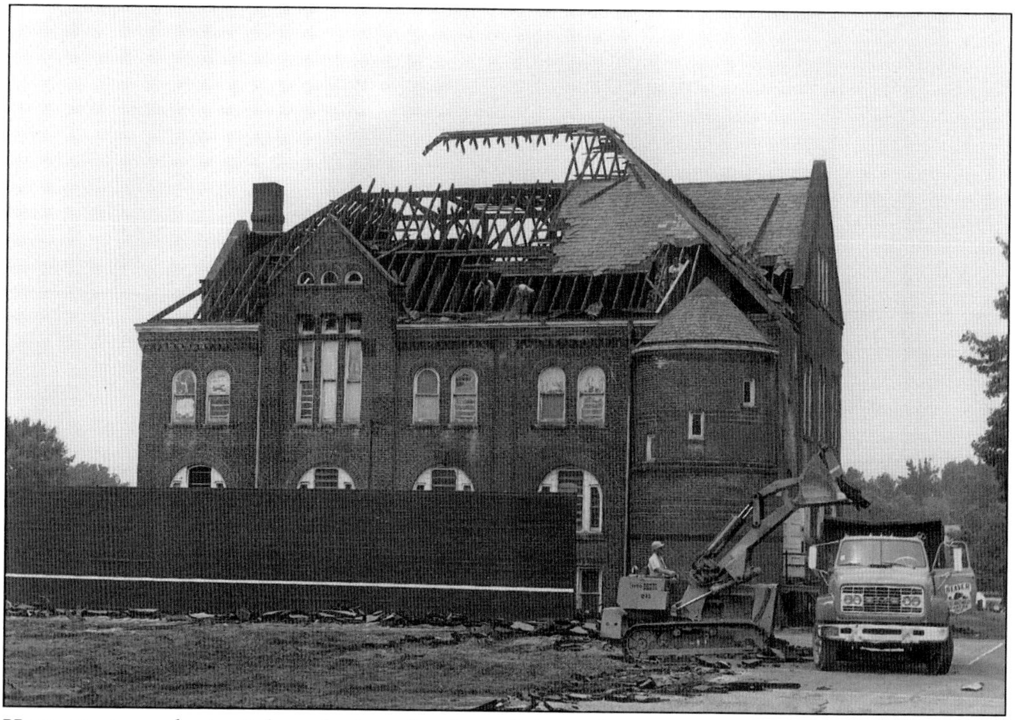

Here are two photos taken during the demolition of Morgan gymnasium. Both point to progress, of course ... even if they also give views of loss. The year is 1972.

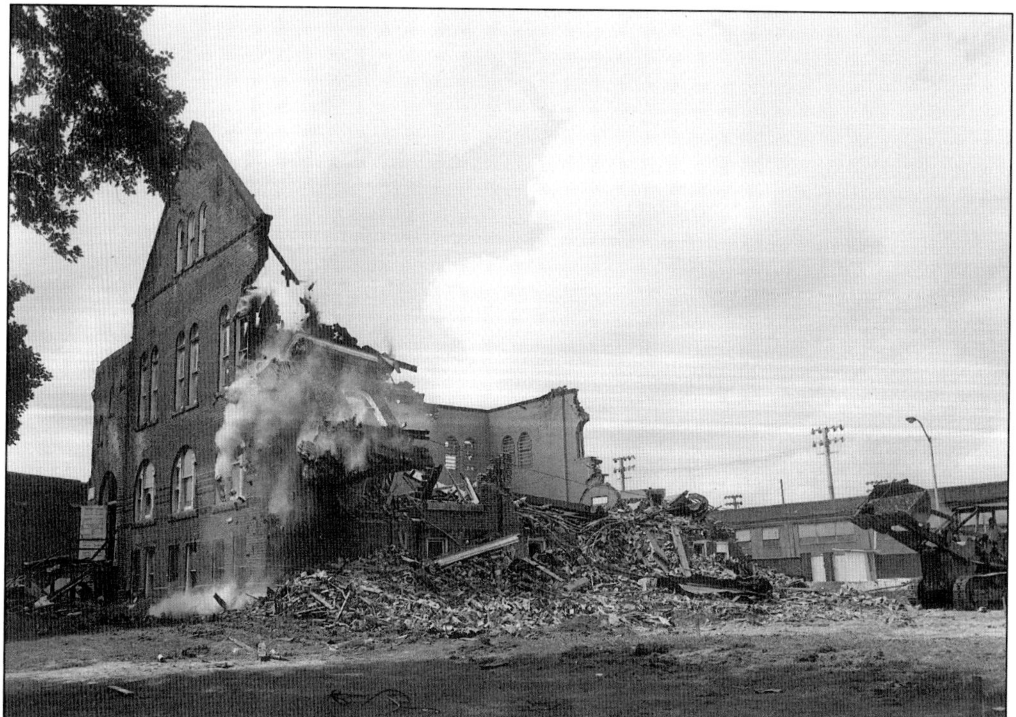

The razing continues.

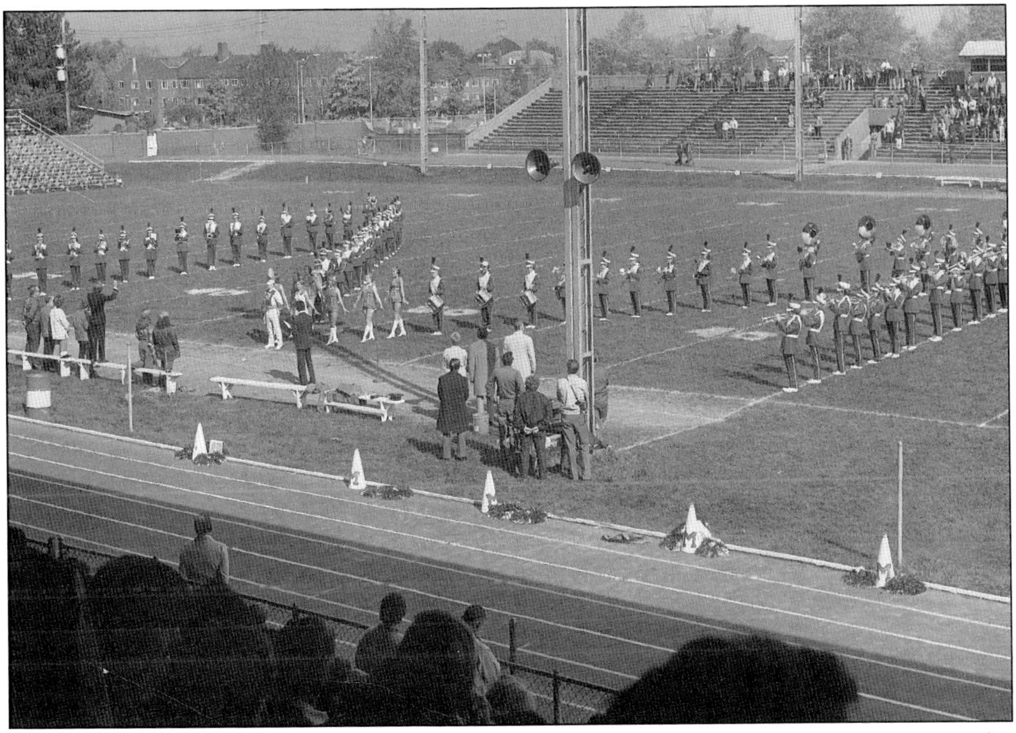

Here you can see the Mount Marchers performing, despite the small crowd across the field. The game was in the 1970s.

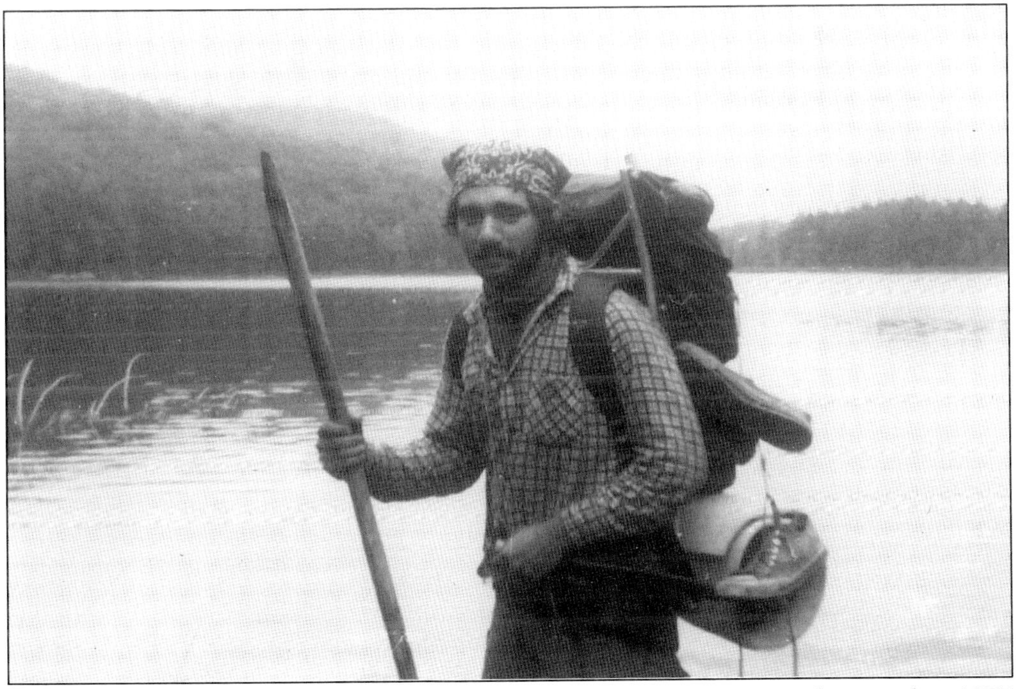

Games of many kinds were played; here is Roger Charriere during the 1977 Wilderness Trip.

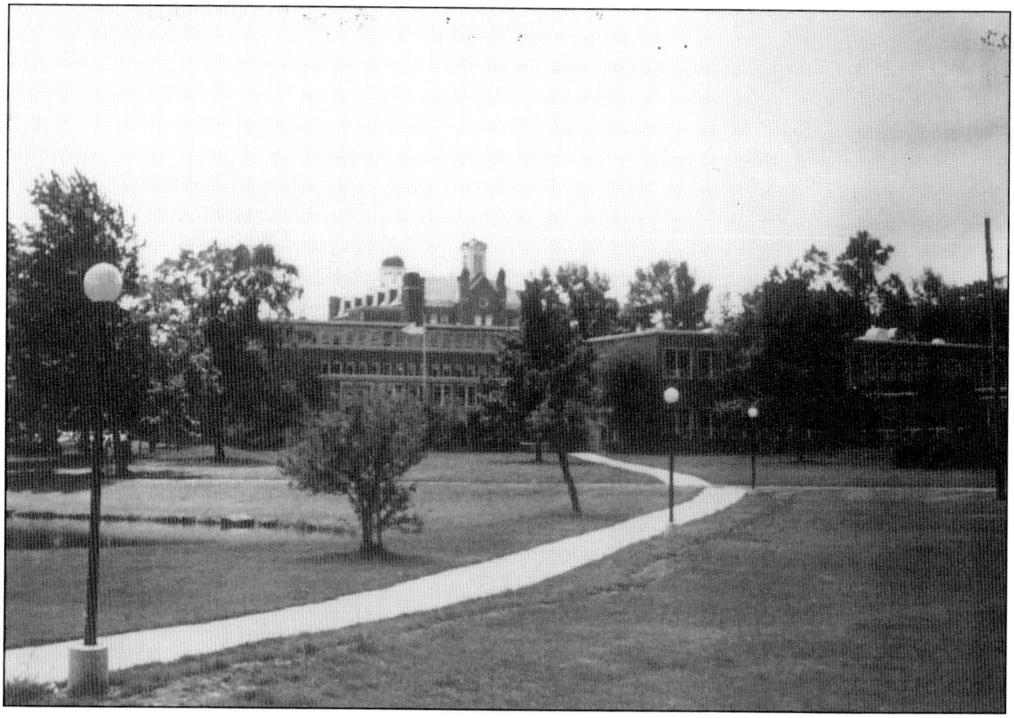

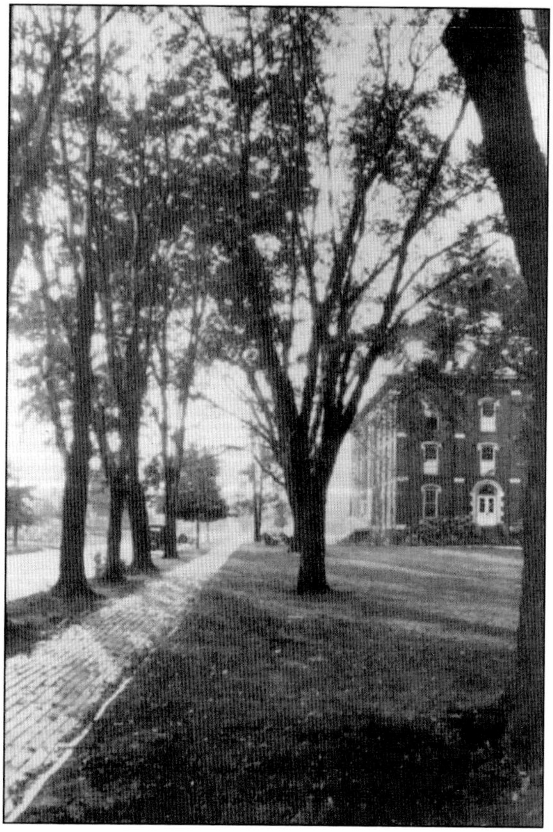

This campus view illustrates one of the key reasons Chapman Hall has always been a dominant building: it's taller than the others!

The walkway along Hartshorn Street ... and the brick sidewalk that leads to Miller Hall.

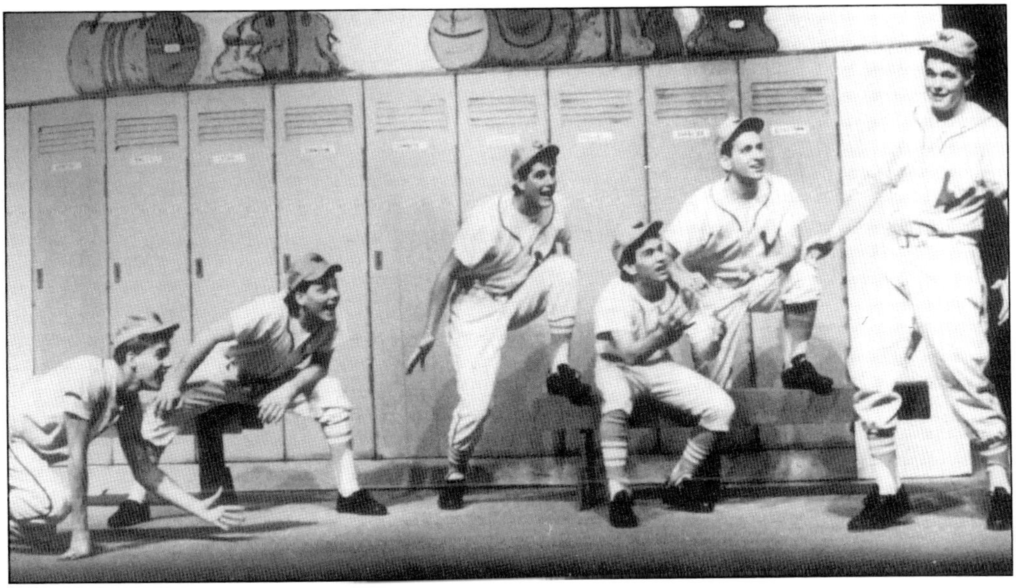

Well, there's not a baseball game going on here, but it is a dramatic game! A Mount Union presentation in 1989 is seen here.

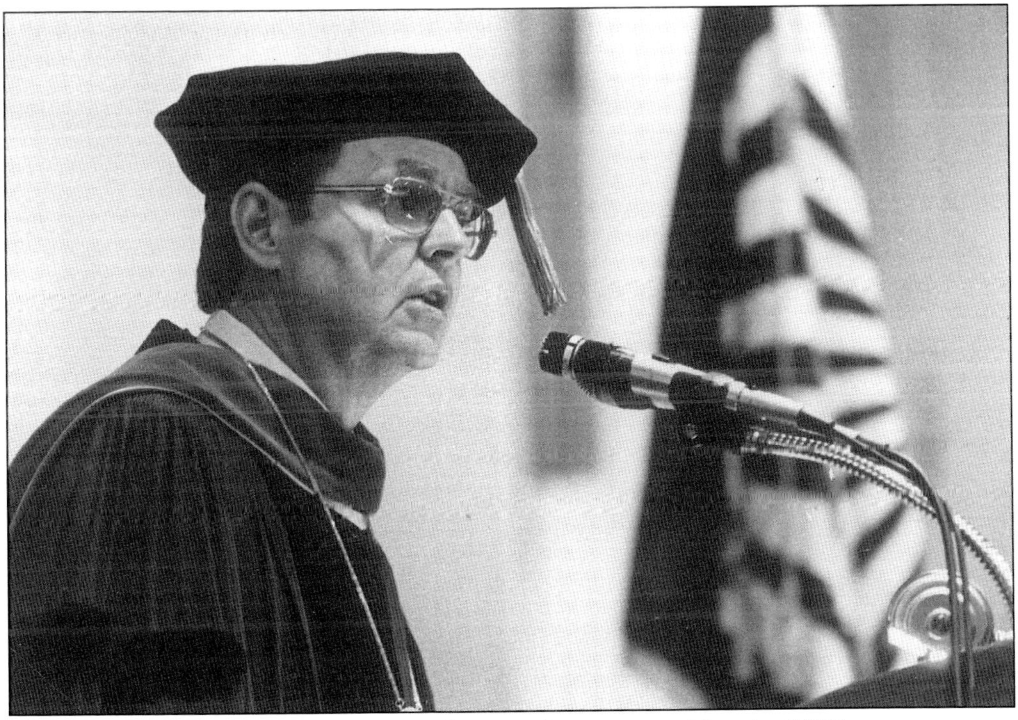

Here is College President Ben Lantz; he was the new president in 1980.

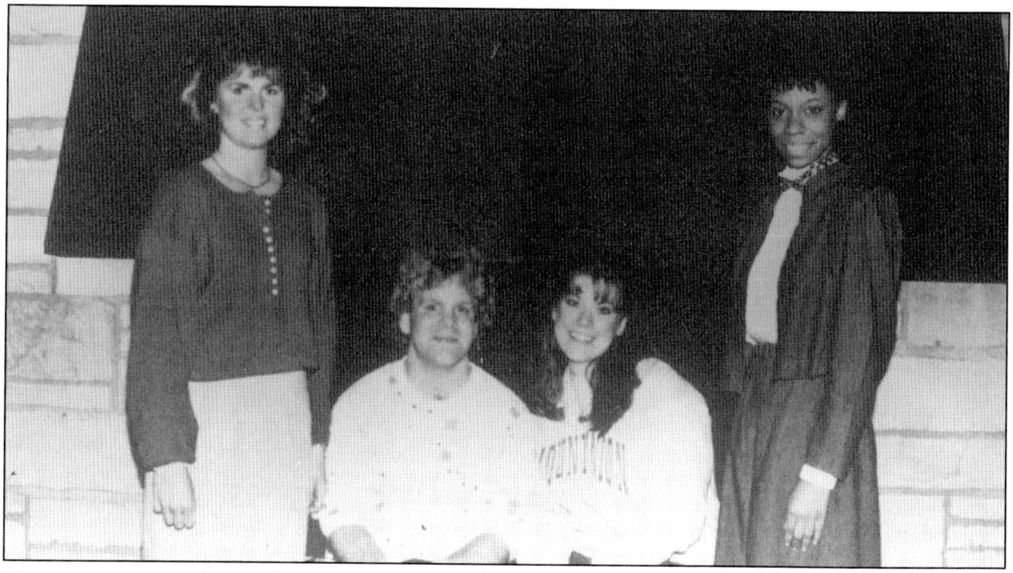

Here are senior-class officers in the late 1980s.

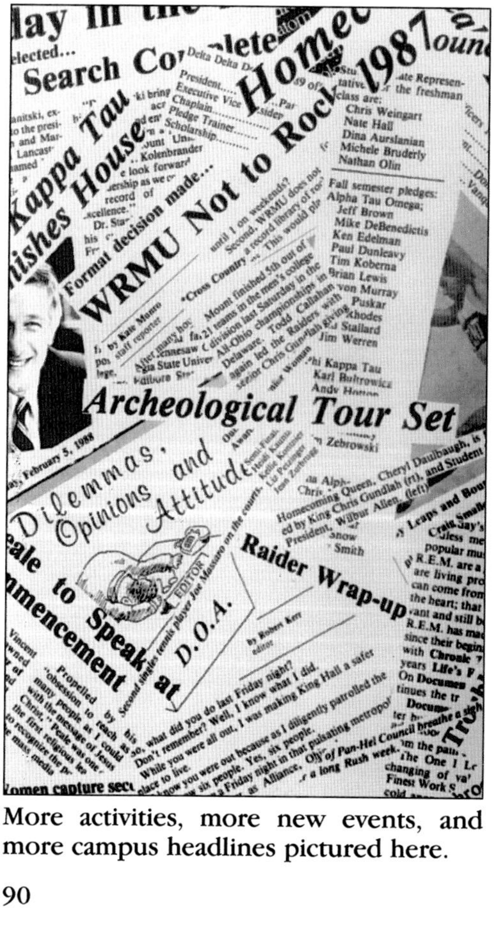

More activities, more new events, and more campus headlines pictured here.

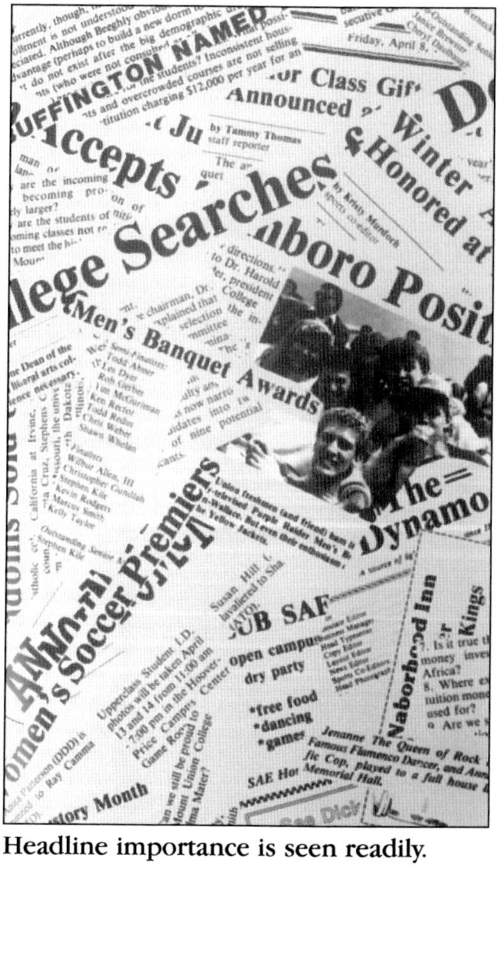

Headline importance is seen readily.

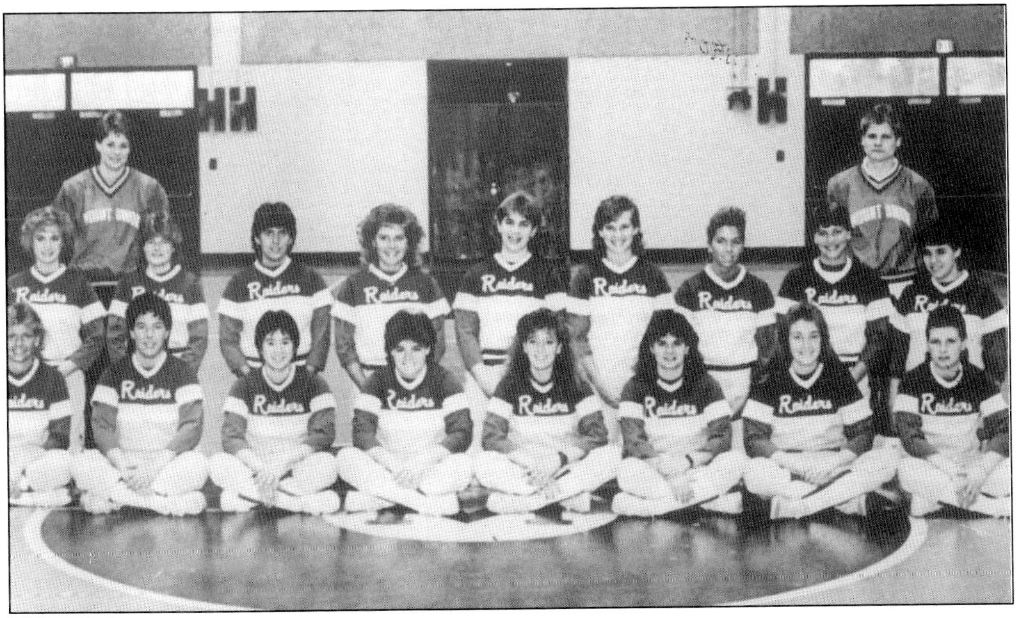

The women's softball team poses here during their 1988 season.

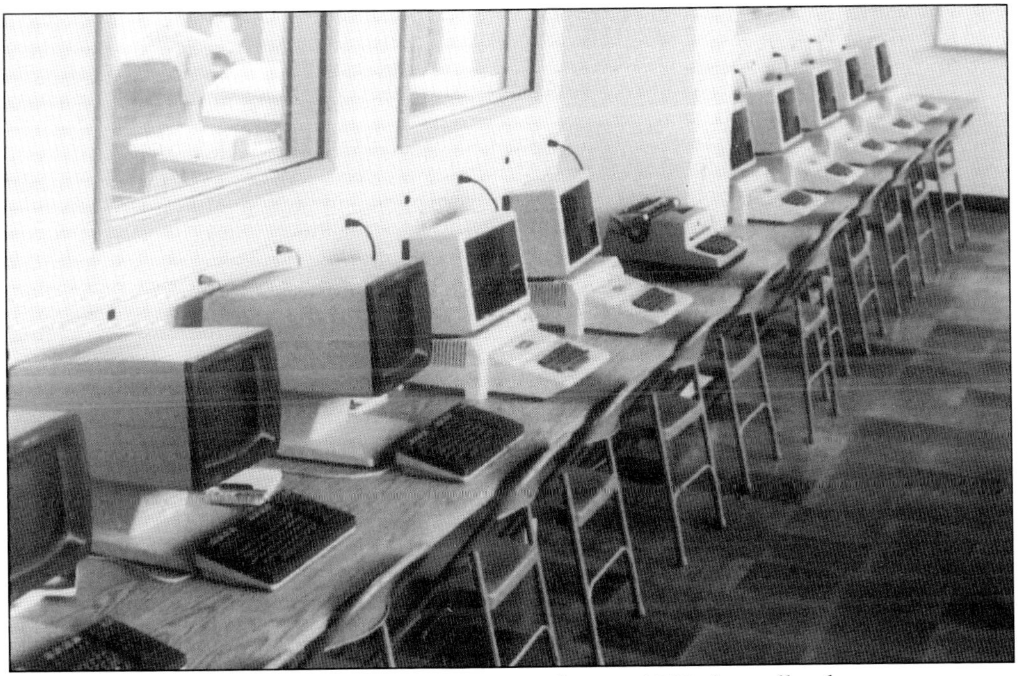

Computers, of course, took over ... but note that in 1983, by golly, there was even a portable typewriter on the table!

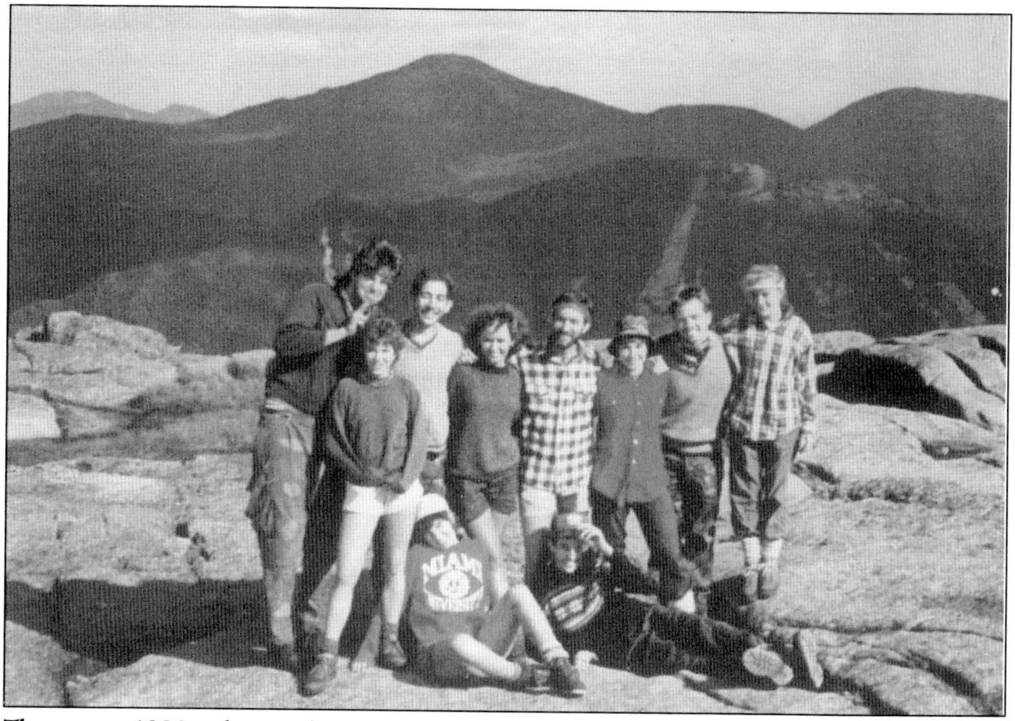

These two 1980s photos show that—although much time is spent on campus—some find far off places ... and perhaps those places have a much bigger "campus" than the one in Alliance!

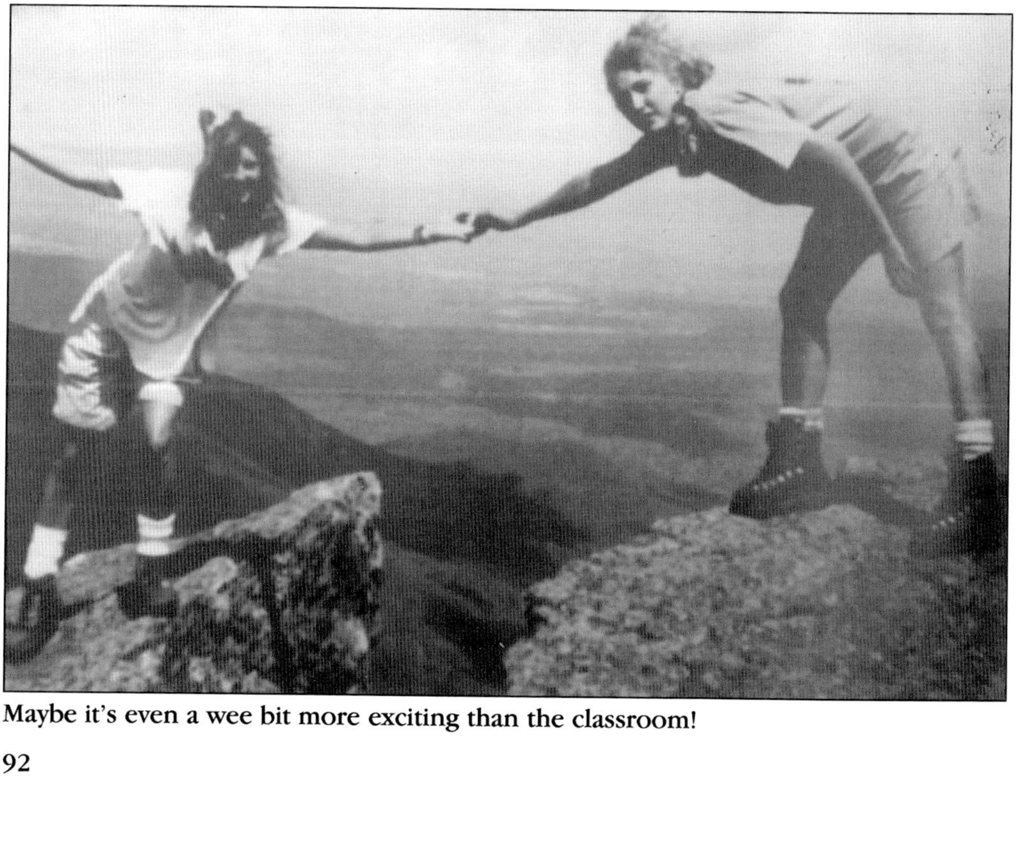

Maybe it's even a wee bit more exciting than the classroom!

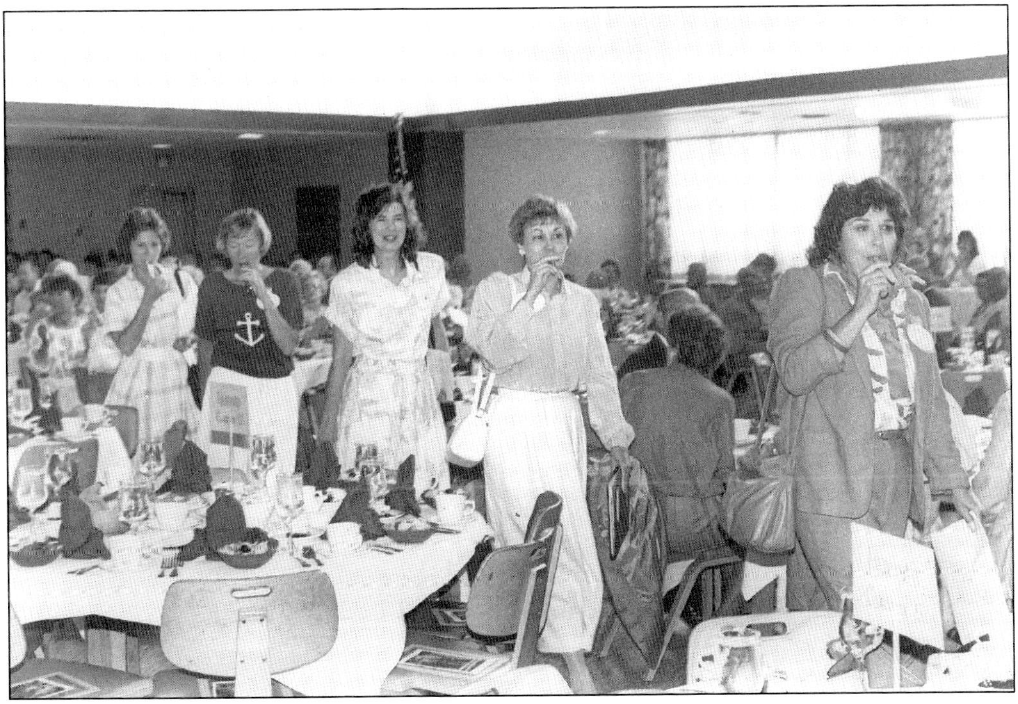

Alumni weekends bring many, and the campus appreciates that. Here is Alumni Weekend for 1987 and note that one meal is inside, the other on the outside, but both help share a happy time.

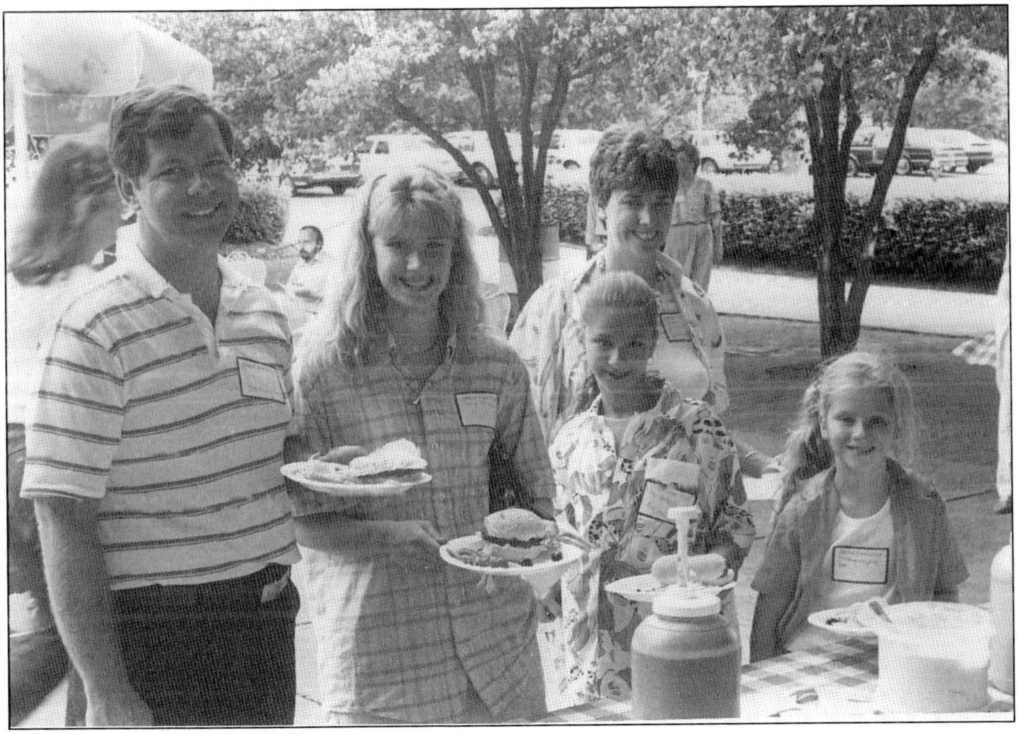

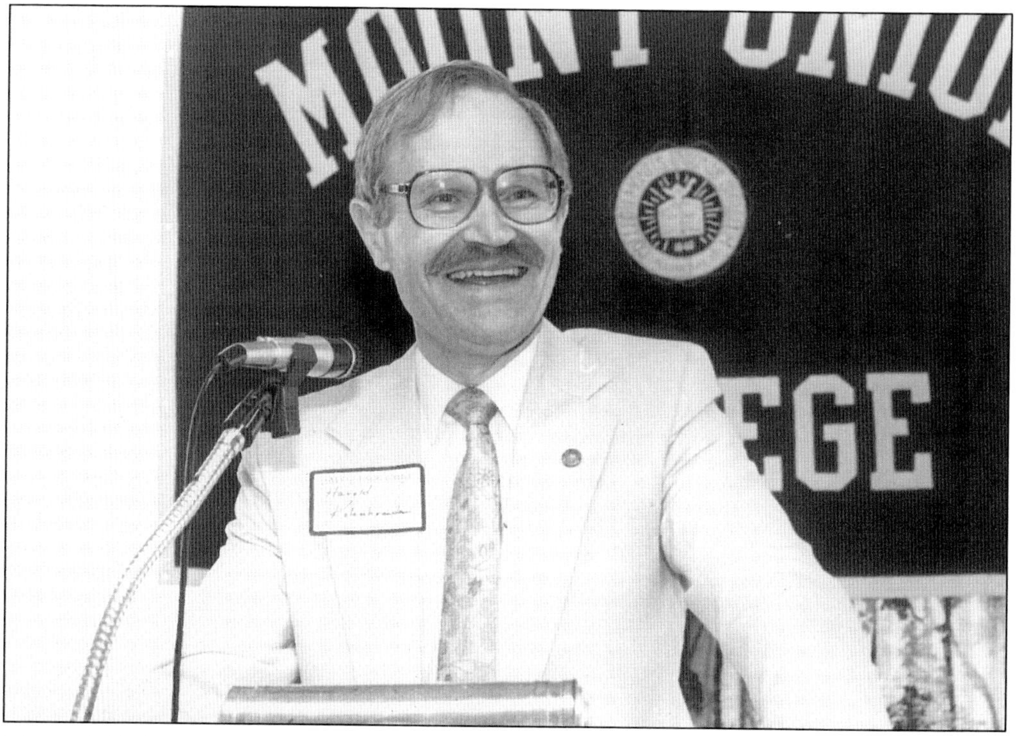

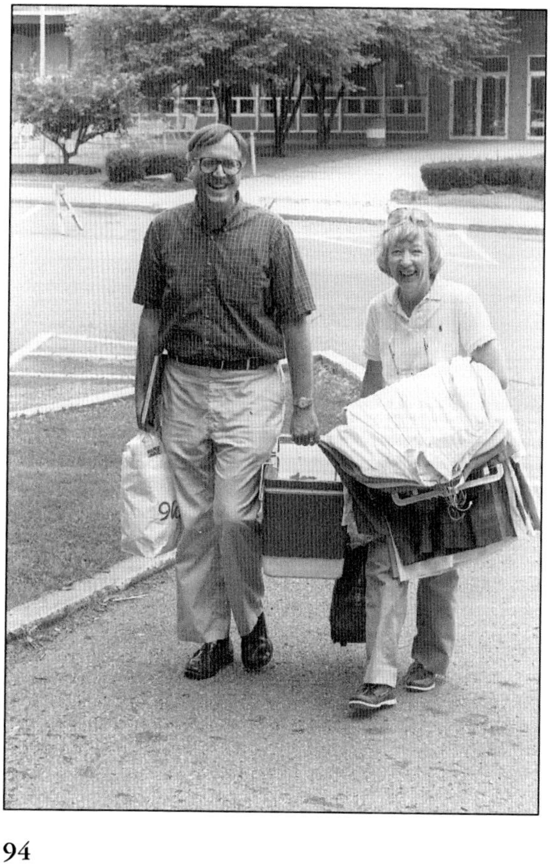

Harold Kolenbrander as President of the College, greets alumni and shares with them.

Bill and Mary Banfield move into one of the dormitories. Why? Because it's one of those Alumni Weekends and they came to be with the sessions.

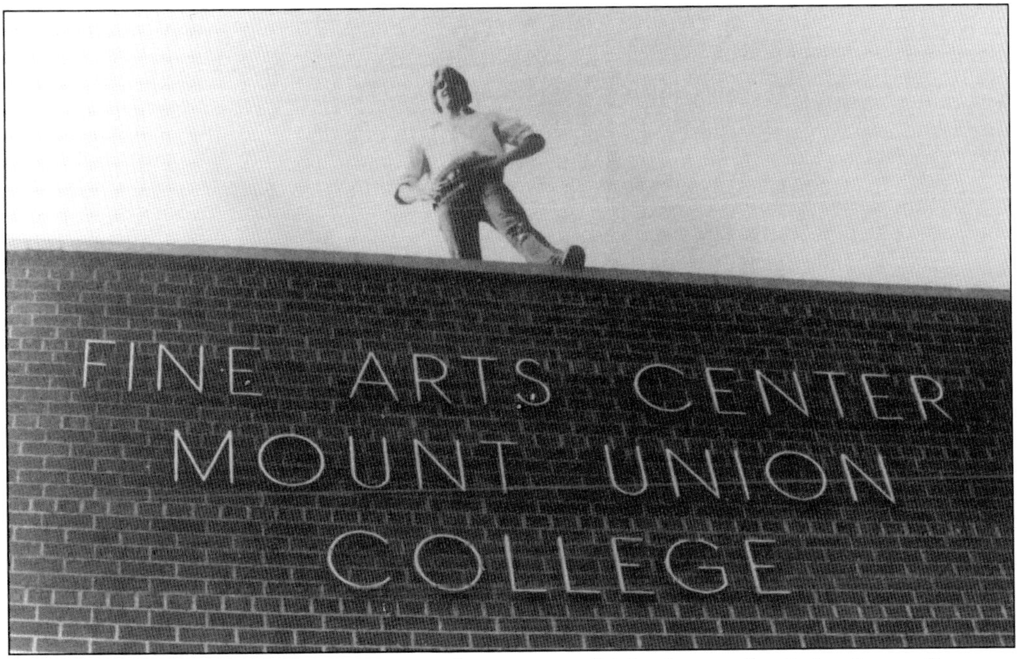

The date is 1980, and we say if it's a "fine picture," it's also an "artistic picture."

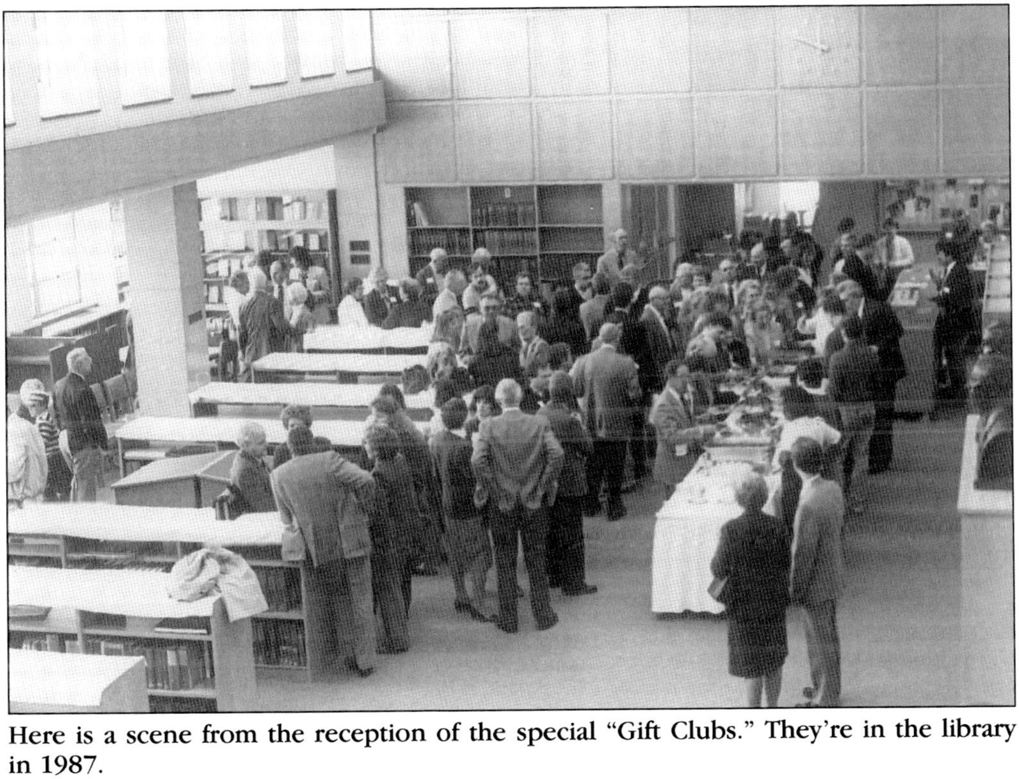

Here is a scene from the reception of the special "Gift Clubs." They're in the library in 1987.

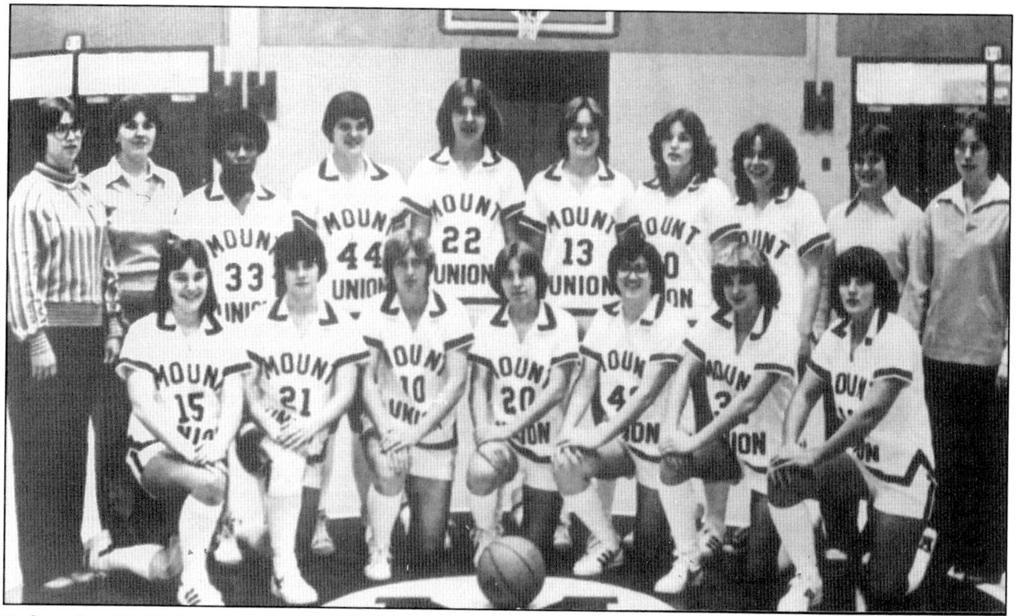

A fine basketball team—women from Mount Union.

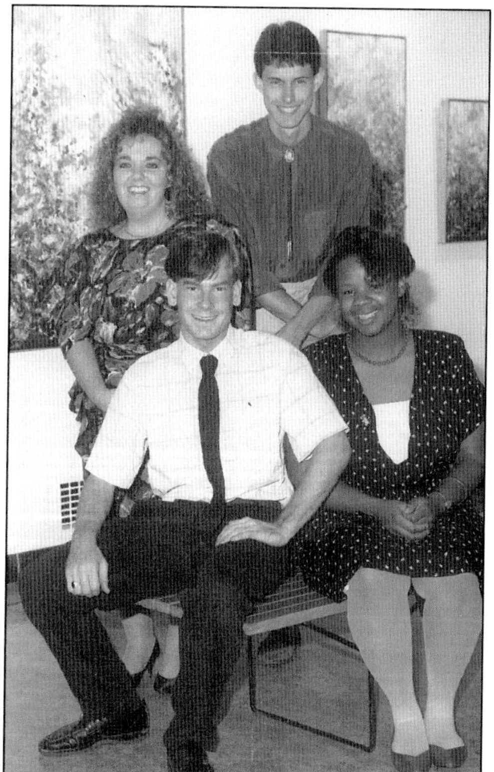

Here are students at the 1991 senior exhibit.

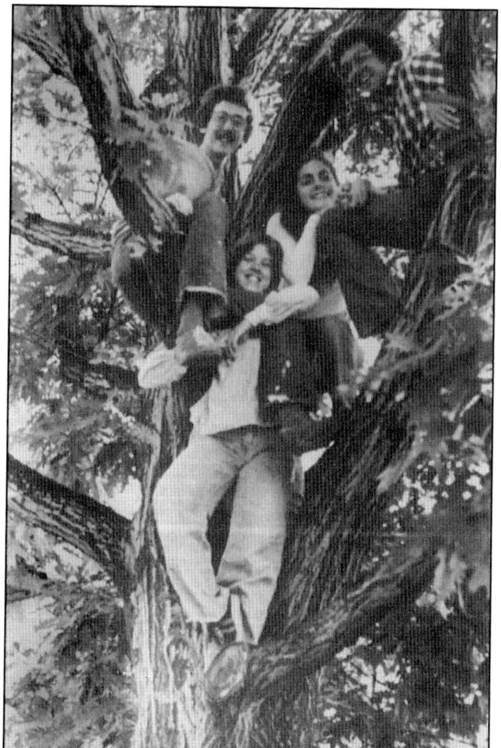

This is not a basketball team, but perhaps a "team" of some sort! Pictured are four student climbers of 1979.

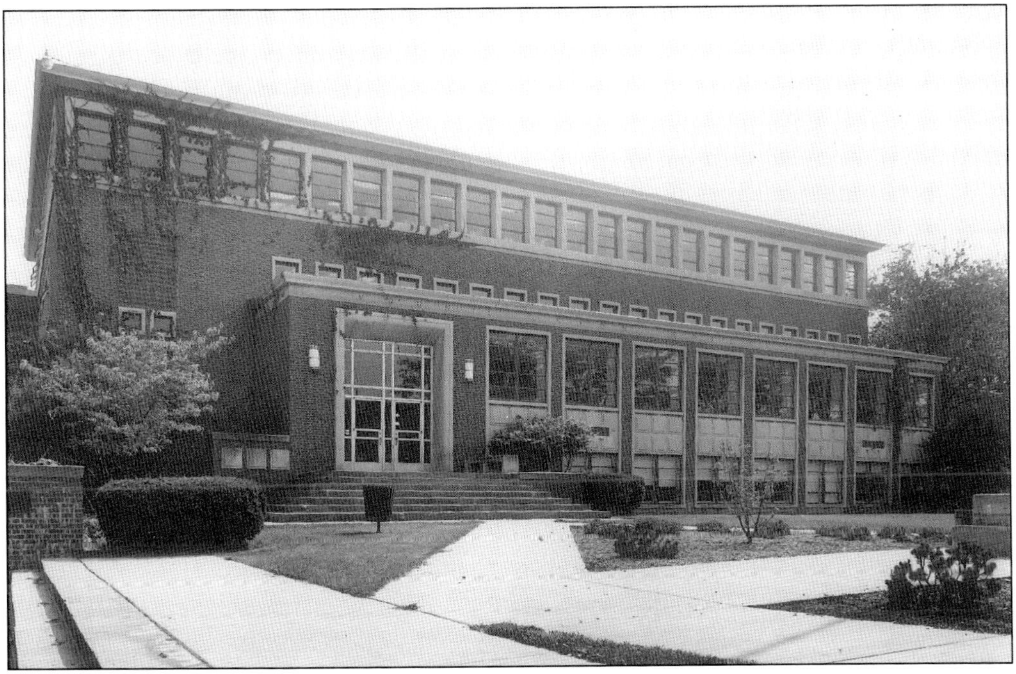

The college library poses here for us in the summer of 1990.

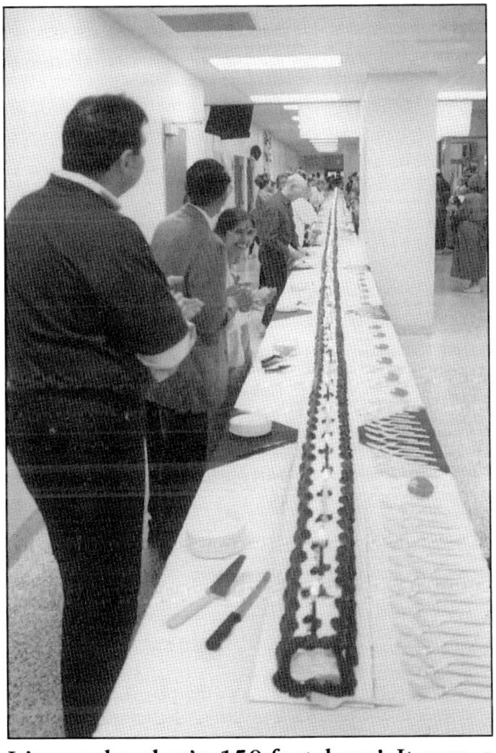

It's a cake that's 150-feet long! It was a part of homecoming and the college's sesquicentennial, 1996.

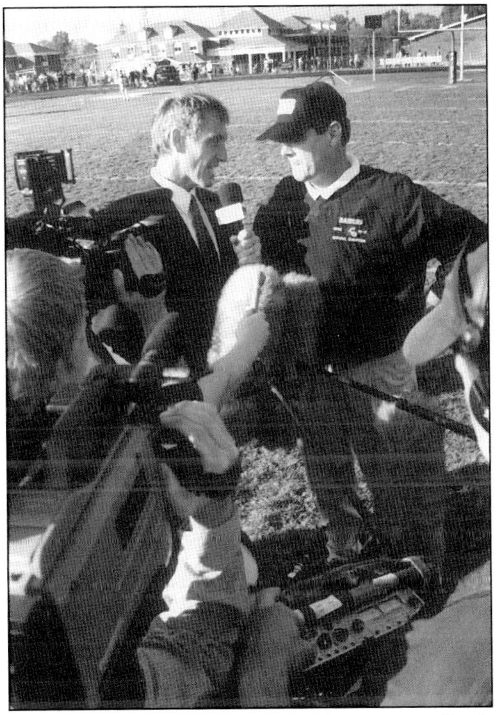

Here's conversation about the game which put Otterbein face-to-face with Mount Union. It turned out to be part of the longest winning streak Mount had.

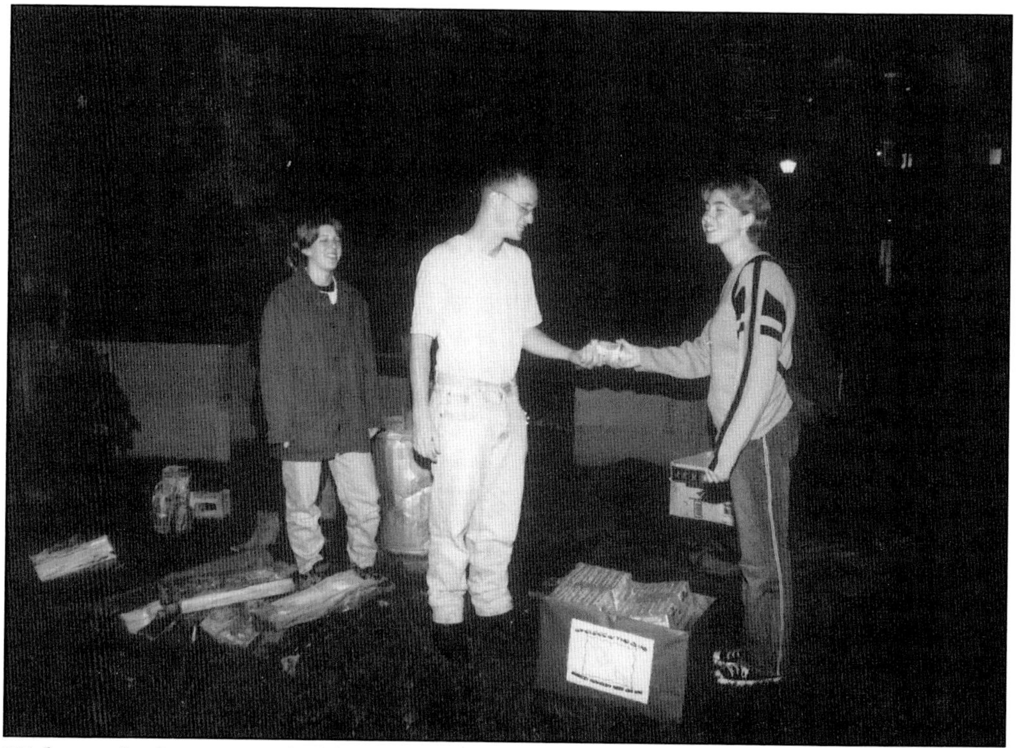

Night on the Streets was held on campus in 1999.

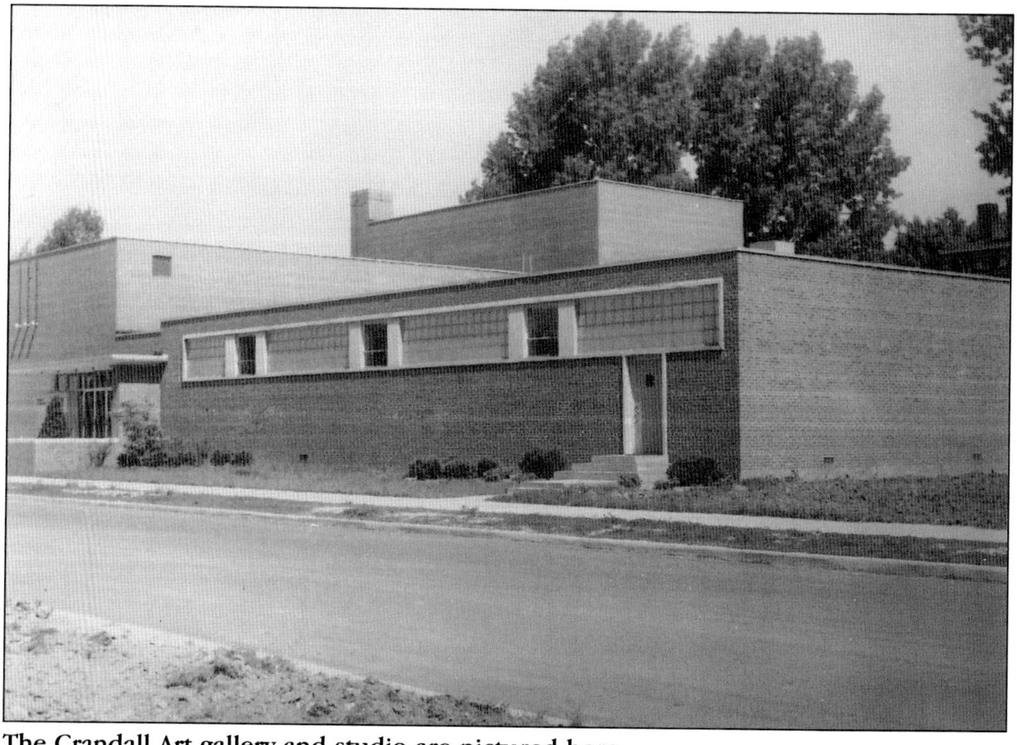

The Crandall Art gallery and studio are pictured here.

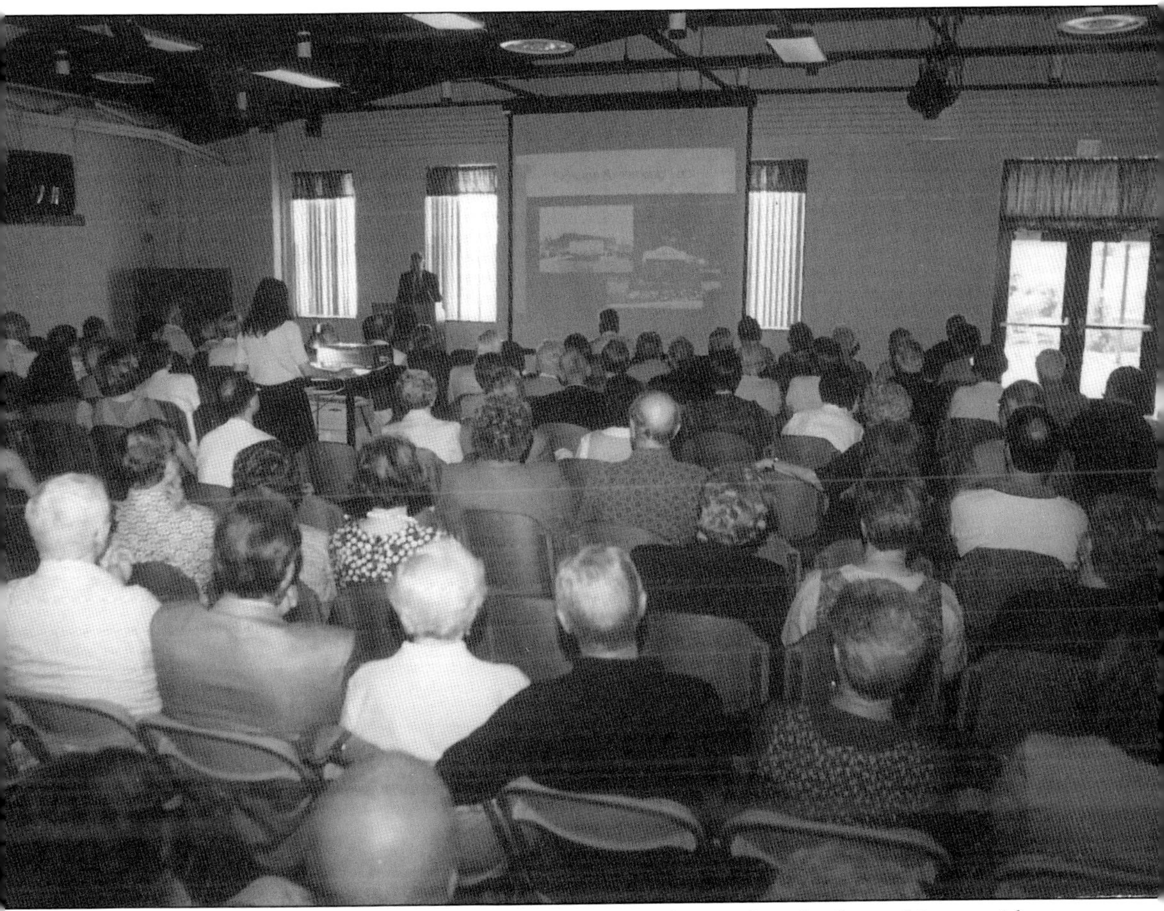

The college is always moving—in its building, its faculty, student body, and its president. Here's a view of his farewell "State of the College" which he gave in 2000.

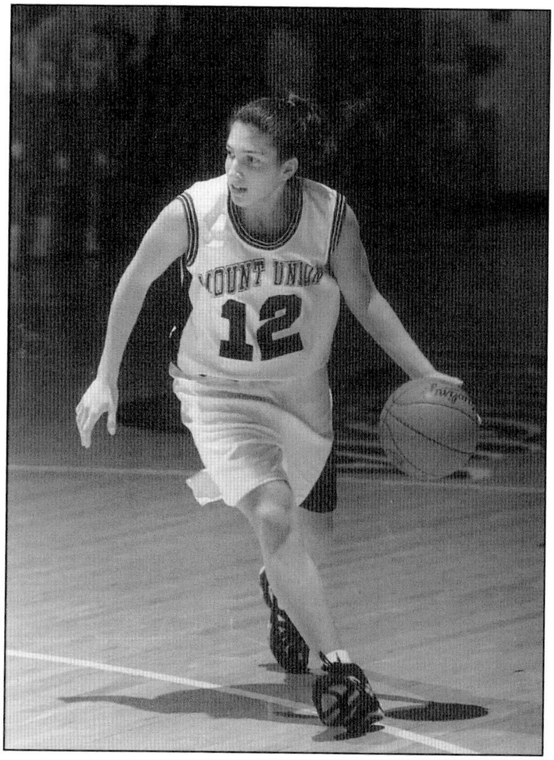

Here is Suzy Venet from the college women's basketball team. This photo was taken in the 1995-96 season.

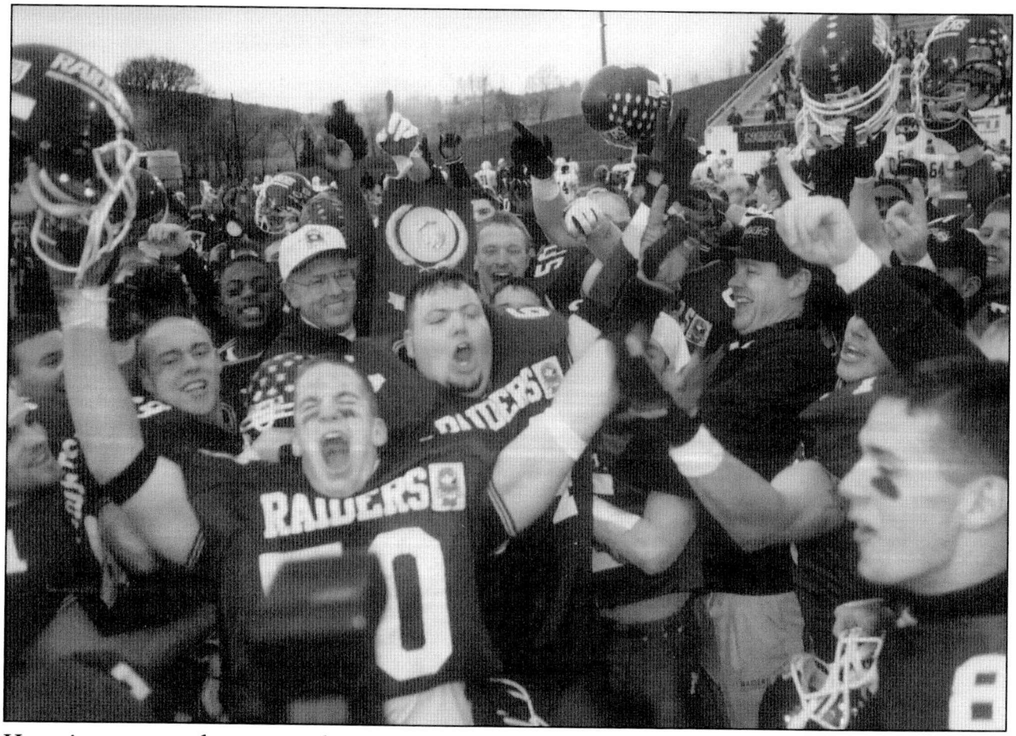

Here is a great photo... with great emotion. The Purple Raiders won the Stagg Bowl game in 1997.

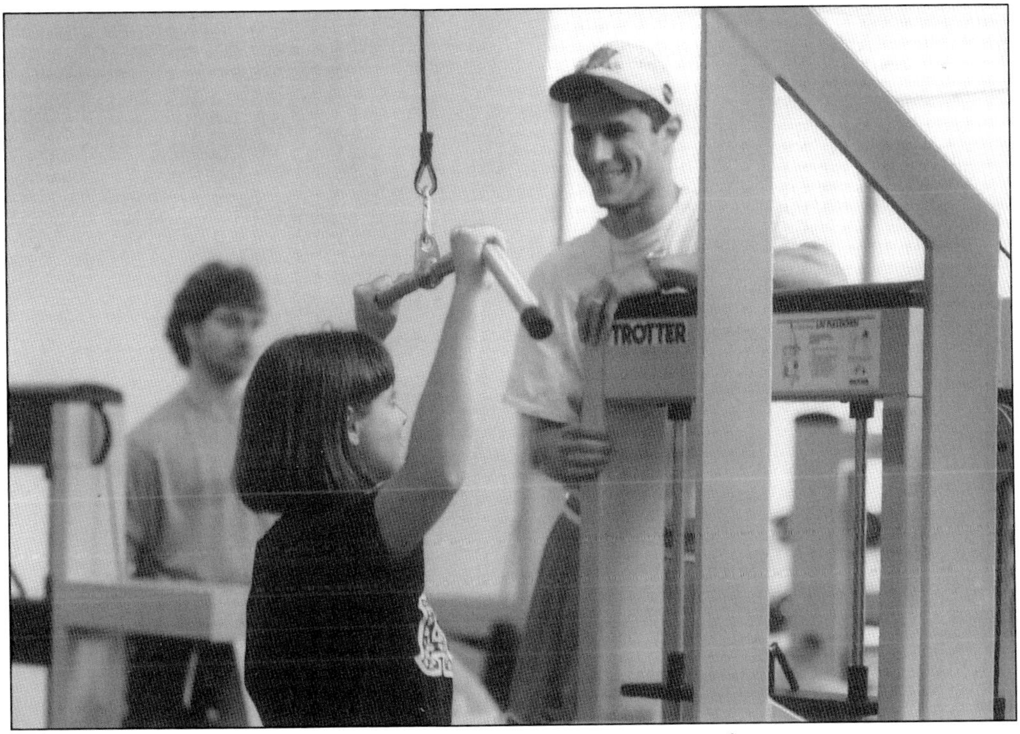

This photo shows the McPherson weight room. That was 1996.

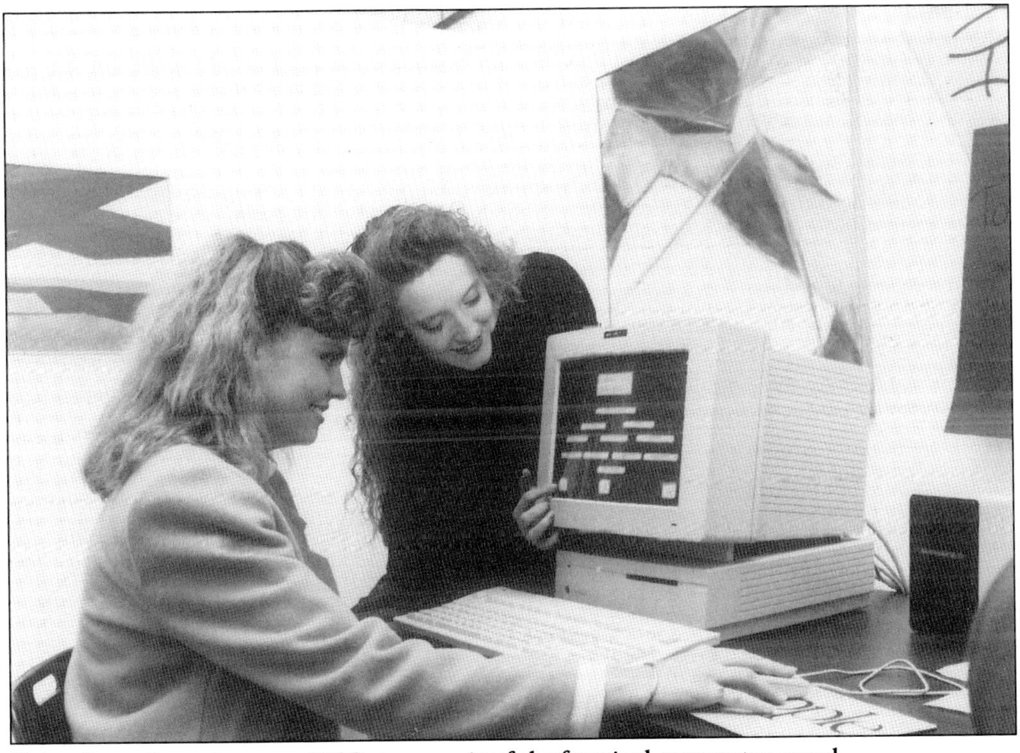

This photo from January 1993, is meaningful of typical computer need.

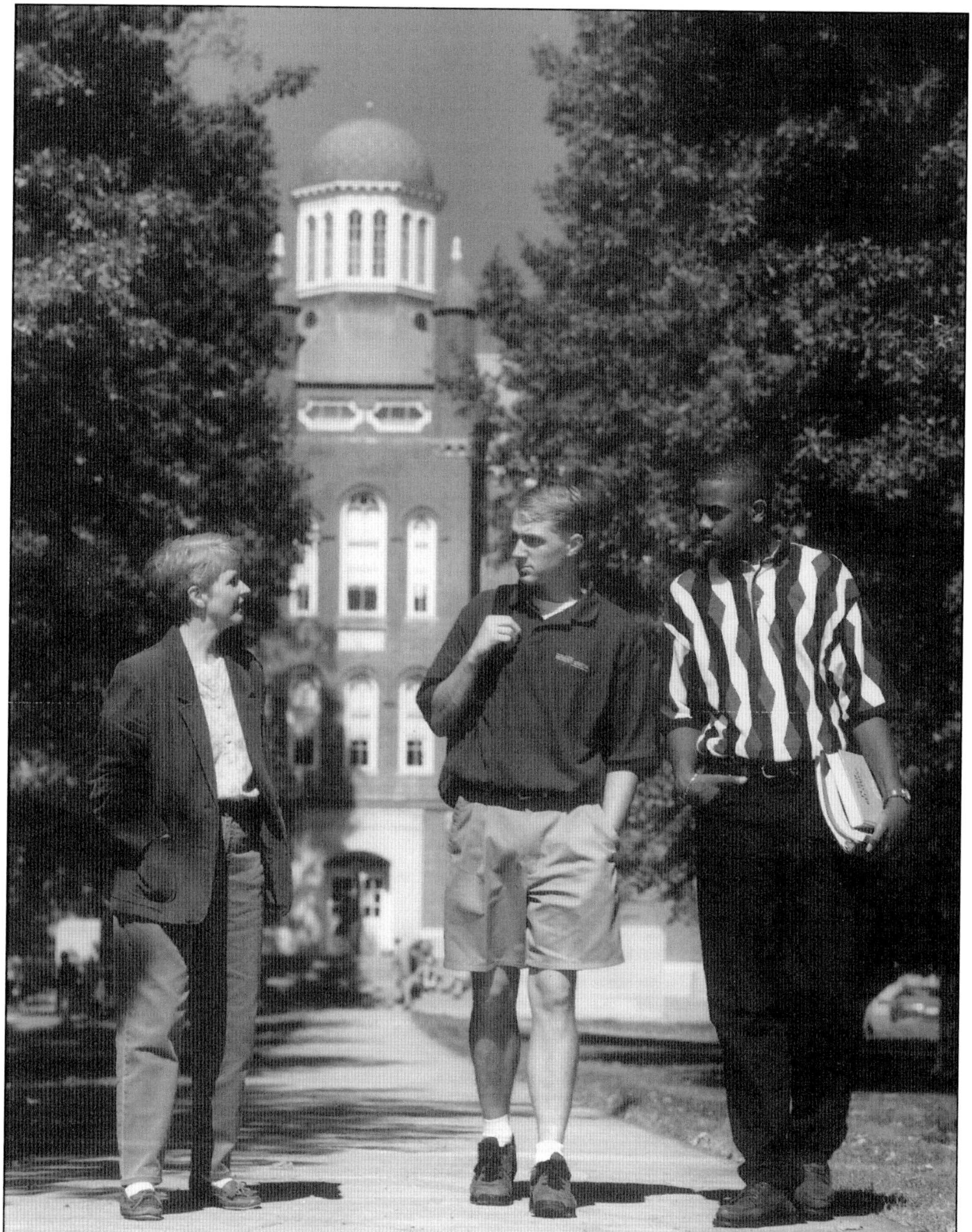

A typical campus scene in 1995: good conversation going on as they walk from Chapman Hall.

Pictured is the Bell Tower on campus.

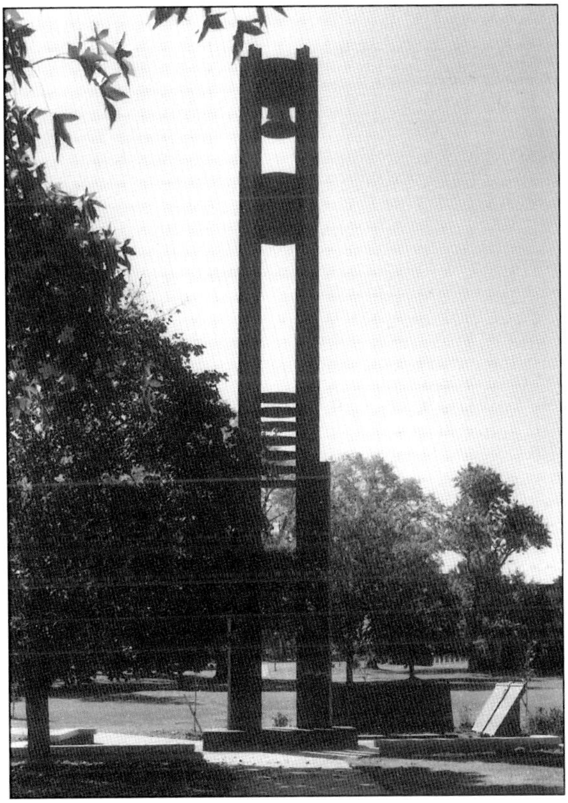

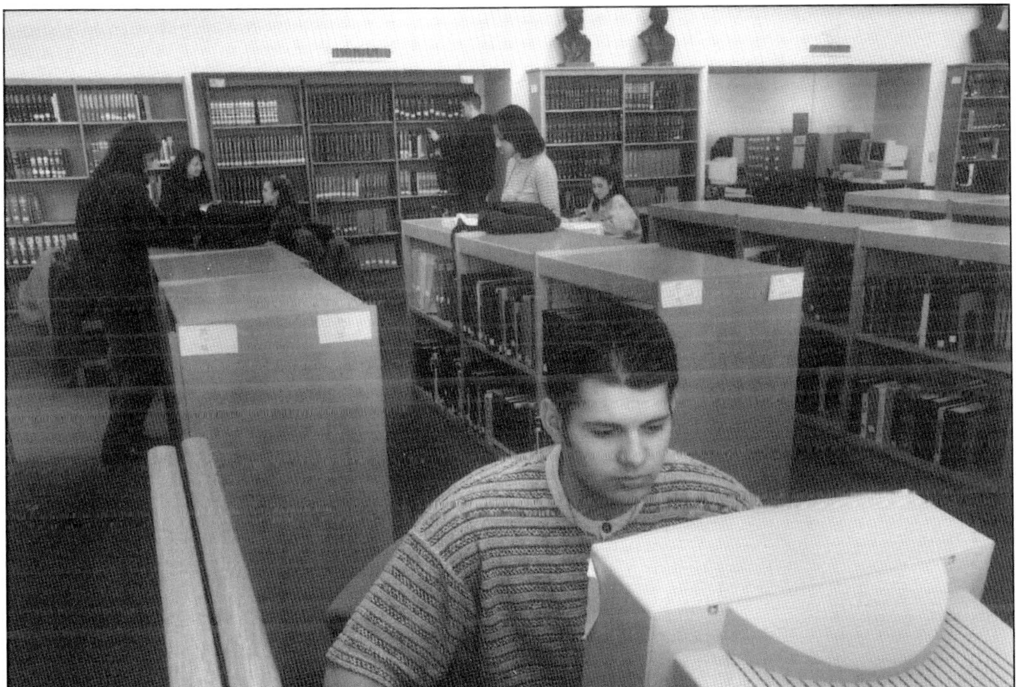

Library books ... in the computer age are seen here.

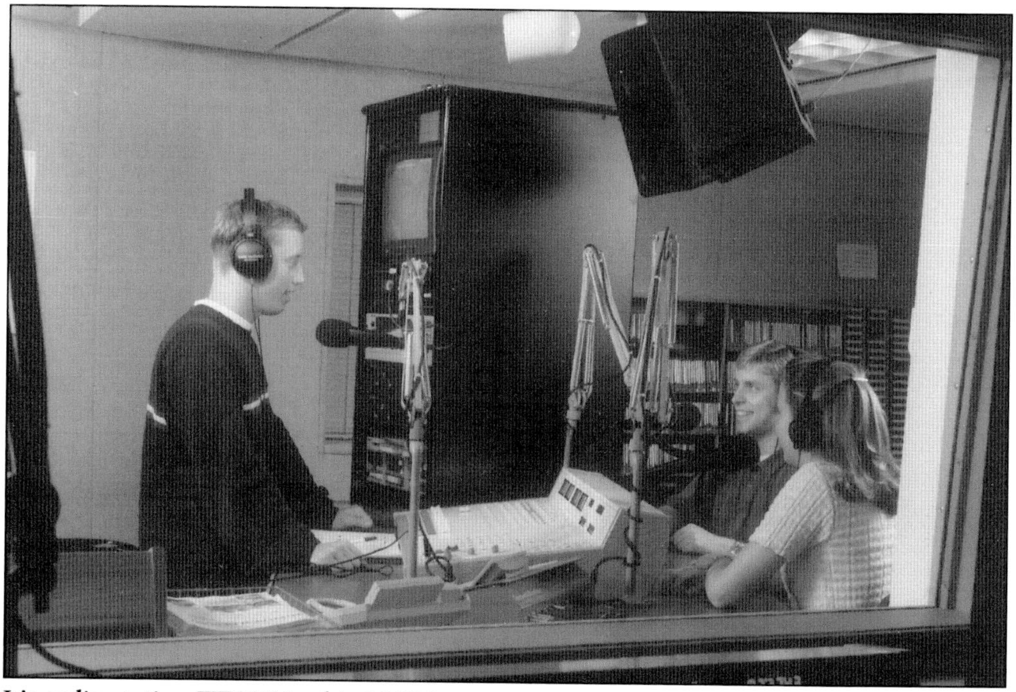

It's radio station WRMU in this 1998 image.

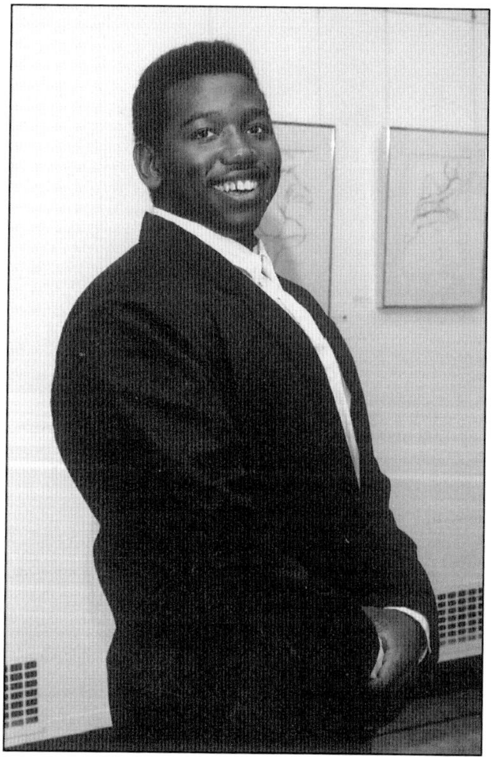

Philip Walker is with the artistry at the Student Art Exhibit in March 1990.

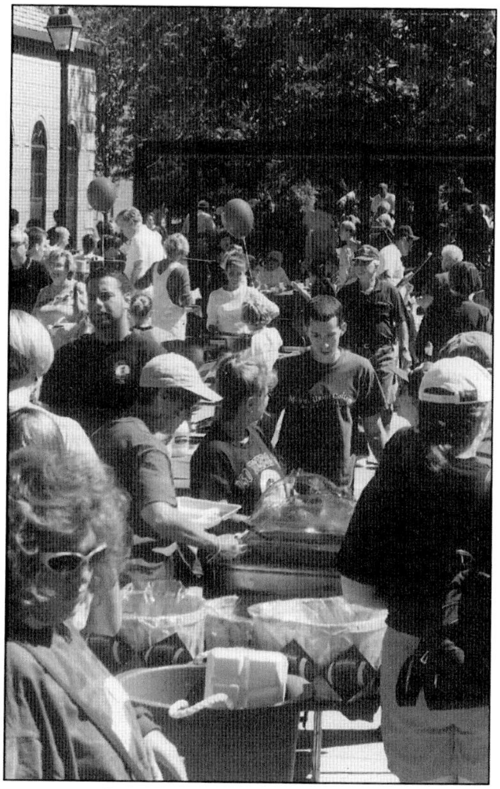

A scene from Community Day in 1999.

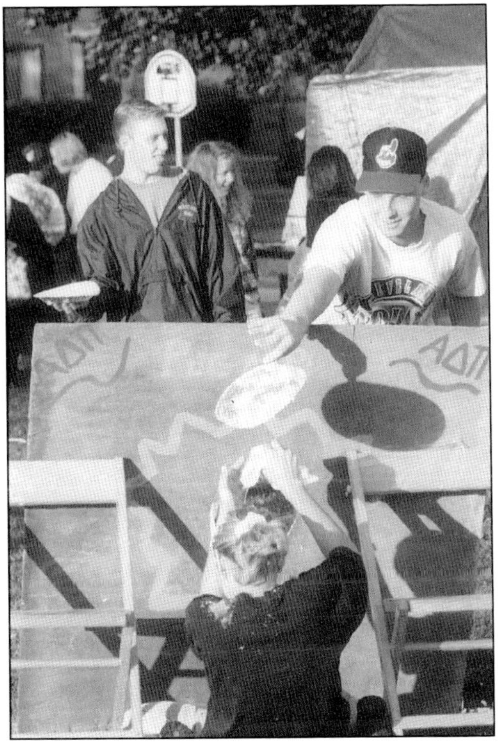

It's the Alpha Delta Pi "Pie Tossing Booth" at the homecoming carnival in 1995.

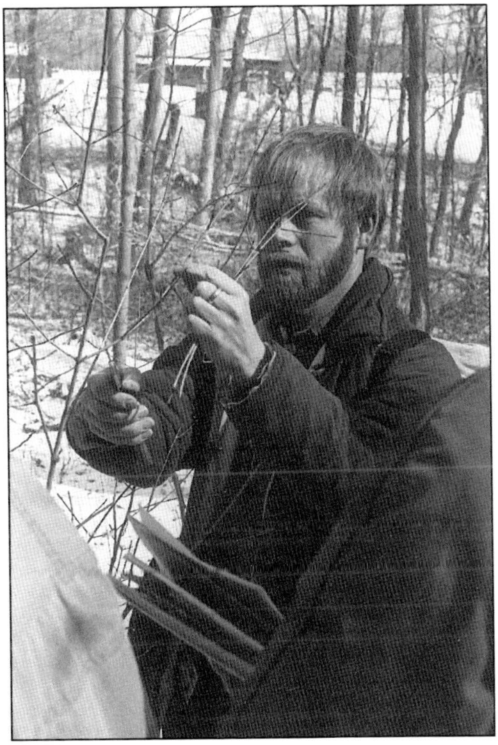

Professor Chuck McClaugherty shows and tells at the nature center.

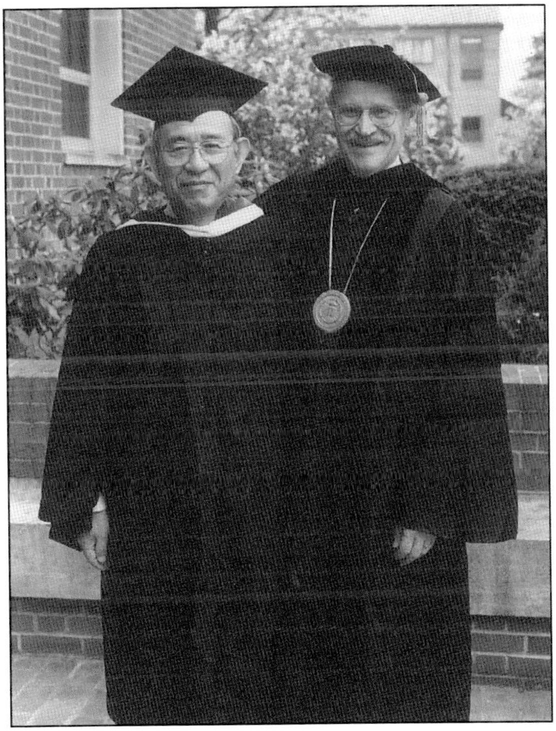

President Kolenbrander with a Baika College representative from Japan. The year is 2000

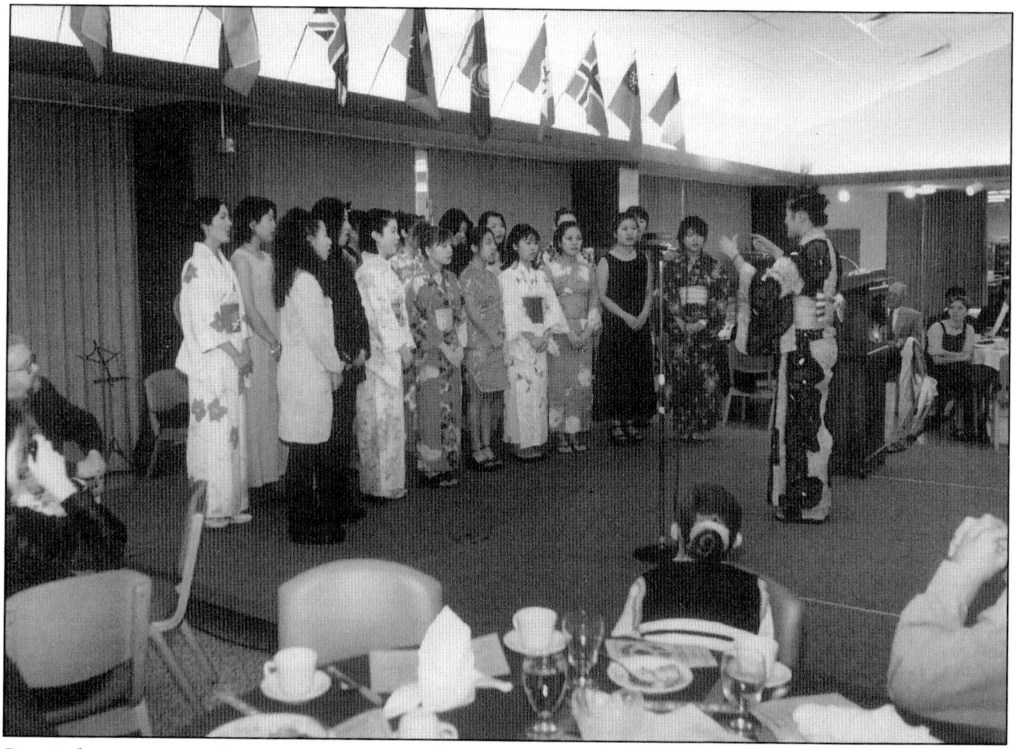

Special programming on campus, this scene is part of the fine activities during "International Week" in 1999.

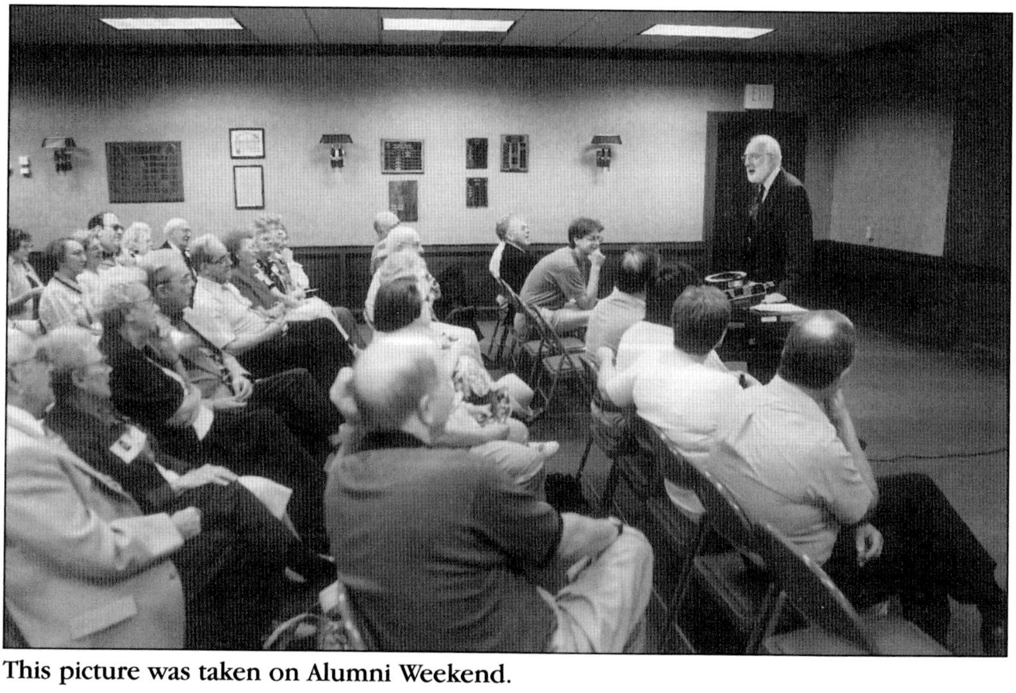

This picture was taken on Alumni Weekend.

Guest lecturers help broaden knowledge. Here is Mario Cuomo giving his Schooler Lecture in the spring of 2000.

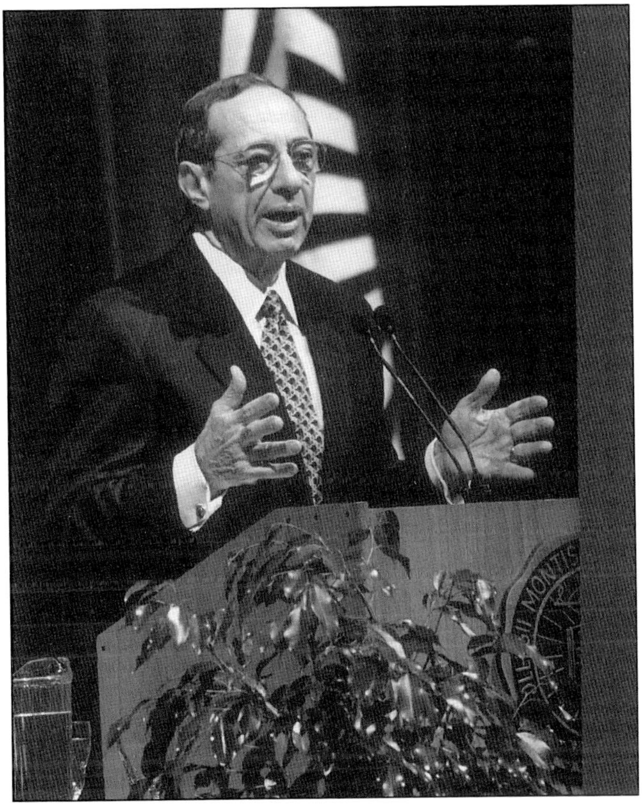

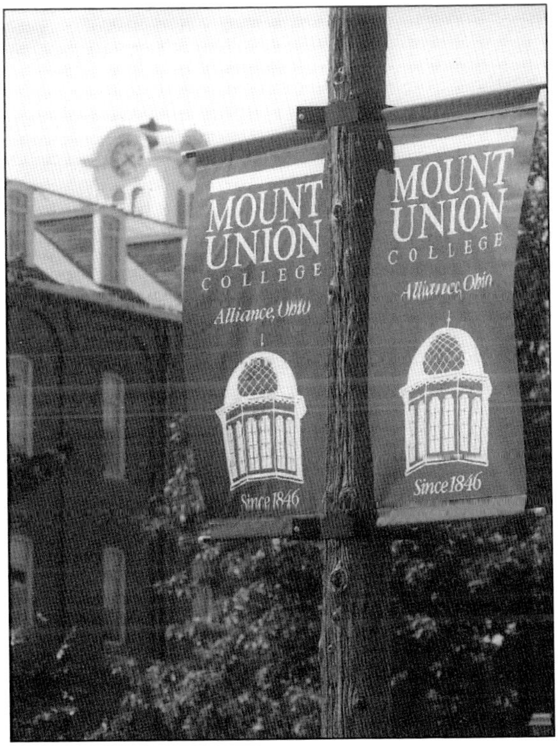

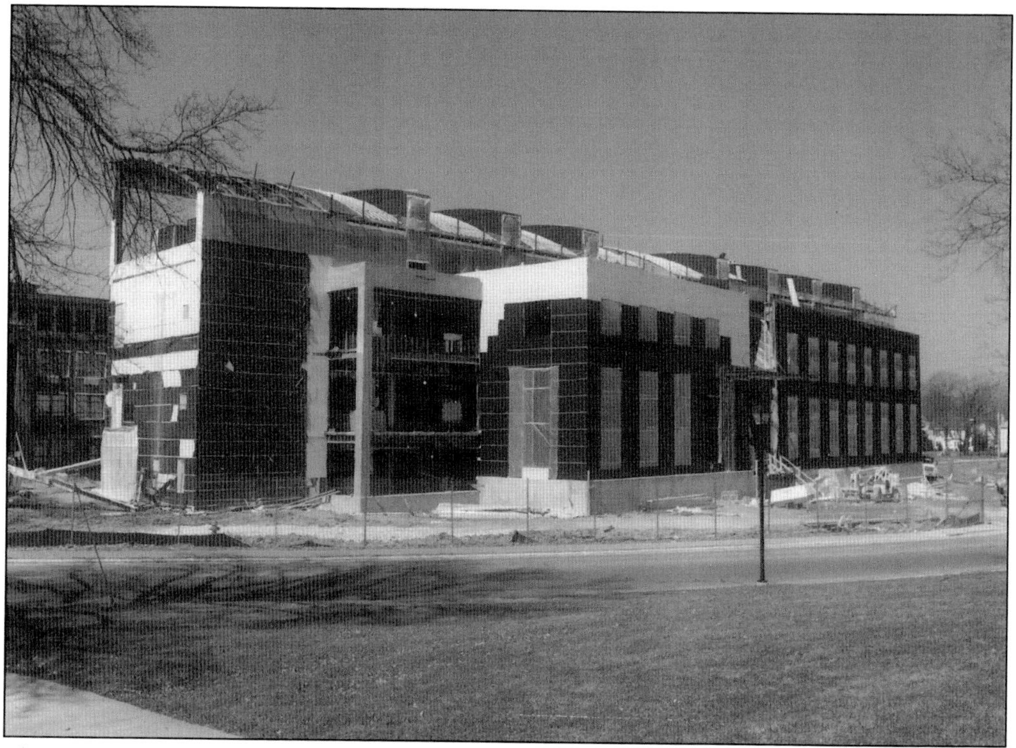

The new Kolenbrander-Harter Information Center under construction in 1999.

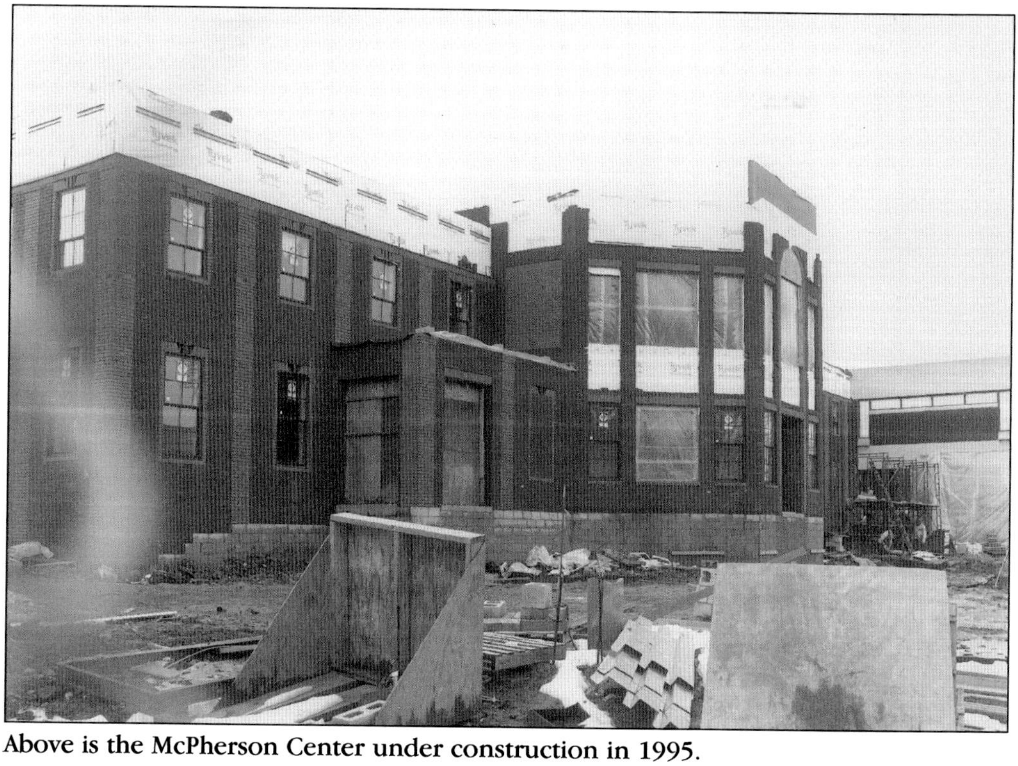

Above is the McPherson Center under construction in 1995.

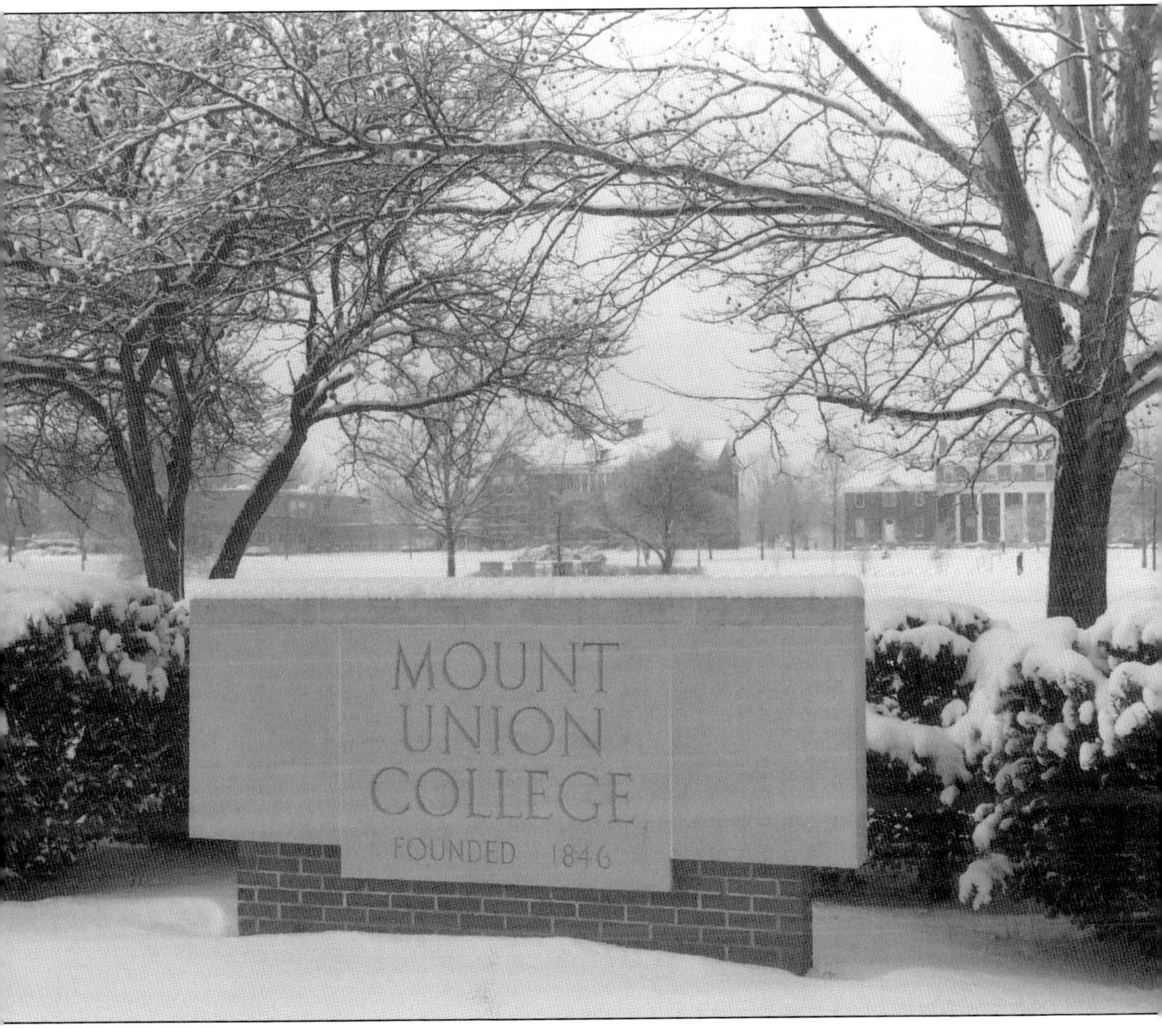

This sign says it all.

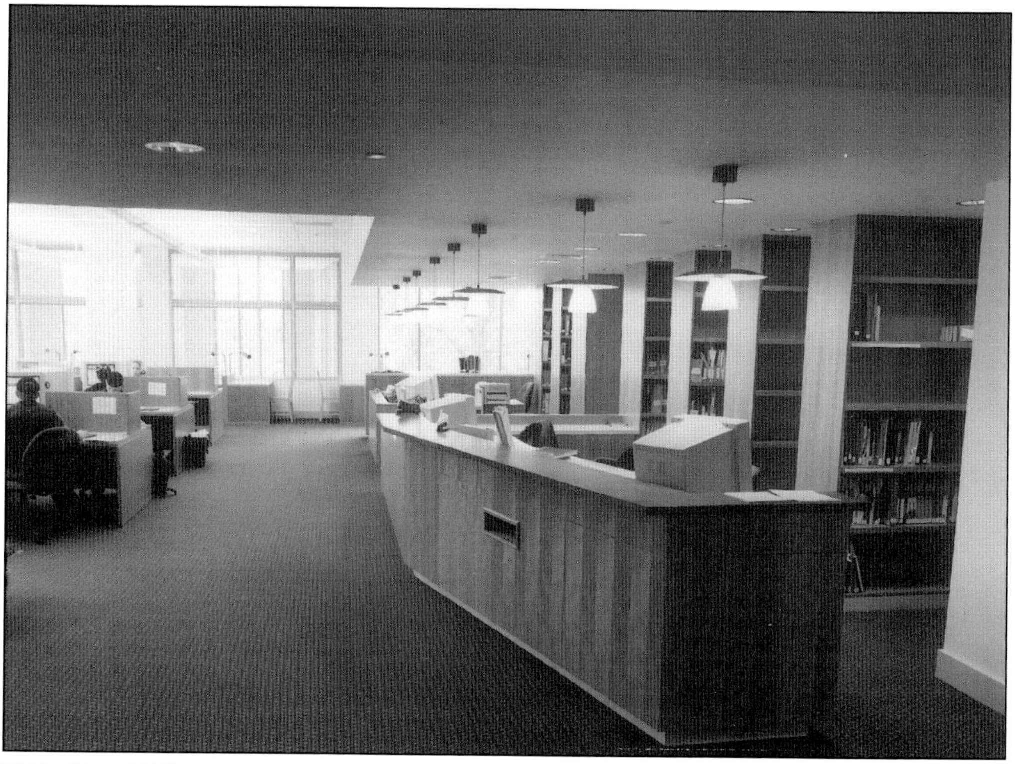

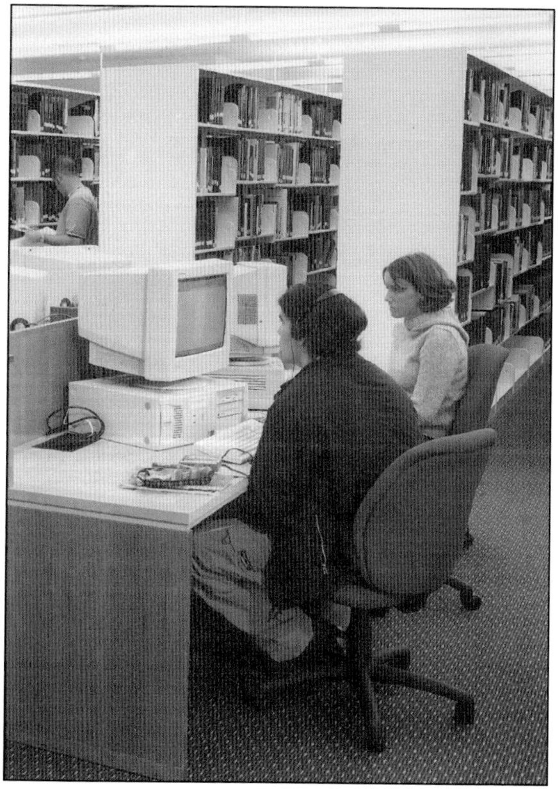

Here is the circulation desk and the reference room at the new Information Center.

Here is a view of students in the library area in the year 2000.

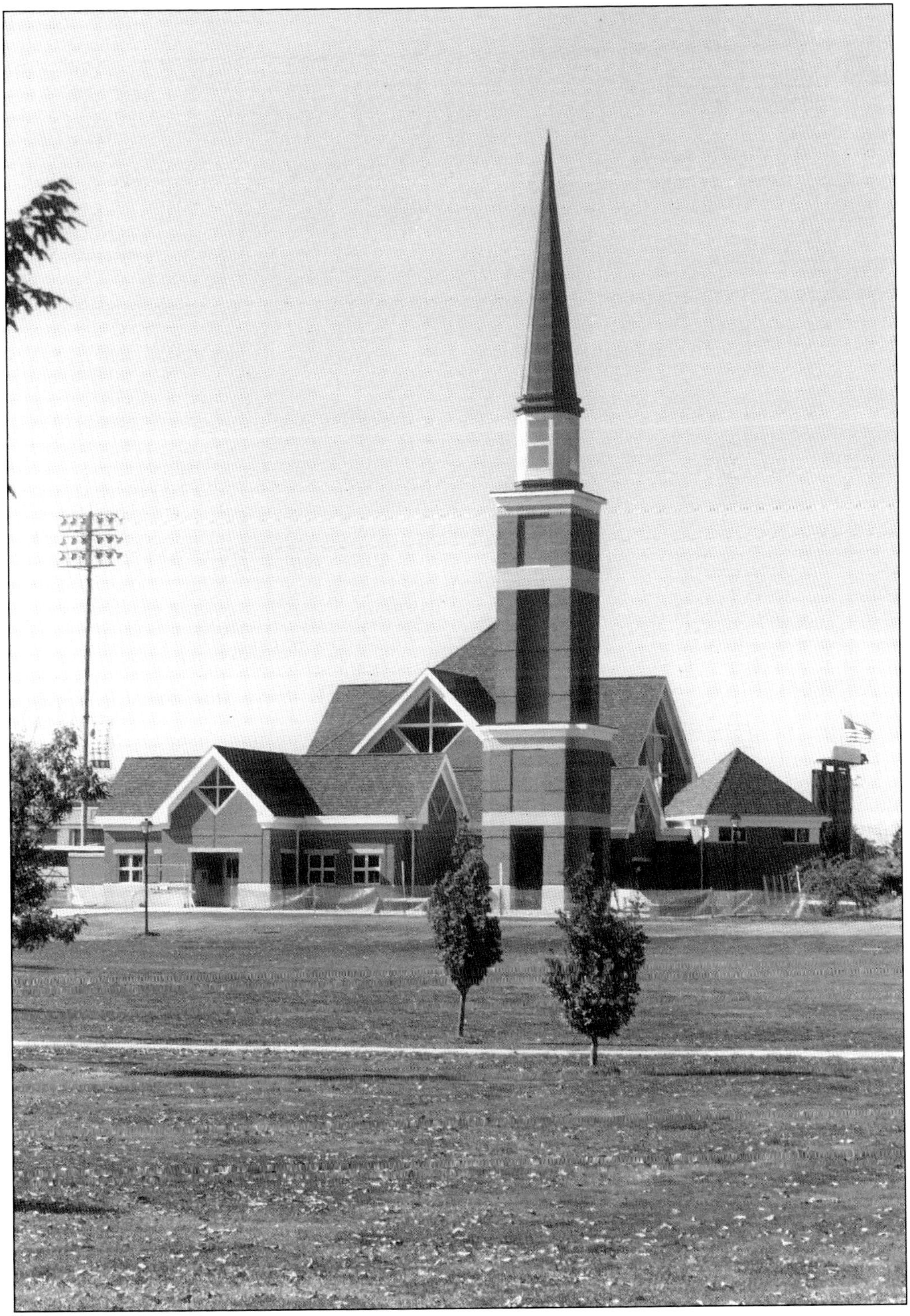
The DeWald Chapel is a fine campus addition.

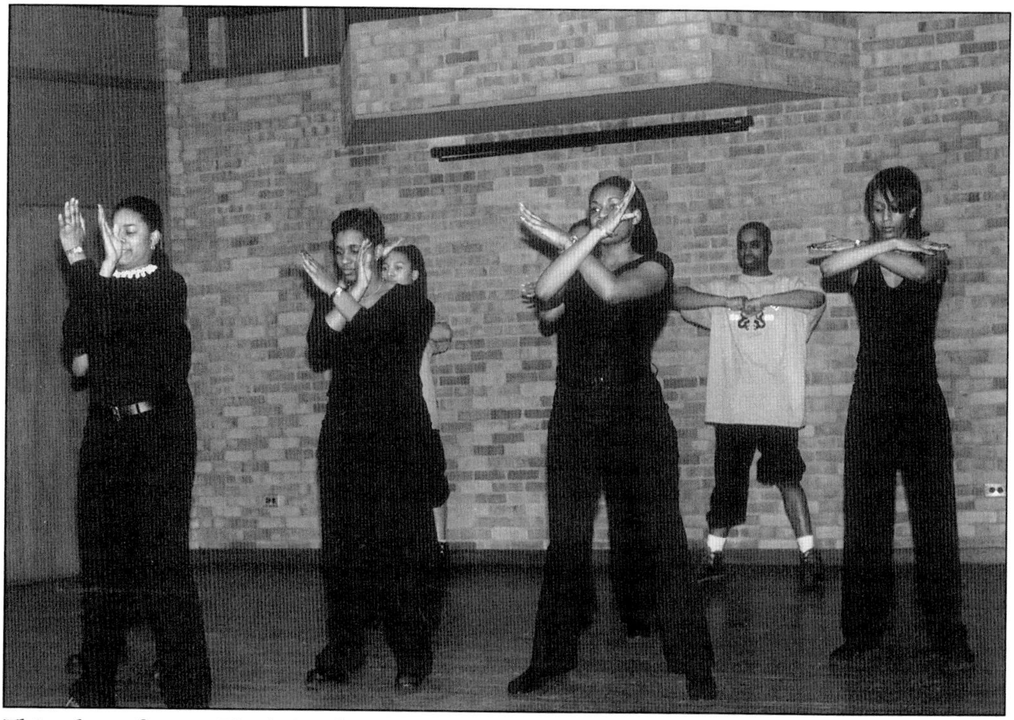

This photo from a Black Student Union production was taken in 2000.

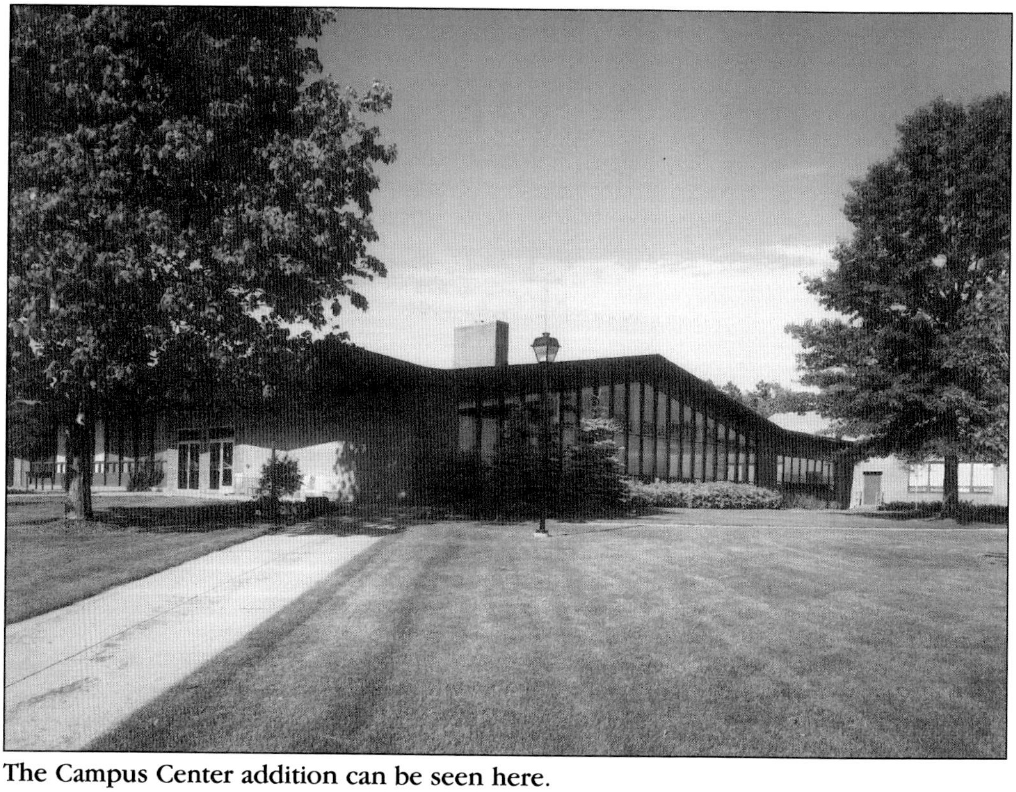

The Campus Center addition can be seen here.

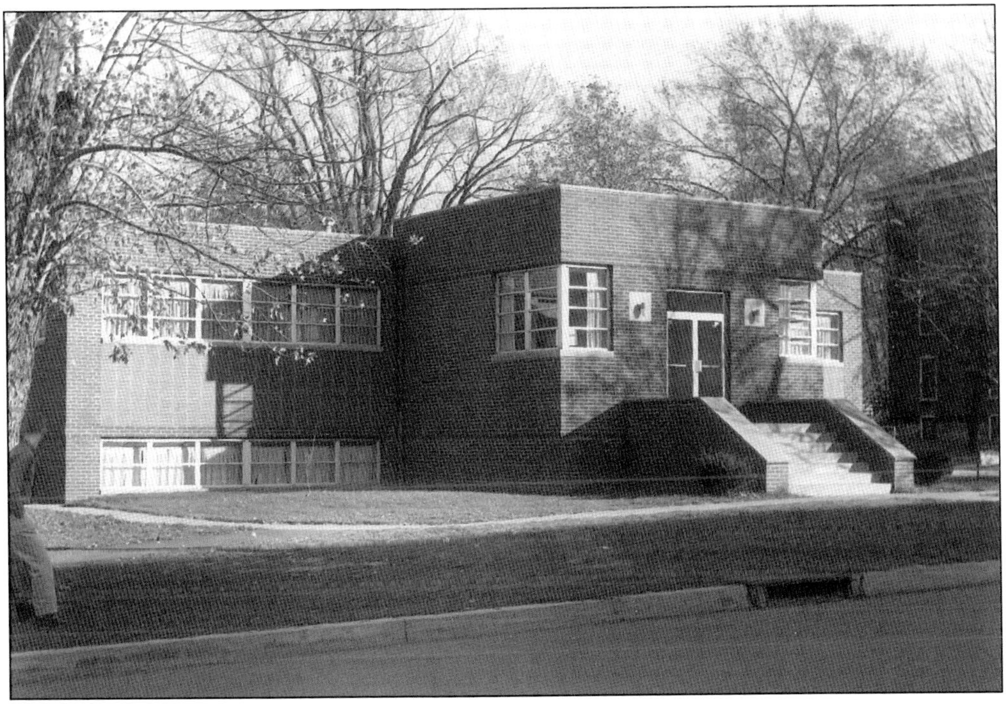

This image shows the Ramsayer Health Center.

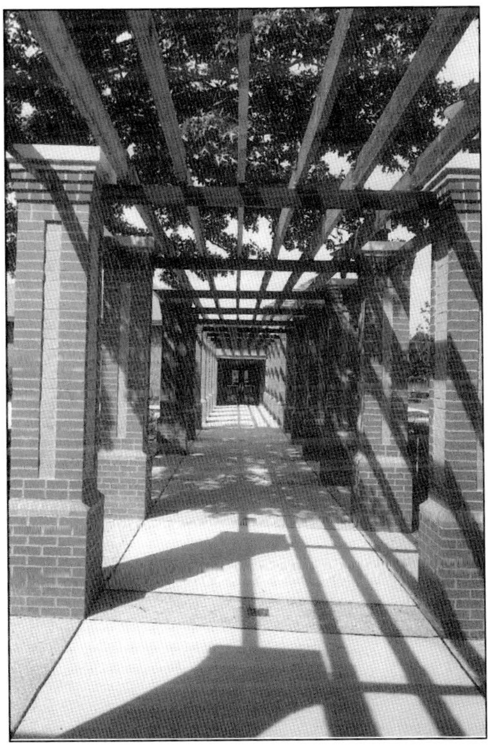

Additions to the campus center provide new views—such as this in 2000.

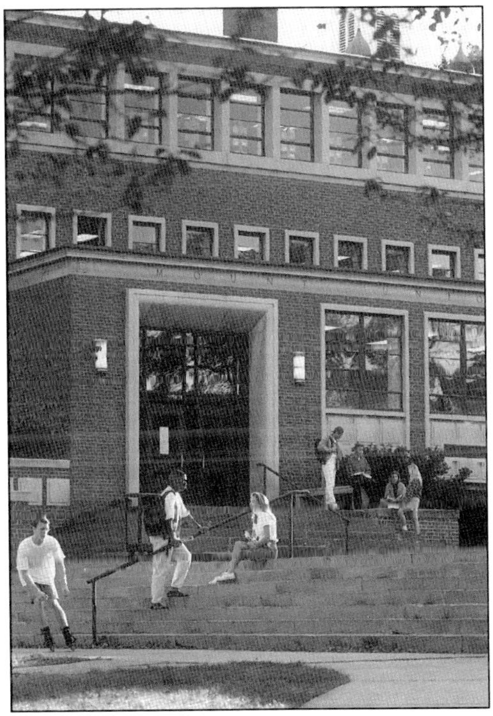

A view of the Library and some who will be entering the library. This photo is from 1995.

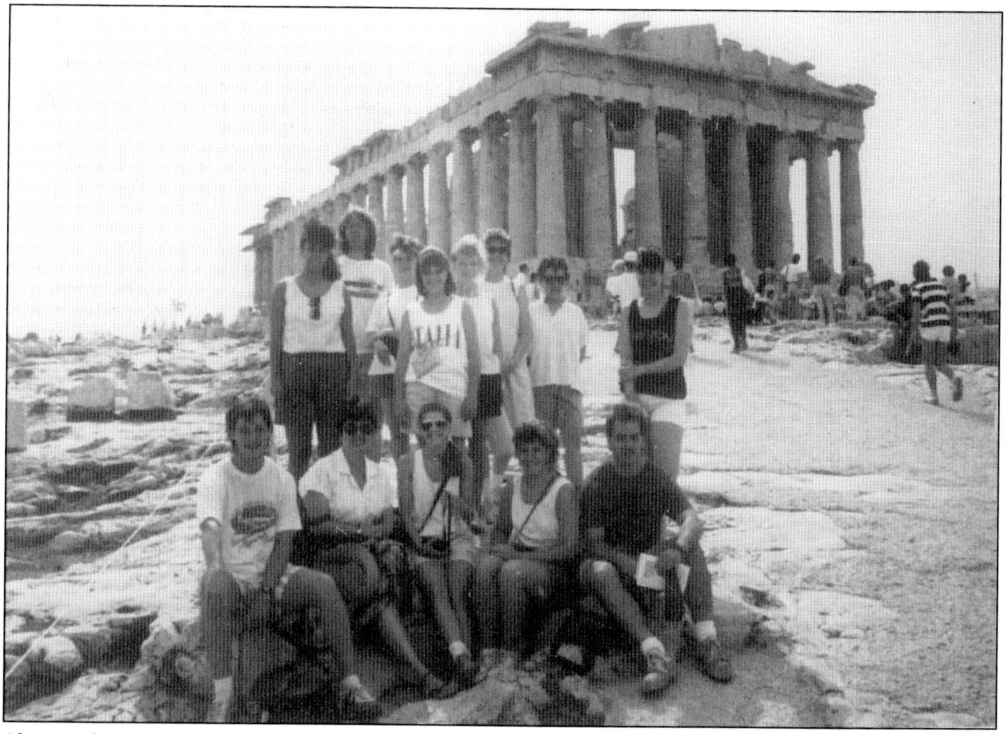

Shown here are two views of an archeological trip visiting Europe and Israel.

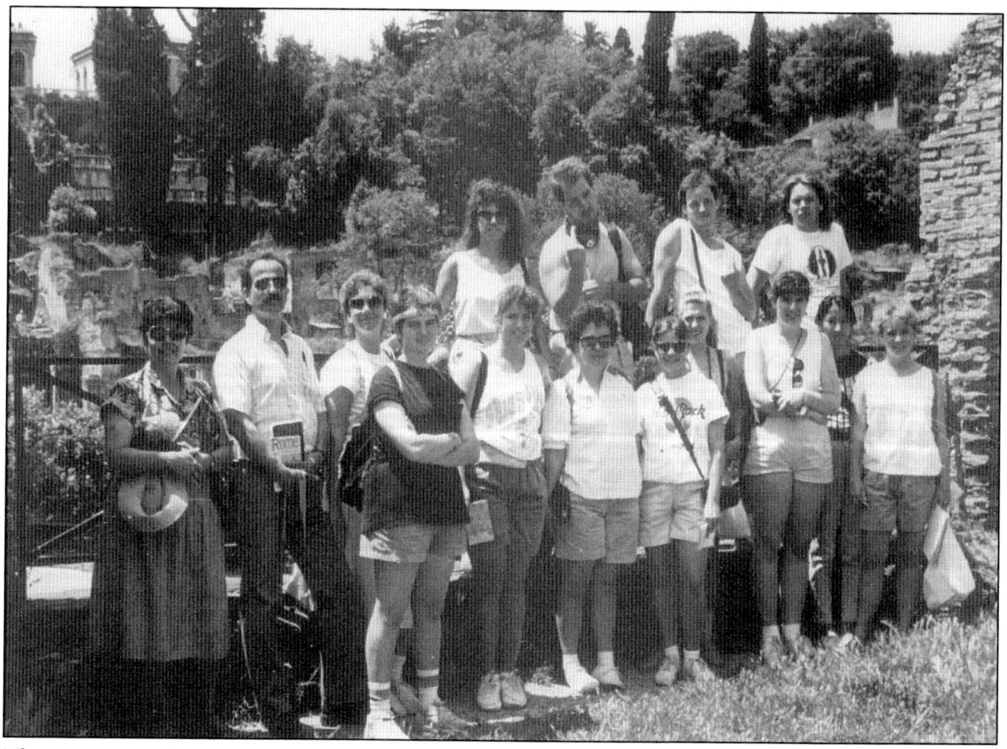

The year is 1988.

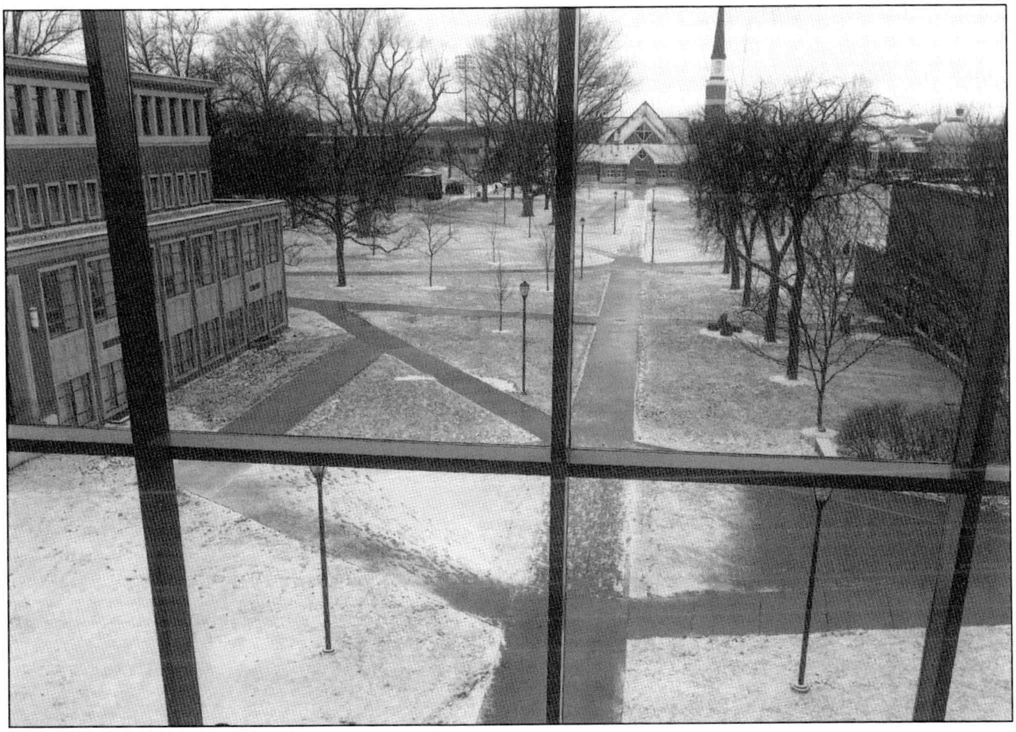

Here is a wintertime view of the campus from the Kolenbrander-Harter Information Center.

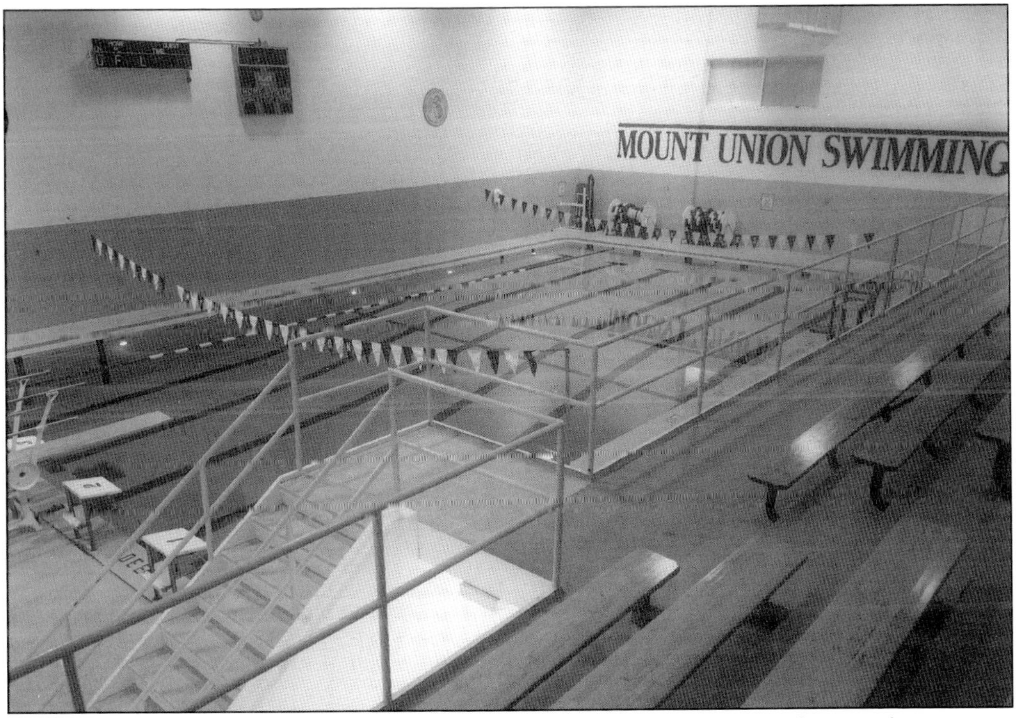

A smooth, important water area and good seating areas for those who watch.

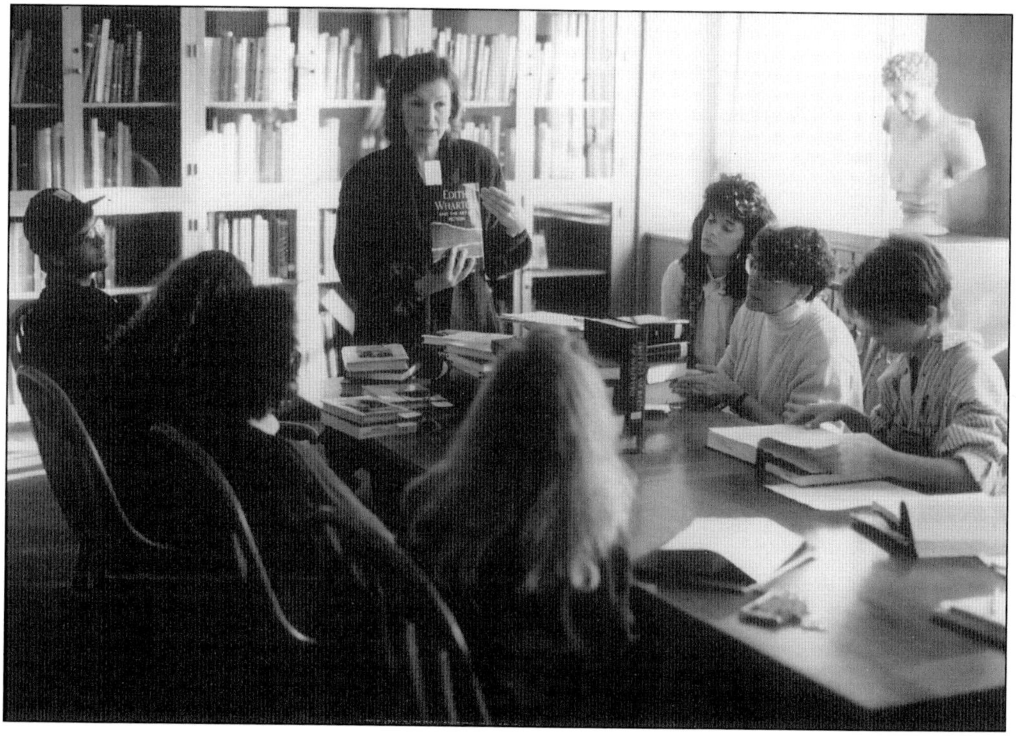

Here is Dr. McMahan teaching literature in the fall of 1990.

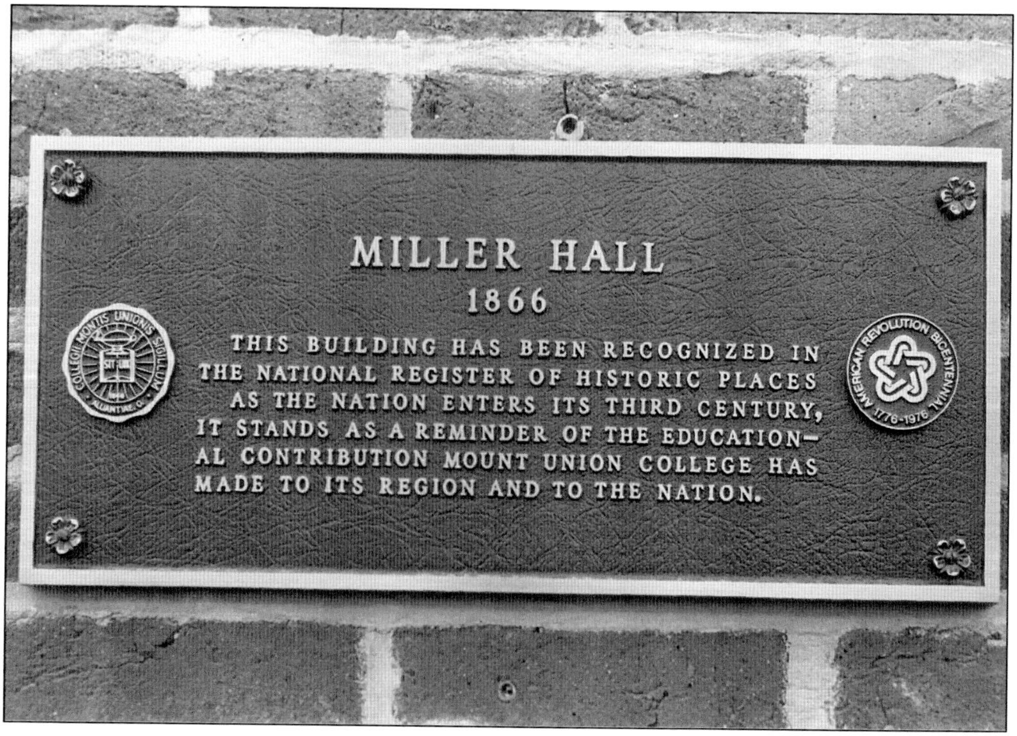

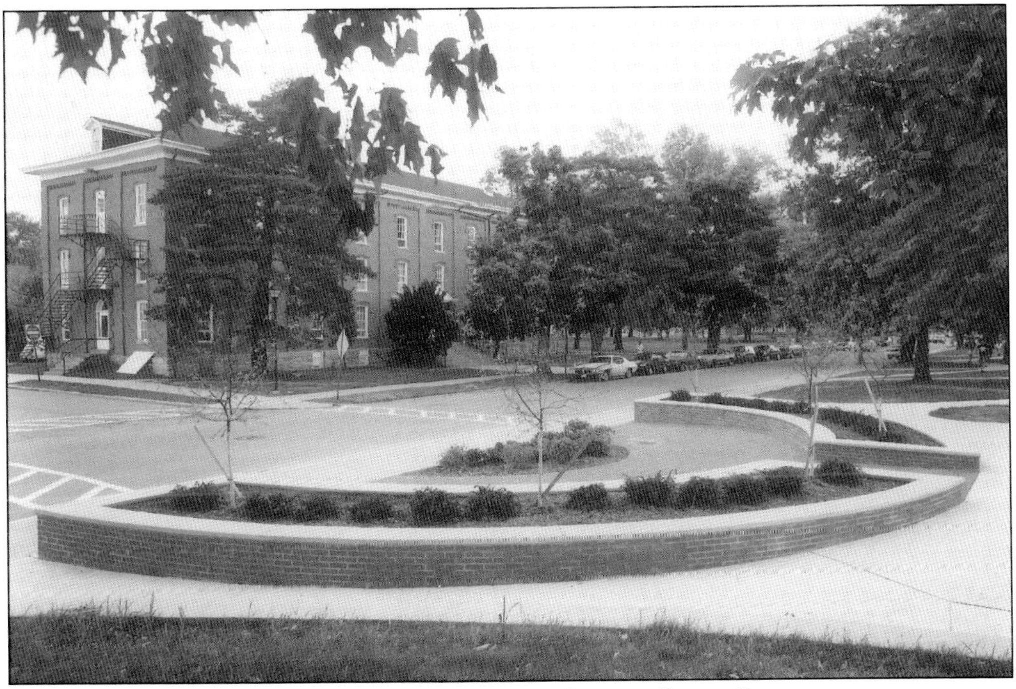

This 1993 view shows the Hoover Plaza, across from Miller Hall.

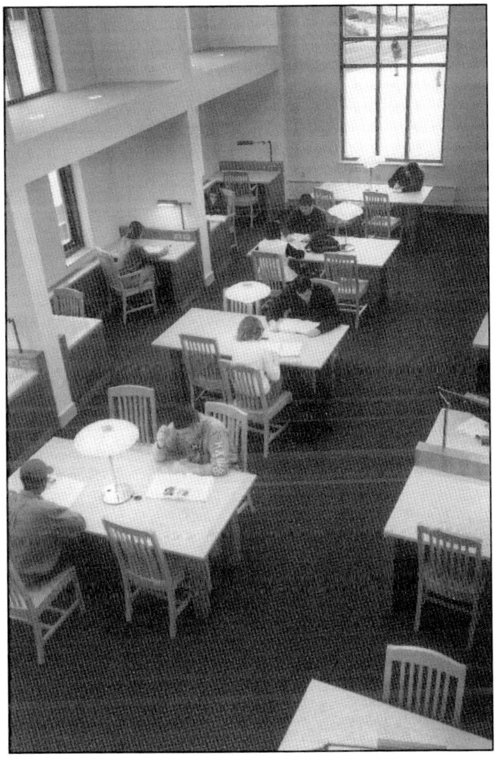

Many fine study areas are in the Kolenbrander-Harter Information Center.

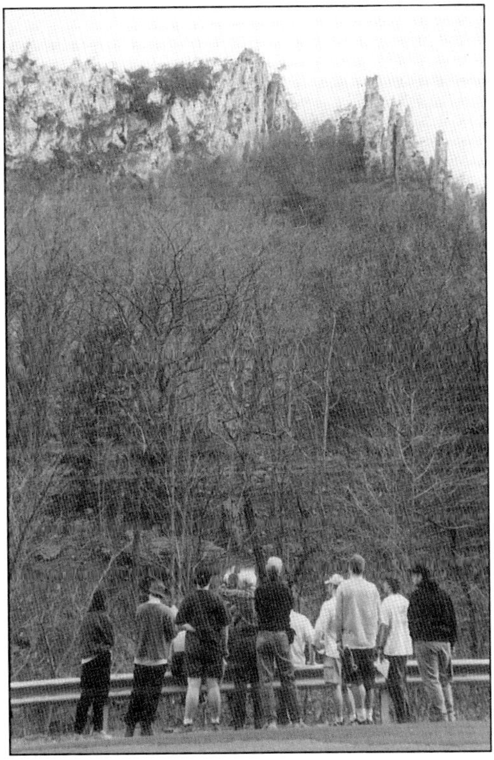

A look during a geology trip to West Virginia; this image was taken in 1998.

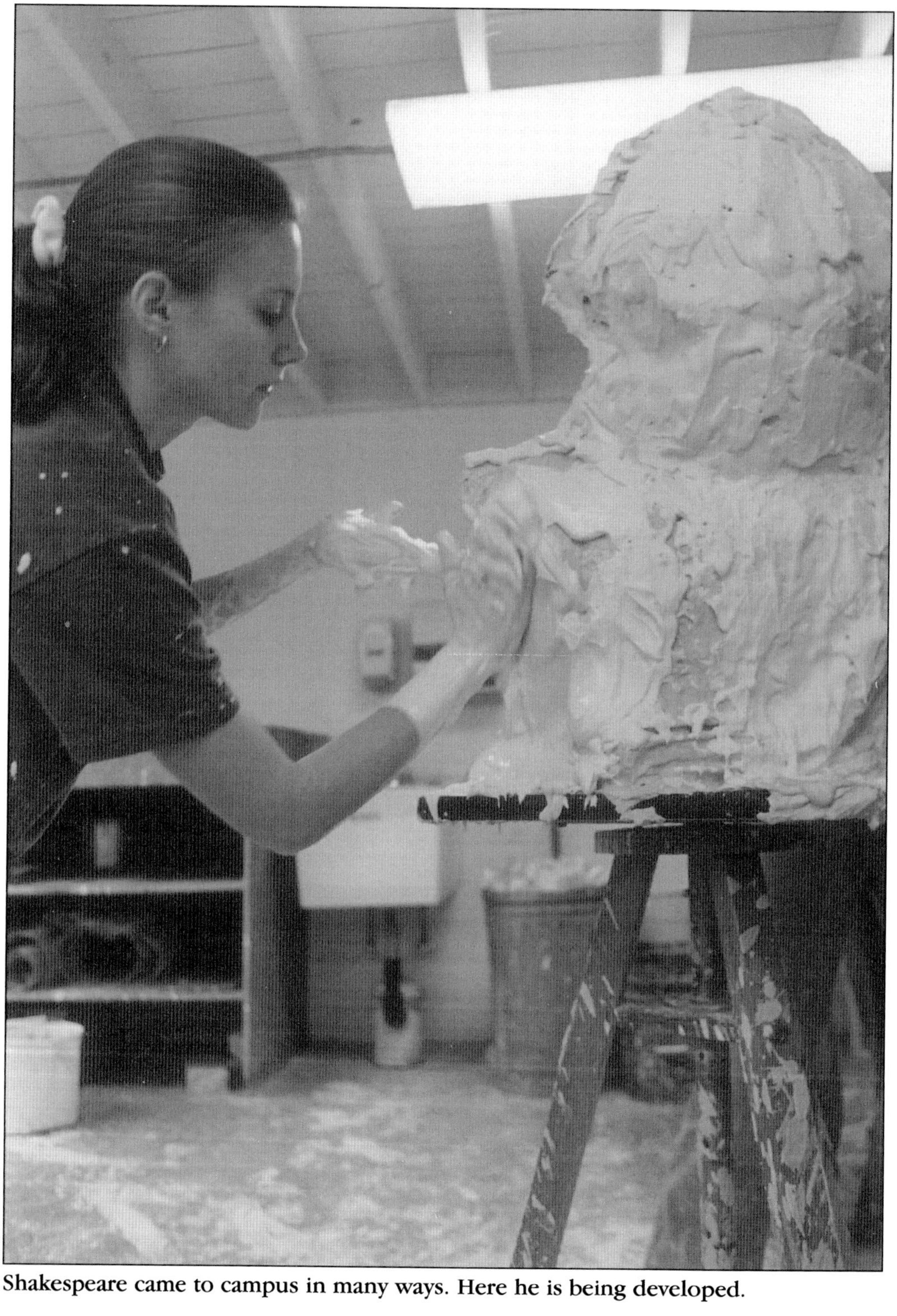

Shakespeare came to campus in many ways. Here he is being developed.

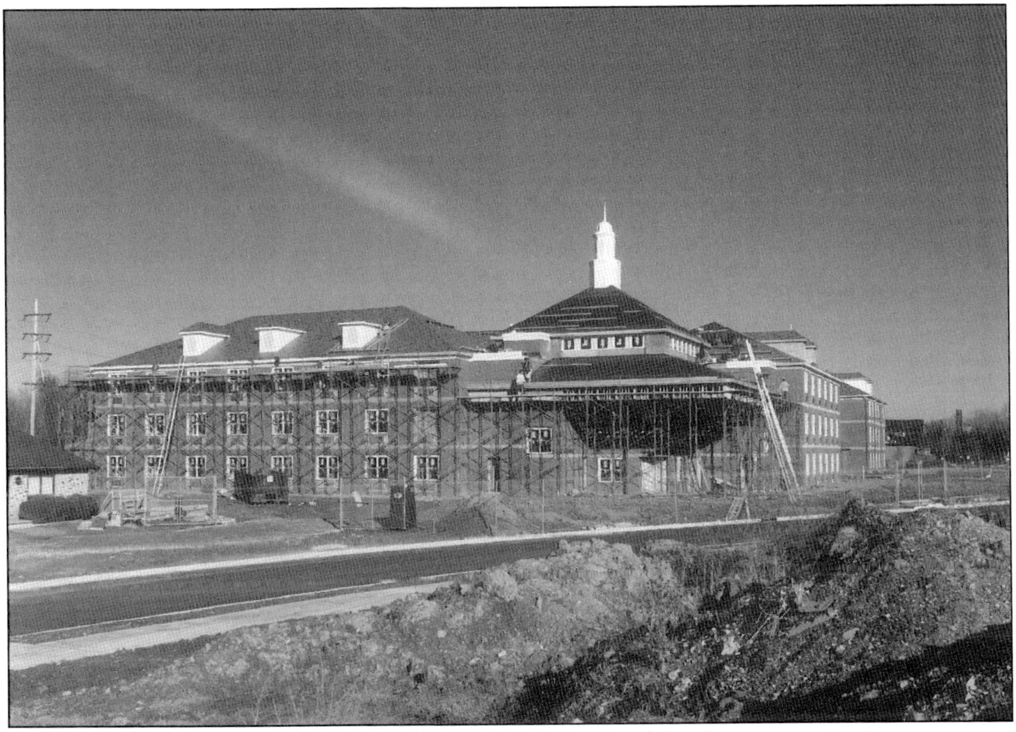

New dormitories under construction here, as new land has been acquired.

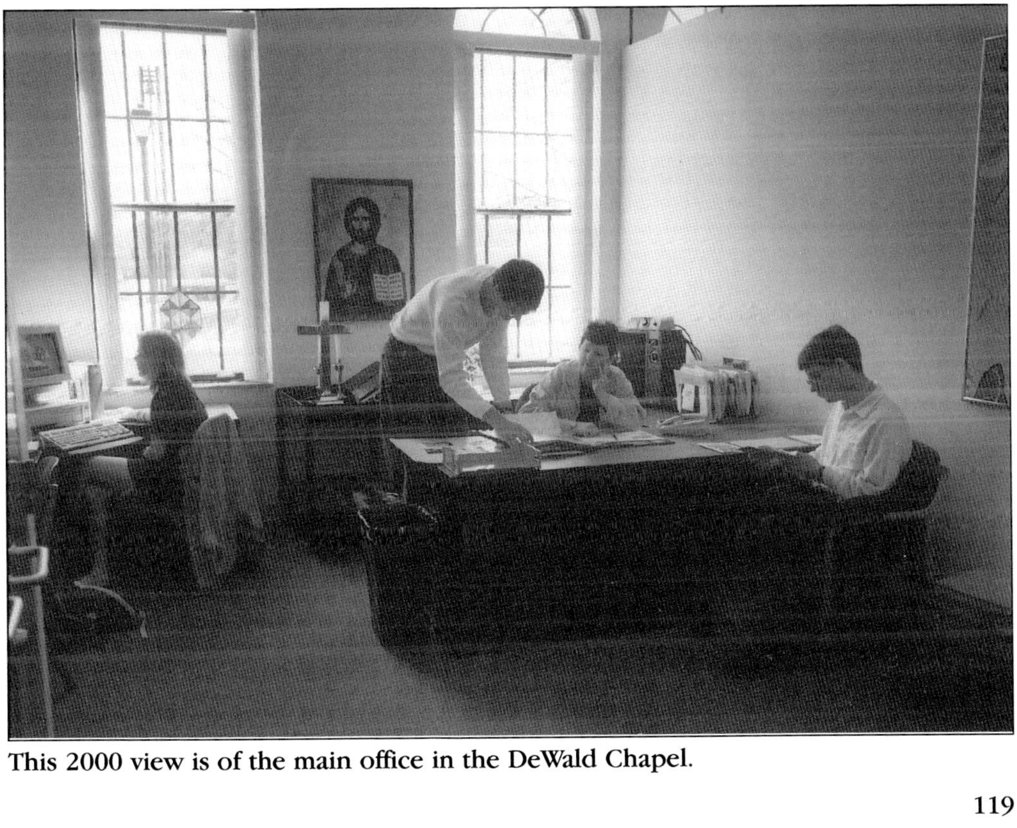

This 2000 view is of the main office in the DeWald Chapel.

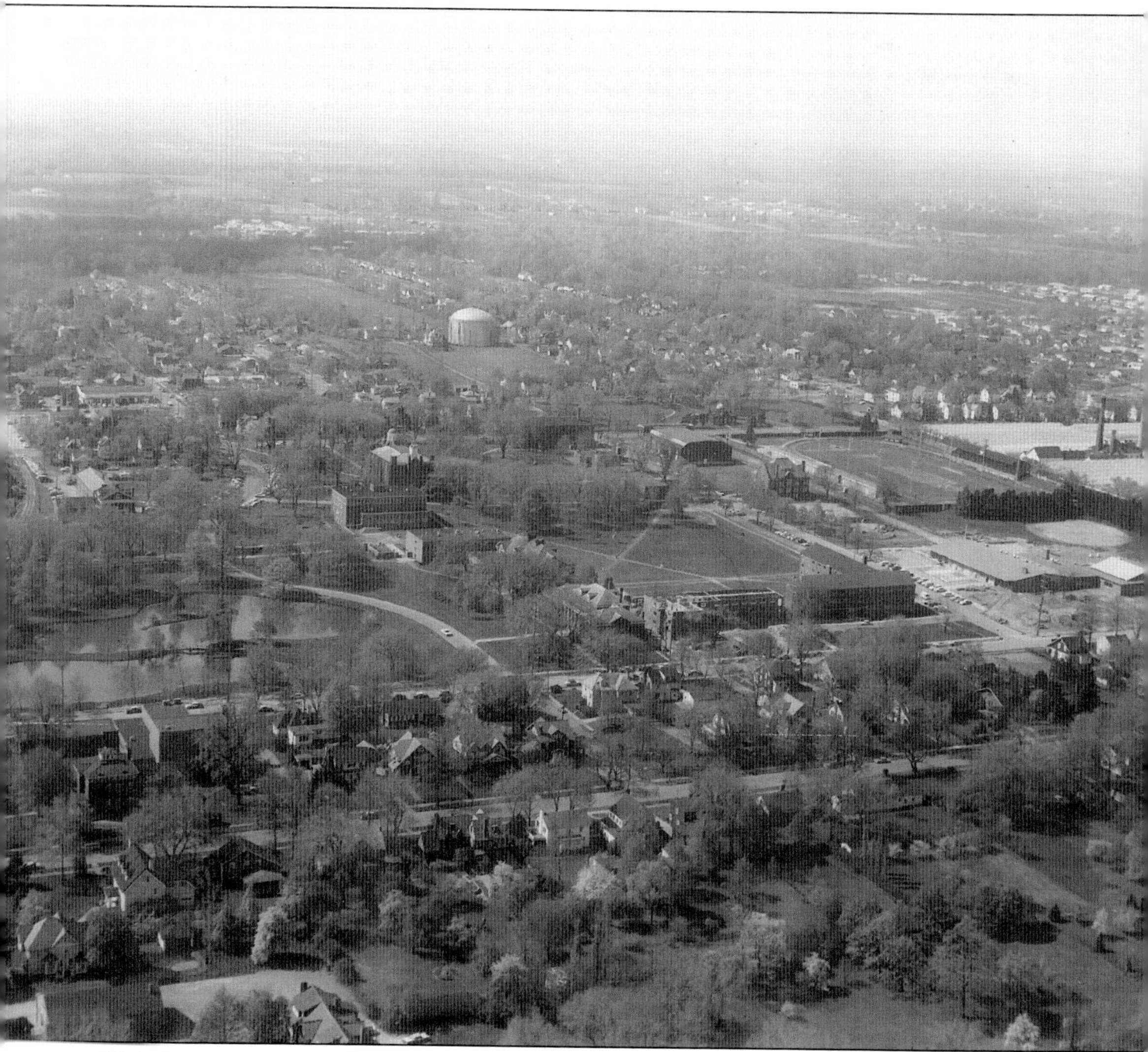

This image is an aerial view of the campus!

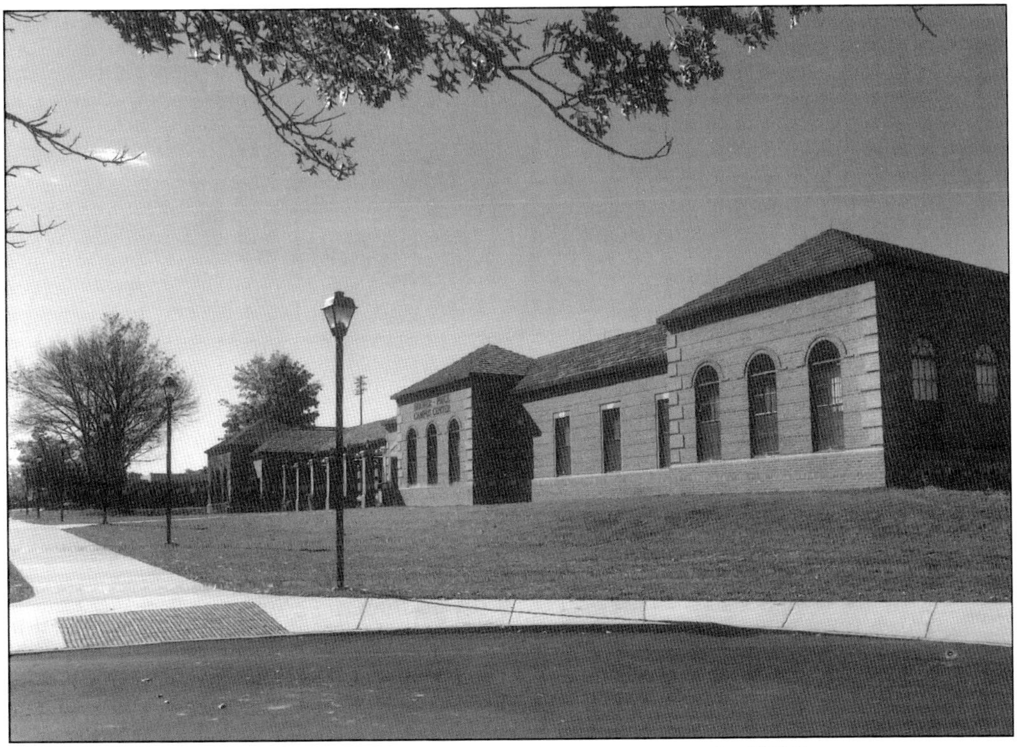

This shows the addition to the Hoover-Price Campus center in 1996.

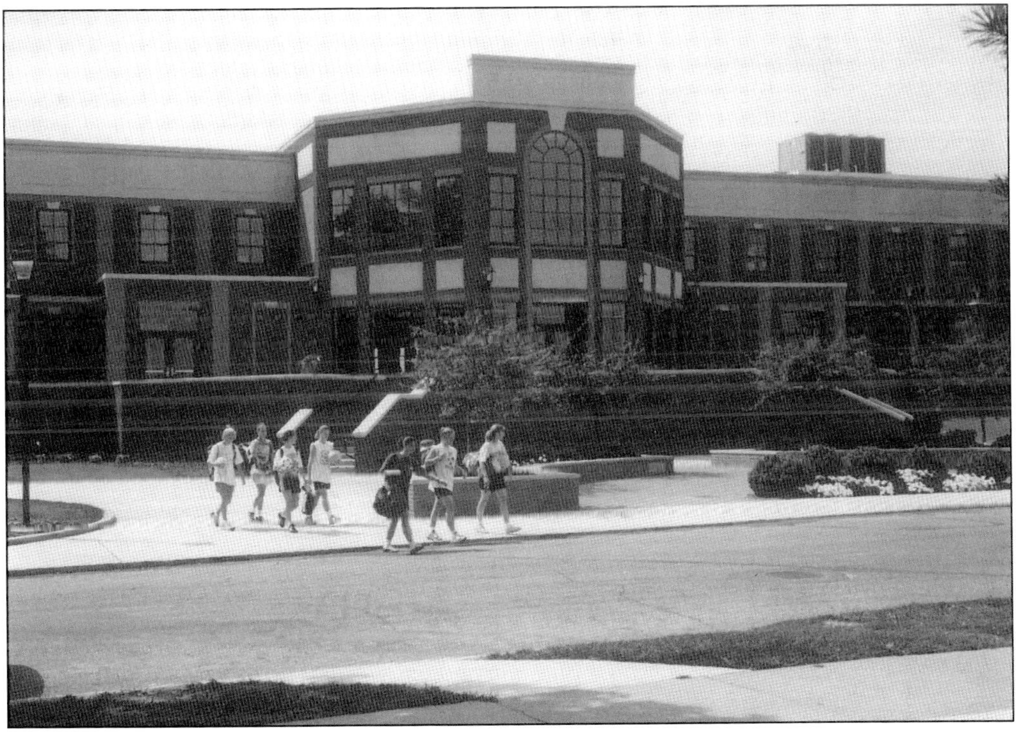

This is the McPherson Wellness Center.

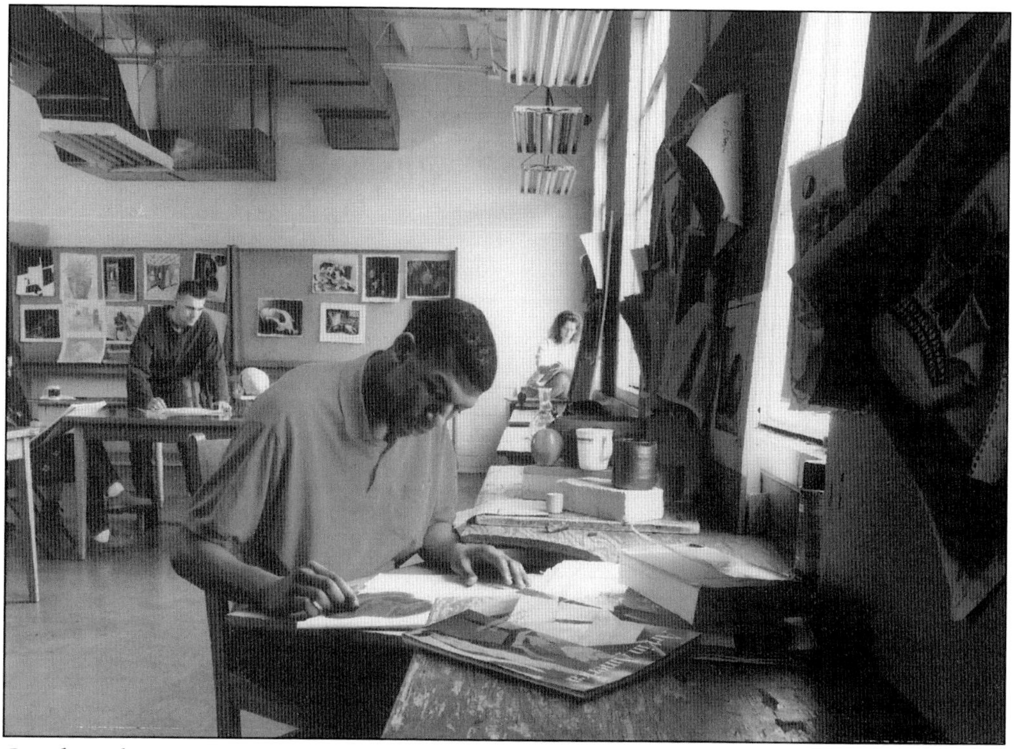

Good working times ... in artistic areas!

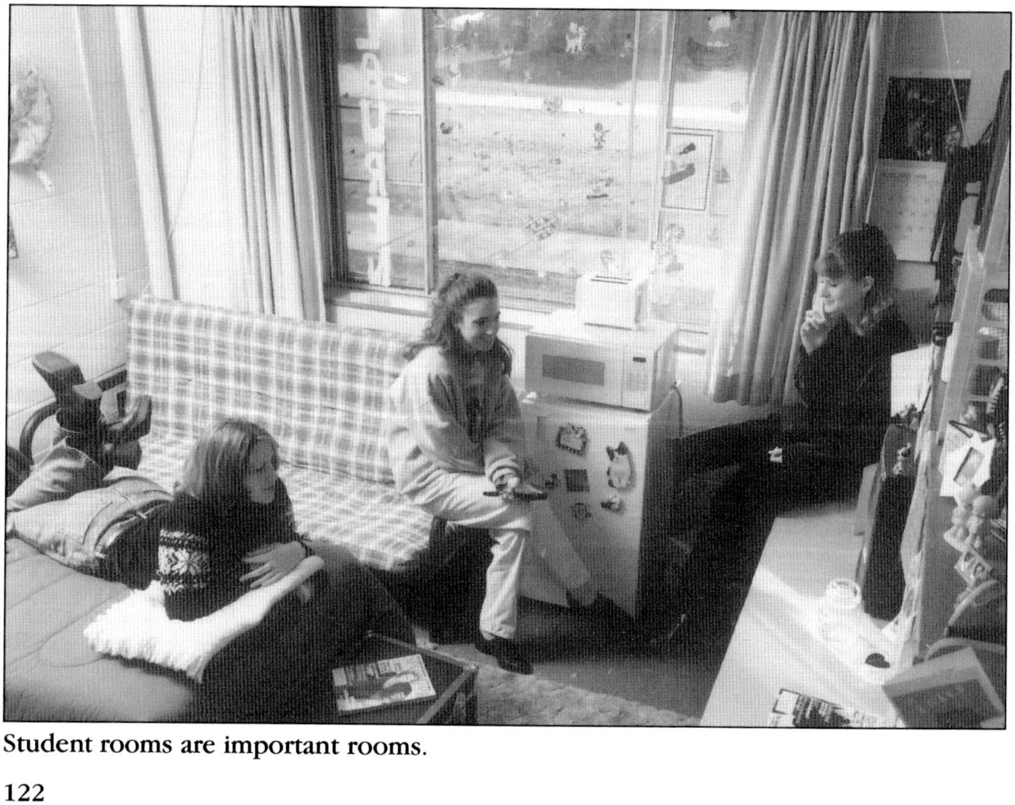

Student rooms are important rooms.

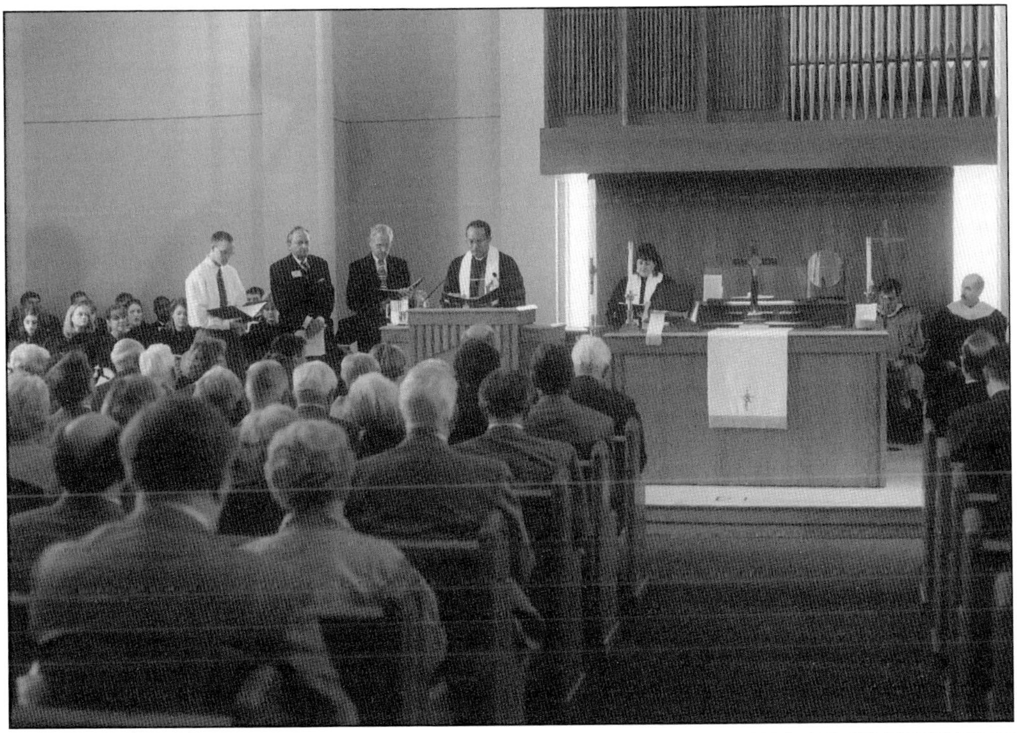

This scene is of the DeWald Chapel dedication service in 2000.

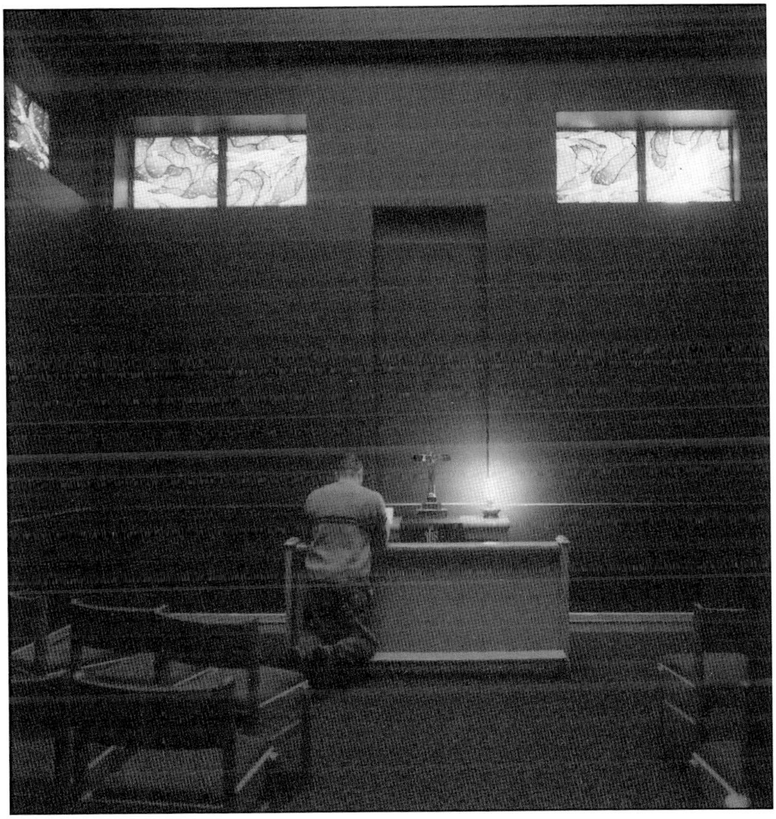

Here is one type of use of the DeWald chapel.

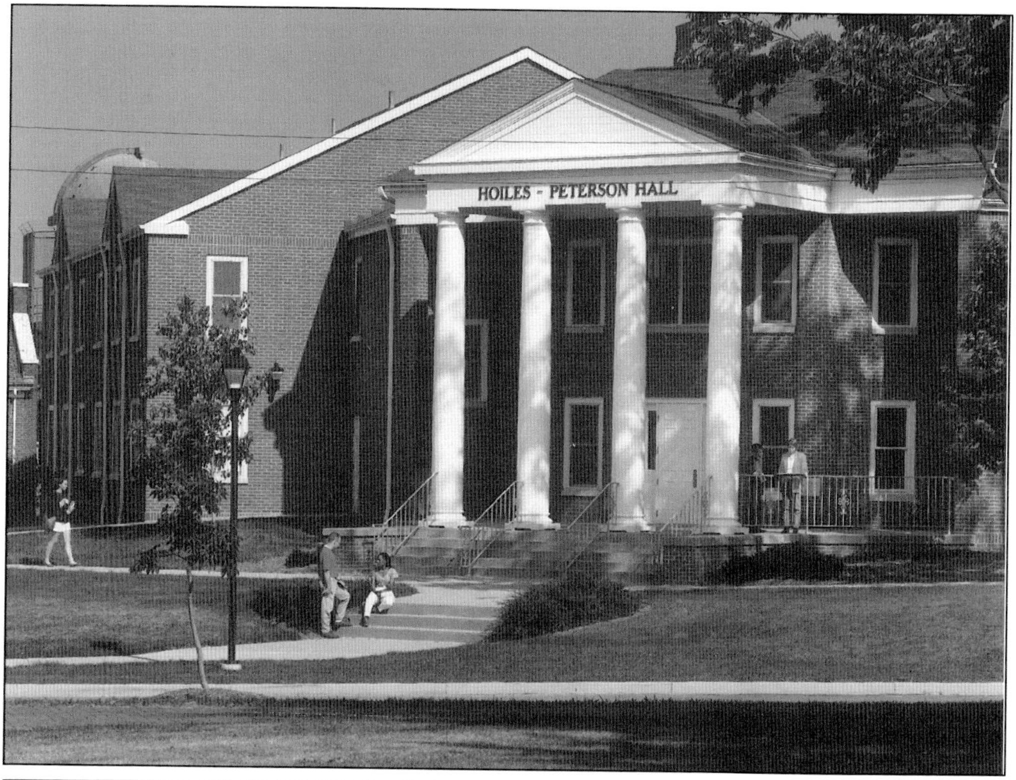

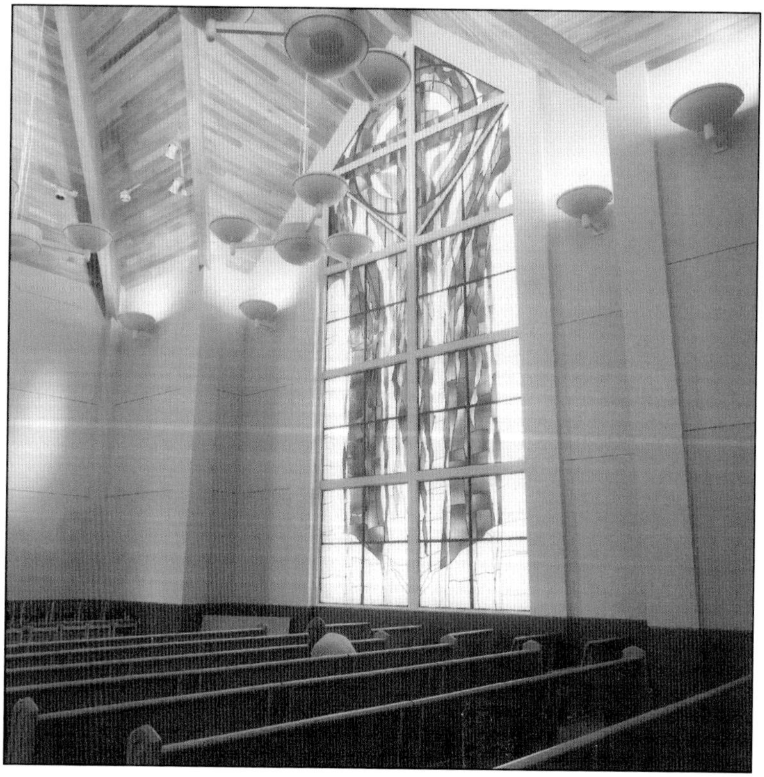

The name now identifies this dormitory, and the name refers to important helpers of M.U.C.

The DeWald chapel is meaningful for all.

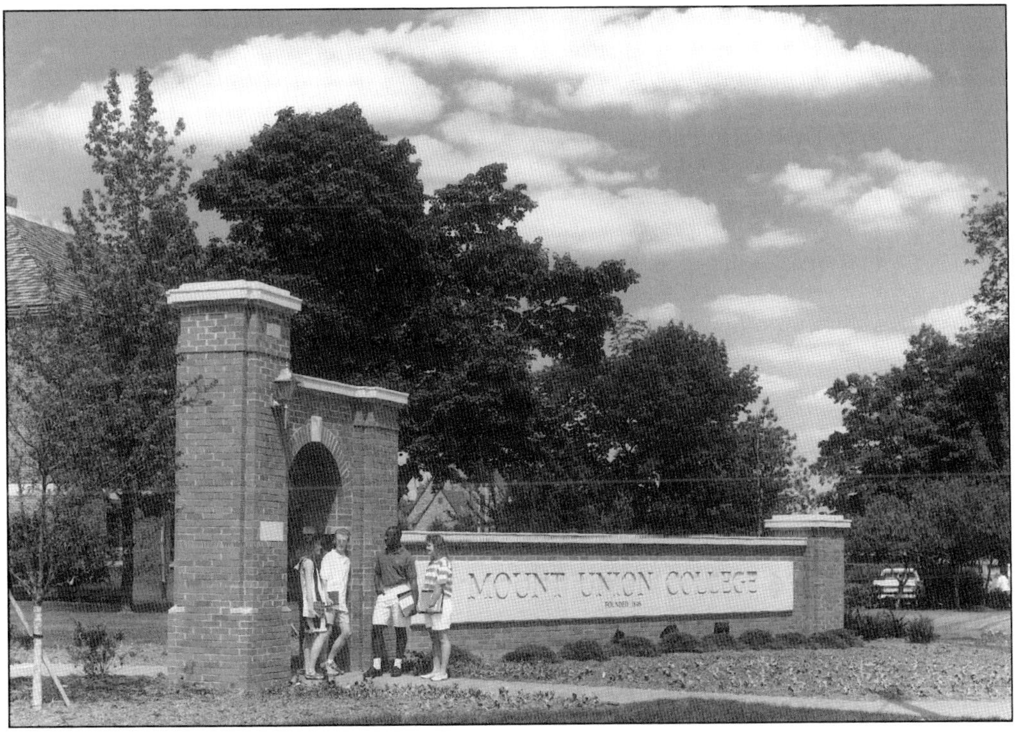

Here is a classic sky to go with this key area on campus.

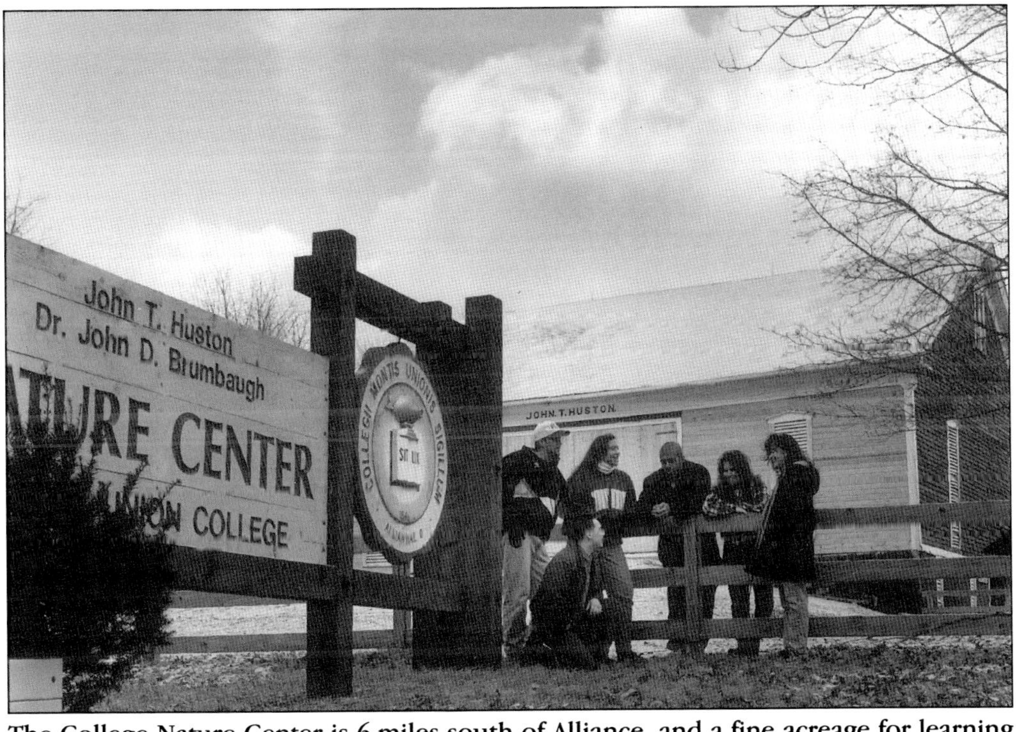

The College Nature Center is 6-miles south of Alliance, and a fine acreage for learning and appreciating.

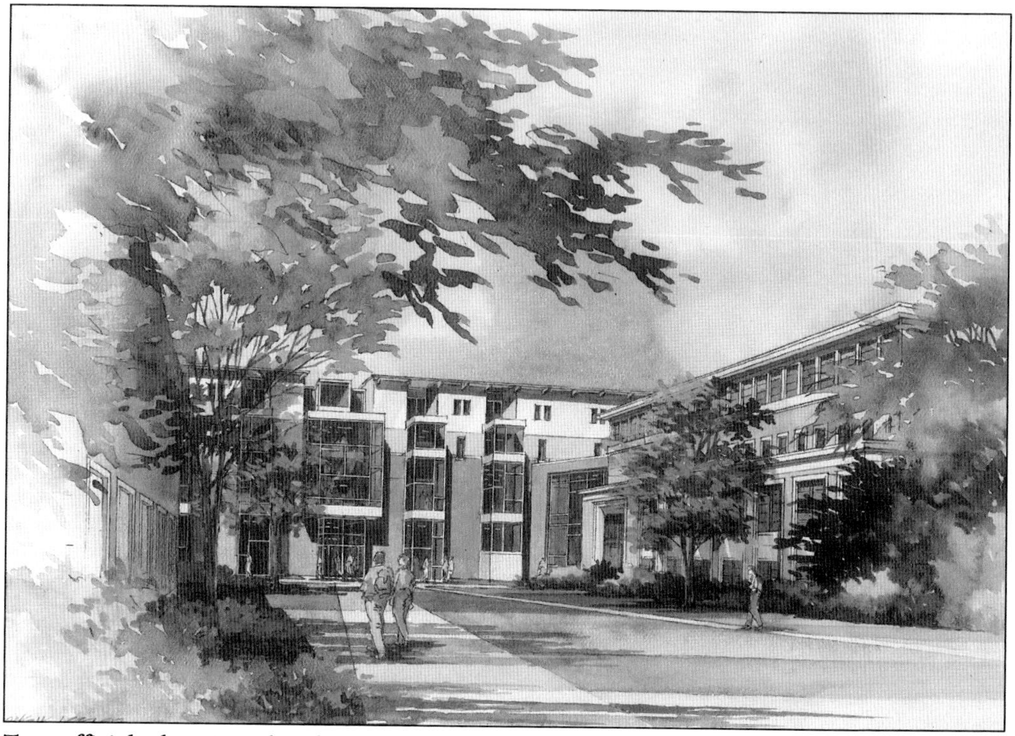

Two official planning sketches of two new buildings: Kolenbrander-Harter tie-in with the library ... and science.

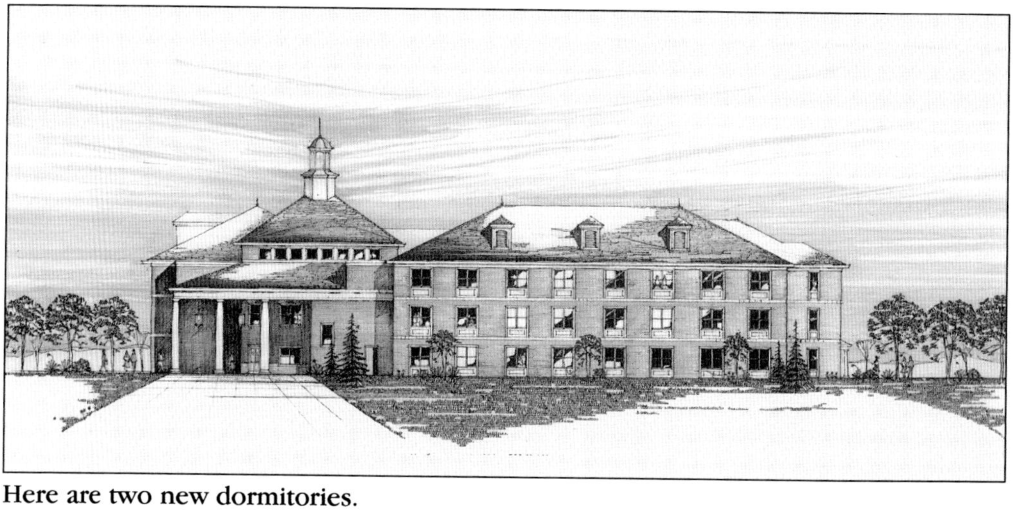

Here are two new dormitories.

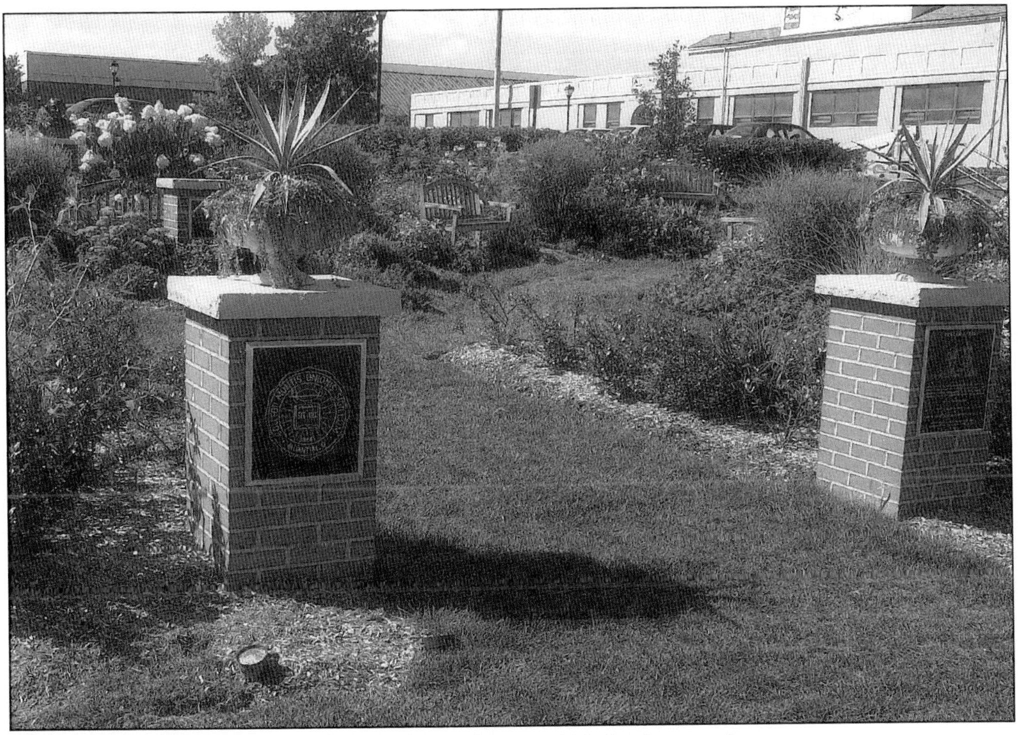

Here are two views of the delightful and beautiful Eckler gardens on campus,

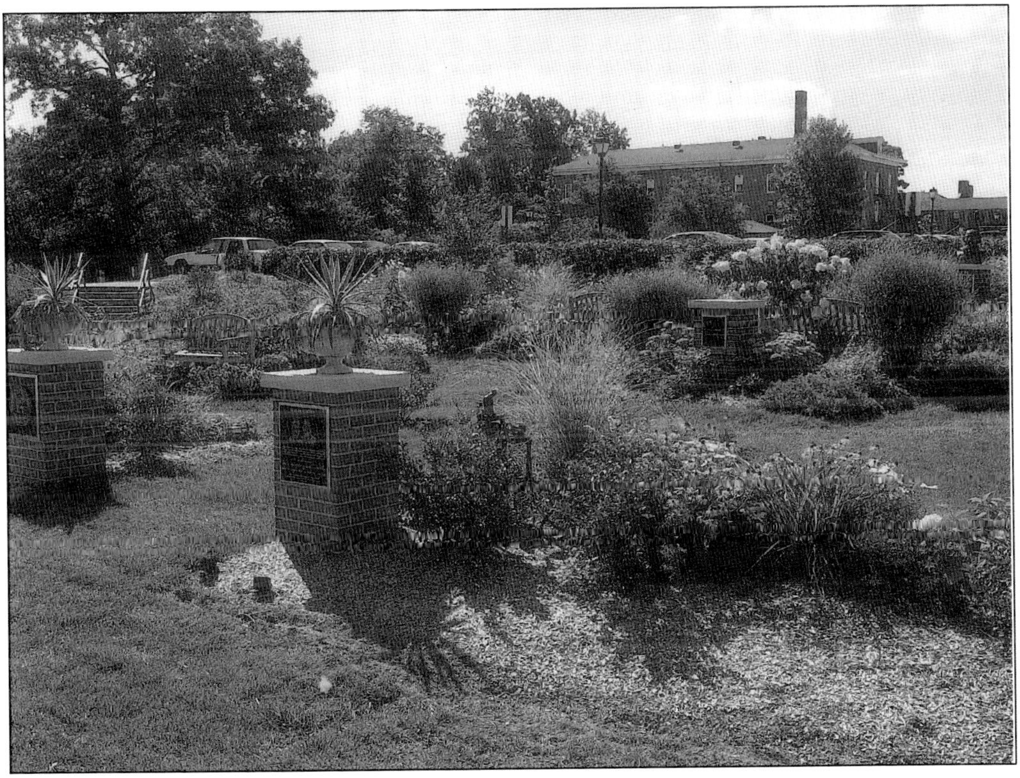

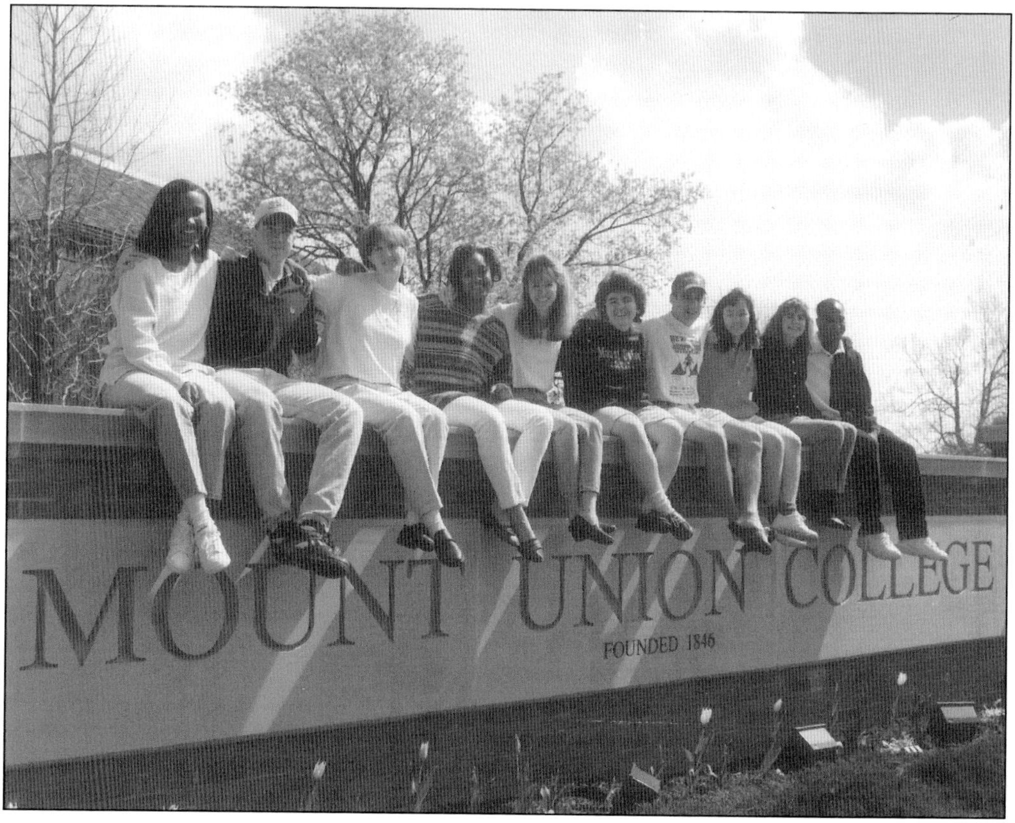

Mount Union College was founded in 1846 . . . and many, many students are pleased to find it today!

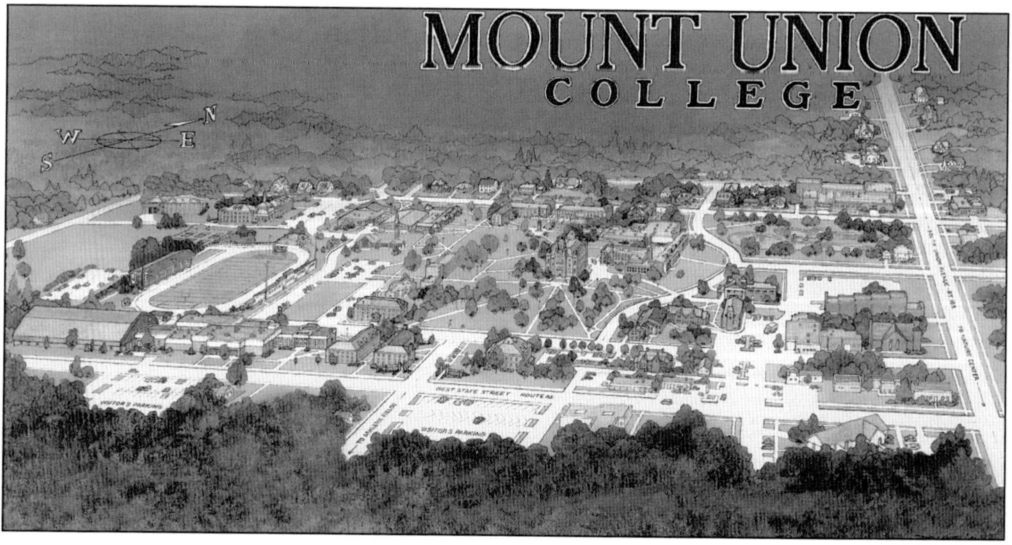